Test Prep
MCSE

Networking Essentials

Second Edition

Covers Exam 70-058

New Riders

201 West 103rd Street, Indianapolis, Indiana 46290

Jay Adamson

MCSE TestPrep: Networking Essentials, Second Edition

Copyright © 1999 by New Riders Publishing

International Standard Book Number: 0-7357-0010-9

Library of Congress Catalog Card Number: 98-87716

Printed in the United States of America

First Printing: December, 1998

00 99 98   4   3   2   1

Trademarks

All terms mentioned in this book that are known to be trademarks or service marks have been appropriately capitalized. New Riders cannot attest to the accuracy of this information. Use of a term in this book should not be regarded as affecting the validity of any trademark or service mark.

Warning and Disclaimer

EXECUTIVE EDITOR
Mary Foote

Acquisitions Editor
Sean Angus

Development Editor
Kezia Endsley

MANAGING EDITOR
Sarah Kearns

COPY EDITOR
Audra McFarland

INDEXER
Craig Small

TECHNICAL EDITOR
Marc Savage

PROOFREADER
Jeanne Clark

LAYOUT TECHNICIAN
Brad Lenser

Contents at a Glance

Table of Contents

About the Author

Jay Adamson, MCSE, MCT, is currently working for SHL Systemhouse as a Technical Architect. His current project is to review and plan the implementation of new hardware and software into the network environments for the clients in the Winnipeg and Manitoba area. He has spent many years in the training industry, developing course material and the delivery of the Microsoft technical curriculum.

Acknowledgments

I would like to thank all of those people who have helped me with this book. It has proven to be a challenge, and without their help, I'm sure it would not have turned out as well as it has.

First, I would like to thank Sean Angus for his tremendous support and understanding. The timing of this proved to be very challenging and Sean gave me a lot of support through the difficult times. I have worked with Sean on many projects and it has always been a pleasure.

Kezia Endsley, the development editor on this book, has been a pleasure to work with. She has great suggestions and is always able to present them in a way that makes you feel that it must have been your own idea. Every time I work with her, I'm always amazed at how quickly she is able to edit a chapter and get it back to me. I'm sure that she often wishes that I were able to work as fast as she does. Thank you, Kezia.

I would also like to thank Marc Savage for his good work as technical editor. He helped to make me more precise when I wasn't as thorough on a topic as I should have been.

There are a lot of people that did not directly contribute to the content of this book that deserve a lot of recognition. First and foremost, I must thank my wife, Sherri, and our two boys, Matthew and Devon. I know there were many evenings and weekends that they spent without me to be there with them. In addition, there were also our many friends that could not directly contribute, but were there to offer support and encouragement.

Finally, I would like to thank each of you who purchased this book. Each book sale tells me that I am able to help another person to get a little closer to certification.

—Jay Adamson

Dedication

I would like to dedicate this book to the memory of my good friend, Cal Lockhart, who has left us all with many, many memories. Thanks, "Thumper."

—Jay Adamson

Tell Us What You Think!

As the reader of this book, *you* are our most important critic and commentator. We value your opinion and want to know what we're doing right, what we could do better, what areas you'd like to see us publish in, and any other words of wisdom you're willing to pass our way.

As the Executive Editor for the Certification team at Macmillan Computer Publishing, I welcome your comments. You can fax, email, or write me directly to let me know what you did or didn't like about this book—as well as what we can do to make our books stronger.

Please note that I cannot help you with technical problems related to the topic of this book, and that due to the high volume of mail I receive, I might not be able to reply to every message.

When you write, please be sure to include this book's title and author, as well as your name and phone or fax number. I will carefully review your comments and share them with the author and editors who worked on the book.

Fax: 317-581-4663

Email: certification@mcp.com

Mail: Mary Foote
          Executive Editor
          Certification
          Macmillan Computer Publishing
          201 West 103rd Street
          Indianapolis, IN 46290 USA

Introduction

The *MCSE TestPrep* series serves as a study aid for people preparing for Microsoft certification exams. The series is intended to help reinforce and clarify information with which the student is already familiar by providing sample questions and tests, as well as summary information relevant to each of the exam objectives. Note that this series is not intended to be the only source for student preparation, but rather a review of information with a set of practice tests that can be used to increase the student's familiarity with the exam questions. Using this series with the *MCSE Training Guide* series can increase the student's likelihood of success when taking the exam.

WHO SHOULD READ THIS BOOK

The *Networking Essentials* book in the *MCSE TestPrep* series is intended specifically for students preparing for Microsoft's Networking Essentials (70–058) exam, which is one of the core exams in the MCSE Microsoft Windows NT 4.0 Track program.

HOW THIS BOOK HELPS YOU

This book provides a wealth of review questions similar to those you will encounter in the actual exam, categorized by the objectives published by Microsoft for the exam. Each answer is explained in detail in the "Answers and Explanations" section for each objective. The "Further Review" section provides additional information that is crucial for successfully passing the exam. The two full-length practice exams at the end of the book help you determine whether you have mastered the skills necessary to successfully complete the exam.

HOW TO USE THIS BOOK

When you feel that you're fairly well prepared for the exam, use this book as a test of your knowledge. After you have taken the practice tests and feel confident in the material on which you were tested, you are ready to schedule your exam. Use this book for a final quick review before taking the test to make sure that all the important concepts are set in your mind.

HARDWARE/SOFTWARE RECOMMENDATIONS

MCSE TestPrep: Networking Essentials, Second Edition is meant to help you review concepts with which you already have training and experience. In order to make the most of the review, you need to have as much background and experience as possible. The best way to do this is to combine studying with working on real networks using the products on which you will be tested. This section gives you a description of the minimum computer requirements you need to build a good practice environment.

The minimum computer requirements to study everything on which you are tested include one workstation running Windows 95, and one server running Windows NT Server—both of which must be connected by a network.

Windows 95 requirements are as follows:

- Any computer on the Microsoft Hardware Compatibility List

- 486DX 33MHz or better (Pentium recommended)

- A minimum of 12MB of RAM (32MB recommended)

- 200MB (or larger) hard disk

- 3.5-inch 1.44MB floppy drive

- VGA (or SuperVGA) video adapter

- VGA (or SuperVGA) monitor

- Mouse or equivalent pointing device

- Two-speed (or faster) CD-ROM drive

- A Windows 9x–compatible Network Interface Card (NIC)

- Presence on an existing network, or use of a hub to create a test network

Windows NT Server requirements are as follows:

- Any computer on the Microsoft Hardware Compatibility List

- 486DX2 66MHz or better (Pentium recommended)

- 16MB of RAM (64MB recommended)

- 340MB (or larger) hard disk

- 3.5-inch 1.44MB floppy drive

- VGA (or SuperVGA) video adapter

- VGA (or SuperVGA) monitor

- Mouse or equivalent pointing device

- Two-speed (or faster) CD-ROM drive

- A Windows NT–compatible Network Interface Card (NIC)

- Presence on an existing network, or use of a hub to create a test network

- Microsoft Windows NT Server

WHAT THE NETWORKING ESSENTIALS EXAM (70–058) COVERS

The Networking Essentials certification exam measures your ability to implement, administer, and troubleshoot information systems that incorporate Microsoft Windows 95 and any products in the Microsoft BackOffice family. It focuses on determining your skill level in four major areas:

- Standards and Terminology (Chapter 1)

- Planning (Chapter 2)

- Implementation (Chapter 3)

- Troubleshooting (Chapter 4)

The Networking Essentials certification exam uses these categories to measure your ability. Before taking this exam, you should be proficient in the job skills discussed in the following sections.

Standards and Terminology

The Standards and Terminology section is designed to ensure that you understand networking terminology and the standards for servers, protocols, hardware, and how communication takes place between computers.

The objectives for standards and terminology are as follows:

- Define common networking terms for LANs and WANs.

- Compare a file and printer server with an application server.

- Compare user-level security with access permission assigned to a shared directory on a server.

- Compare a client/server network with a peer-to-peer network.

- Compare the implications of using connection-oriented communications with connectionless communications.

- Distinguish whether SLIP or PPP is used as the communications protocol for various situations.

- Define the communication devices that communicate at each level of the OSI model.

- Describe the characteristics and purpose of the media used in IEEE 802.3 and IEEE 802.5 standards.

- Explain the purpose of NDIS and Novell ODI network standards.

Planning

The Planning section of the Networking Essentials exam measures your knowledge of cabling, topologies, protocols, devices, and WAN communication services. You are tested on various items, such as which type of cable to use in different topologies and environments, which protocols to use, and which devices to implement according to the specific needs.

The objectives for planning are as follows:

- Select the appropriate media for various situations. Media choices include twisted-pair cable, coaxial cable, fiber-optic cable, and wireless.

  Situational elements include cost, distance limitations, and number of nodes.

- Select the appropriate topology for various token-ring and Ethernet networks.

- Select the appropriate network and transport protocol or protocols for various token-ring and Ethernet networks. Protocol choices include DLC, AppleTalk, IPX, TCP/IP, NFS, and SMB.

- Select the appropriate connectivity devices for various token-ring and Ethernet networks. Connectivity devices include repeaters, bridges, routers, brouters, and gateways.

- List the characteristics, requirements, and appropriate situations for WAN connection services. WAN connection services include X.25, ISDN, Frame Relay, and ATM.

Implementation

The Implementation section measures your skills in areas such as creating a management plan for security, accounts, and performance; setting up a disaster recovery plan; selecting the appropriate hardware and software; and installing and configuring the hardware and software.

The objectives for implementation are as follows:

- Choose an administrative plan to meet specified needs, including performance management, account management, and security.

- Choose a disaster recovery plan for various situations.

- Given the manufacturer's documentation for the network adapter, install, configure, and resolve hardware conflicts for multiple network adapters in a token-ring or Ethernet network.

- Implement a NetBIOS naming scheme for all computers on a given network.

- Select the appropriate hardware and software tools to monitor trends in the network.

Troubleshooting

The Troubleshooting section of the Networking Essentials certification exam measures your skills in identifying common errors, diagnosing and resolving connectivity problems, and resolving network performance problems.

The objectives for troubleshooting are as follows:

- Identify common errors associated with components required for communications.

- Diagnose and resolve common connectivity problems with cards, cables, and related hardware.

- Resolve broadcast storms.

- Identify and resolve network performance problems.

Thank you for choosing *MCSE TestPrep: Networking Essentials, Second Edition.* We're sure you'll find this a valuable review tool. For more study aids, check your bookstore for *MCSE Training Guide: Windows 98* or *MCSE Fast Track: Windows 98*, published by New Riders Publishing. Good luck with your exam!

CHAPTER 1

Standards and Terminology

The Standards and Terminology portion of the exam helps ensure that you have a good solid base to plan and implement a network, whether it is a LAN or a WAN. These questions test your knowledge of cable type, cable length, connectors, and any other media needed to connect your computers. Without a good understanding of the different types of available media and which types should be used in certain circumstances, you may cost yourself a lot of time and money by having to redesign your network.

In addition to media considerations, you must also understand user accounts and security issues, as well as how they are integrated.

After you have decided how your network is to be configured for accounts and security, you still face many other considerations, including the protocol to be used, the server types to be used, and the kind of dial-in protocol to be used.

To tie it all together, you will be tested on your knowledge of the Open Systems Interconnection (OSI) reference model and the Institute of Electrical and Electronics Engineers (IEEE) 802.3 and IEEE 802.5 standards. The OSI was developed by the International Standards Organization (ISO) to set up global standards for communications and information exchange. The IEEE is an organization of engineering and electronics professionals and has developed a standard for the Physical and Data Link layers of LANs.

Without a familiarity of the issues covered in this chapter, it would be very difficult to plan and implement an efficient and cost-effective network.

OBJECTIVES

The following Microsoft test objectives are covered in this chapter:

Define common networking terms for LANs and WANs. (Practice questions start on page 3.)

▶ The purpose of this objective is to make sure people working in the networking field understand the difference between a local area network (LAN) and a wide area network (WAN). These terms are the main topics of discussion throughout this chapter.

Compare a file and printer server with an application server. (Practice questions start on page 14.)

▶ This objective makes sure you are aware of the different types of servers in the field of networking.

Compare user-level security with access permission assigned to a shared directory on a server. (Practice questions start on page 24.)

▶ This exam objective is designed to encourage you to know the different permissions available to assign to users or groups on a shared directory.

continues

Compare a client/server network with a peer-to-peer network. (Practice questions start on page 31.)

▶ This objective makes sure you are familiar with the two main network classification models.

Compare the implications of using connection-oriented communications with connectionless communications. (Practice questions start on page 39.)

▶ This exam objective addresses whether a person understands how a connection-oriented type of communication differs from a connectionless form of communication.

Distinguish whether SLIP or PPP is used as the communications protocol for various situations. (Practice questions start on page 45.)

▶ The purpose of this objective is to make sure you understand where, when, and for what reasons one would use SLIP or PPP as a communications protocol.

Define the communication devices that communicate at each level of the OSI model. (Practice questions start on page 52.)

▶ The purpose of this exam objective is to make sure that you are able to identify what devices on a network work within what levels of the OSI model.

Describe the characteristics and purpose of the media used in IEEE 802.3 and IEEE 802.5 standards. (Practice questions start on page 59.)

▶ This question is asked to assess whether a person is aware of two of the more popular implementations of the IEEE 802.x set of standards.

Explain the purpose of NDIS and Novell ODI network standards. (Practice questions start on page 65.)

▶ This objective is included to make sure that a person is aware of the differences between the NDIS standard used by Microsoft networks and the ODI standard used by Novell Networks.

DEFINING COMMON NETWORKING TERMS FOR LANS AND WANS

1. You are trying to decide which type of network you will use at your office, and you want the type that will provide communication and avoid collisions on the cable. Which of the following is the best choice?

   A. Token-Ring

   B. CSMA/CD

   C. Ethernet

   D. CSMA/CA

   E. ARCnet

2. You have purchased a MAU (Multistation Access Unit) from your computer supplier and now must decide what type of network card you should install in the workstations. Which of the following would be the most appropriate?

   A. Fast SCSI Wide

   B. Token-Ring

   C. ArcServe

   D. Ethernet

   E. None of the above

3. Your company has a LAN in its downtown office and has now set up a LAN in the manufacturing plant in the suburbs. To enable everyone to share data and resources between the two LANs, what type of device(s) are needed to connect them? Choose the most correct answer.

   A. Modem

   B. Cable

   C. Hub

   D. Router

   E. Multiplexer

4. You have just been contracted to install a Windows NT network in an office that is located in a strip mall. The office is located next to the power plant of the building, so a UPS (uninterruptible power supply) has already been installed. What type of cable should you use for the network cabling? Choose the best answer.

   A. T1

   B. UTP

   C. Fiber-optic

   D. PSTN

   E. STP

5. Ethernet and Token-Ring are the two most commonly used network architectures in the world. Jim has heard of the different topologies for networks and wants to choose the architecture that will provide him with the most options. Which of the following would that be? Choose the most correct answer.

A. Token-Ring, because it currently can run at both 4Mbps and 16Mbps. This means that it can be used in any topology.

B. Ethernet, because it is cabled using fiber-optic cable.

C. Token-Ring, because it uses a MAU.

D. Ethernet, because it can be set up with most topologies and can use multiple transfer speeds.

E. Neither Token-Ring nor Ethernet is the proper choice. Only ARCnet can be used in all topologies.

6. Your office has just expanded its building by adding an additional 2000 square feet. Because the distance from the server falls outside the specs of the cabling that you have, what device should you use to connect the new area to the LAN? Choose the best answer(s).

A. Repeater

B. Passive hub

C. Active hub

D. Bridge

E. Gateway

7. Stephanie is in charge of a small network and wants to make it simple but secure. The users want to have full control over their data and still be able to share data with the rest of the office. The networking knowledge of the office staff is basic. Which network(s) would be the best for Stephanie to set up?

A. Peer-to-peer

B. Master domain

C. Server-based

D. WAN

E. Share-level

8. Brad is in charge of a small network and wants to make it simple but secure. The users want to have full control over their data and still be able to share data with the rest of the office. The networking knowledge of the office staff is excellent. Which network(s) would be the best to set up?

A. Peer-to-peer

B. Master domain

C. Server-based

D. WAN

E. Share-level

9. Alice is setting up a small network in her home so that she can study for her MCSE exams. She doesn't have a lot of money to spend on hardware, so she wants to use a network topology that requires the least amount of hardware possible. Which topology should she select?

A. Star

B. Ring

C. Token-Ring

D. Ethernet

E. Bus

10. **Alex is required to provide information on how many people are using the network at any one time. Which network will enable him to do so?**

  A. Server-based

  B. Token-Ring

  C. Ethernet

  D. Star

  E. Peer-to-peer

ANSWER KEY

1. A	5. D	9. E
2. B	6. A-C	10. A
3. D	7. C	
4. E	8. A	

DEFINING COMMON NETWORKING TERMS FOR LANS AND WANS

1. You are trying to decide which type of network you will use at your office, and you want the type that will provide communication and avoid collisions on the cable. Which of the following is the best choice?

A. Token-Ring

1. CORRECT ANSWER: A

The Token-Ring architecture provides communication on a network and also avoids "collisions." For a computer to transmit data, it must first have possession of the token. The computer with the token transmits the data to a destination computer. When that data is received, the recipient computer modifies the token and releases it to the wire of the network. The next computer that wants to send data receives the token and then transmits its data. In a Token-Ring network, no more than one token exists on the wire at one time. Figure 1.1 illustrates how the token-passing process works.

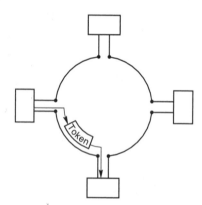

FIGURE 1.1

The token is passed from one computer to the next to enable each computer to transmit data on the network.

Other network types instruct their computers to "listen" on the wire. Carrier-sense multiple access with collision detection (CSMA/CD) is a type of access control used with bus topologies. If a computer does not see another transmission on the wire, it sends its transmission.

The other method for determining which computer can transmit on the network in a bus topology is carrier-sense multiple access with collision avoidance. CSMA/CA waits a period of time after detecting the last signal on the network before transmitting its data. This wait period makes CAMS/CA slower and, therefore, less popular than CSMA/CD. This works fine in most cases, but the possibility exists that two computers are listening and thus will send their transmissions at the same time. When such a collision occurs, the computers end up retransmitting their data.

2. You have purchased a MAU (Multistation Access Unit) from your computer supplier and now must decide what type of network card you should install in the workstations. Which of the following would be the most appropriate?

B. Token-Ring

2. CORRECT ANSWER: B

Recall that the term MAU is an abbreviation for Multistation Access Unit. This device is used in Token-Ring networks to connect all the computers on the network. Generally, a MAU has 16 ports to which computers are connected. If the network has more than 16 computers, multiple MAUs can be connected to act as a single unit.

A *hub* is similar to a MAU in that the computers of the network are all connected to it. However, the internal workings of a MAU are that of a "ring," whereas a hub is like an intersection. Tokens pass in a circular motion on the "ring" inside the MAU, which means that the token can be passed from one computer to the next. The intersection within a hub is simply a point for communication to pass through.

3. Your company has a LAN in its downtown office and has now set up a LAN in the manufacturing plant in the suburbs. To enable everyone to share data and resources between the two LANs, what type of device(s) are needed to connect them? Choose the most correct answer.

D. Router

3. CORRECT ANSWER: D

The most commonly used device to connect networks that are not closely situated is the router. The router translates data into a format that may be transmitted across telephone lines to another router, which then retranslates the packets of information into network data.

A number of different telephone lines can be used, depending on how fast the user desires the communication. The router to be used must be matched to the line speed, otherwise communication may be unpredictable.

Bridges can also be used to connect to remote LANs. The main difference between a router and a bridge is that two distinct subnets to the network are present when routers are used. When bridges are used, the two remote networks look as if they make up a single subnet.

Another device that is used to connect a computer with a remote LAN is the *modem*. This device enables one computer to connect to another by dialing into it over the telephone lines. However, this permits only one computer to connect to another computer or LAN; it does not allow multiple computers to connect through a single connection. The other drawback of using modems is that the communication tends to be much slower.

Other devices—including multiplexers, MAUs, hubs, and repeaters (used to extend a network and regenerate signals)—are all used on the local network to either connect the computers or increase the signal strength.

4. You have just been contracted to install a Windows NT network in an office that is located in a strip mall. The office is situated next to the power plant of the building, so a UPS (uninterruptible power supply) has already been installed. What type of cable should you use for the network cabling? Choose the best answer.

E. STP

4. CORRECT ANSWER: E

STP stands for shielded twisted-pair. Network cabling can refer to a number of different types of cable. Because the office in this case is close to a power plant, it is better to use a cable that shields the signal from EMF (electro-magnetic interference) that could be emitted from the power cables.

In most instances, UTP (unshielded twisted-pair) cable meets and exceeds the needs of any LAN. However, because the power supply is so close to this office, it is worth the small additional expense to upgrade from UTP to STP cable. Fiber-optic cable could also be used, but because there is no mention of extreme security needs, its cost makes it an unlikely choice.

5. Ethernet and Token-Ring are the two most commonly used network architectures in the world. Jim has heard of the different topologies for networks and wants to choose the architecture that will provide him with the most options. Which of the following would that be? Choose the most correct answer.

   D. Ethernet, because it can be set up with most topologies and can use multiple transfer speeds.

Ethernet is the most commonly used architecture today. This is due to its versatility and relatively low cost. Most Ethernet networks run at 10Mbps, 100Mbps, or both. 10Mbps and 100Mbps hubs can be connected through a switch to accommodate multiple transfer rates on the same network.

The servers can be connected to the 100Mbps hub, and the workstations can be connected to the 10Mbps hubs. As the need arises, the 10Mbps hubs could be replaced with 100Mbps hubs, and the overall speed on the LAN would increase (providing that the network interface cards [NICs] in each of the workstations are capable of switching from 10Mbps to 100Mbps).

6. Your office has just expanded its building by adding an additional 2000 square feet. Because the distance from the server falls outside the specs of the cabling that you have, what device should you use to connect the new area to the LAN? Choose the best answer(s).

   A. Repeater
   C. Active hub

Although certain types of cabling enable you to use longer lengths, a limit still exists as to how far signals can travel before the signal must be boosted. Repeaters and active hubs do just that.

A *repeater* regenerates and retimes a signal on the bus network. This means that the signal can travel much farther without losing data and without being timed out. An *active hub* does the same thing as a repeater, except that it acts as the central point through which all network traffic must pass, as in a star topology. Because active hubs and repeaters both regenerate signals, an active hub is sometimes referred to as a multiport repeater. Unlike a passive hub, the active hub needs electrical power to operate. A wiring panel or punch-down block is an example of a passive hub; it acts merely as a connection point and does not alter the signal in any way.

7. Stephanie is in charge of a small network and wants to make it simple but secure. The users want to have full control over their data and still be able to share data with the rest of the office. The networking knowledge of the office staff is basic. Which network(s) would be the best for Stephanie to set up?

  C. Server-based

The key points to this question are that the users want to be able to share data and that they have a basic networking knowledge. Without a good understanding of how a network operates as far as creating shares and setting up security, potential exists for lost data. In a peer-to-peer network, each user is the "administrator" of his own computer. Therefore, it is essential that each user be comfortable with managing his data.

In the case of a server-based network, all data is stored on a central server. The administrator of the server sets up shares that each user can access, and sets specific permissions depending on each person or group's needs. Each user can then concentrate on the data that he is creating or working with and need not be concerned about other people accessing his computers. If any changes must be made to expand or restrict someone's access to files or folders, the administrator makes those changes.

If the users were all knowledgeable on how a network operates, it could be advantageous to use a peer-to-peer network. Because the LAN may be very small, the company may feel that having a computer simply for sharing data is a waste.

8. Brad is in charge of a small network and wants to make it simple but secure. The users want to have full control over their data and still be able to share data with the rest of the office. The networking knowledge of the office staff is excellent. Which network(s) would be the best to set up?

  A. Peer-to-peer

Please see the explanation for question 7. Because the readers have a good understanding of networking techniques, peer-to-peer networking is the best bet.

9. Alice is setting up a small network in her home so that she can study for her MCSE exams. She doesn't have a lot of money to spend on hardware, so she wants to use a network topology that requires the least amount of hardware possible. Which topology should she select?

  E. Bus

Three basic topologies exist for setting up a network: bus, star, and ring. In addition to these are hybrids that enable you to combine topologies. Figure 1.2 illustrates the three main topologies.

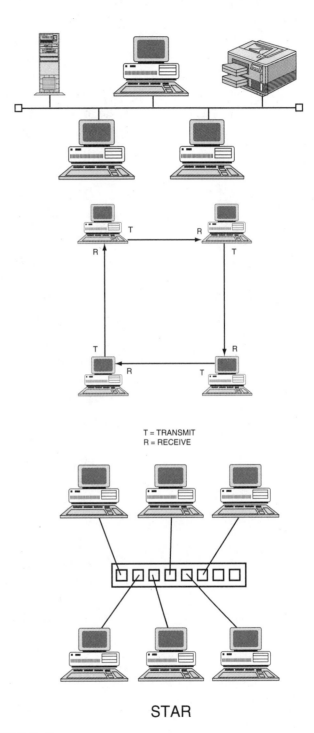

T = TRANSMIT
R = RECEIVE

STAR

FIGURE 1.2
The bus, ring, and star topologies are the most common configurations.

The bus topology is made up of a single cable (known as a *trunk*), to which each of the computers on the network is connected. At each end of the trunk is a device known as a *terminator* that absorbs the signal when it reaches the end of the cable. If the signals were not absorbed by the terminator, the signal would continue to bounce back and forth between the ends of the trunk and would not allow any other computers to send signals.

The one drawback of the bus system is that all cables on the network must be plugged into something. If one cable end is unconnected, the entire network (subnet) will not operate.

In the star topology, each of the computers is connected to a central device called a *hub*. All signals are transmitted to the other computers through the central hub. The star network originated from the use of central mainframe servers.

The drawback of the star configuration is that significantly more cable is required because all computers must be connected to the hub. In addition, if the hub fails, the network also goes down. If only one computer, or the cable to a computer on the network fails, however, the rest of the network continues to operate normally.

As the name implies, the ring topology is configured as a ring or circular cable. Because no end to the cable exists, terminators are not needed. The signals pass from one computer to the other, with each computer acting as a repeater.

The major drawback of the ring topology is that because the signal passes through each computer, the entire network fails if one of the computers fails. Although the Token-Ring architecture appears to be a star topology, it is actually a ring inside the MAU. The ring topology also offers advantages, the biggest being that if a computer connected to a port on the MAU fails, it will not bring the rest of the network down.

10. Alex is required to provide information on how many people are using the network at any one time. Which network will enable him to do so?

   A. Server-based

10. CORRECT ANSWER: A

Microsoft Windows NT enables the administrator to see who has logged on to the network and see which accounts are accessing resources on the server. The Event Viewer enables the administrator to view the logs and see who has logged on to the network. Server Manager can display who is using which resources, and for how long they have been using them.

The peer-to-peer network does not allow any centralized monitoring of the network.

COMPARING FILE AND PRINTER SERVERS WITH APPLICATION SERVERS

1. Joan is working in a peer-to-peer network and wishes to grant the other people in her network access to some files on her computer. She is running Windows NT Workstation 4 on her computer and has created user accounts for everyone in her network on her computer. After creating the accounts, she then assigns the appropriate permissions for these accounts to the files on her computer. Will these measures grant everyone on the network access to the files as she wishes? Select the most correct answer.

   A. Everyone on the network will have the appropriate access.

   B. Everyone on the Internet will have access to the documents on her computer.

   C. No one except Joan will have access to the resources on her computer.

   D. Only administrators will have access.

   E. Joan cannot set permissions for individuals.

2. Peter has a computer that he wants to use as a file and printer server, but he isn't sure of all the hardware requirements he will need. His computer currently has a single 266MHz processor with 128MB of RAM and a RAID 5 disk array with 20GB of disk space. The network is Ethernet at 10Mbps. Does this setup meet the requirements for a file and printer server? Choose the best answer.

   A. Peter must increase the amount of memory from 128MB to at least 512MB.

   B. The processor should be upgraded to 400MHz, or the system should be upgraded to have at least two processors.

   C. The network speed should be increased to 100Mbps.

   D. The drive should be switched from RAID 5 to RAID 1.

   E. Nothing should be done to this file and printer server.

3. You have been talking to some software vendors about a possible solution for an application you want to set up on a web server. What kind of client would be best for accessing this application on the web server? Choose the best answer.

   A. Windows NT Workstation

   B. Windows 95

   C. Windows 98

   D. Thick client

   E. Thin client

4. **You have been given the task of selecting a server that will act as your print server. This box will serve a color laser, two color inkjets, and a printer pool consisting of four monochrome laser printers. Approximately 100 users will access these print queues, and both PostScript and PCL documents will be sent to the queues. Which of the following options is the best bet, given these circumstances?**

   A. A server with two Pentium II 200MHz processors with 128MB of RAM, and 2GB of free disk space on the default spool partition

   B. A server with two Pentium II 200MHz processors with 128MB of RAM, and 1GB of free disk space on the spool partition that is not located on the default partition

   C. A server with 512MB of RAM, a single 266 Pentium II processor, and 1GB of free disk space on the default spool partition

   D. A server with 2GB of free disk space on the spool partition that is not in the default location, 256MB of RAM, and two Pentium II 266MHz processors

   E. A server with 512MB of RAM, a single 400MHz Pentium II processor, and 1GB of free disk space on the default spool partition

5. **Paul has had numerous complaints about file access being slow on the file server. Part of the problem is that 42 new people have been hired in the last three months to work in the company's new** graphics department. **What should Paul do to fix the file access speed? Choose the best answer.**

   A. Change the disk drives.

   B. Add more memory.

   C. Increase the speed of the network adapter.

   D. Add another processor.

   E. Add more disk space.

6. **Disk failure is probably the single most feared occurrence that an administrator faces. If the processor or network card fails, they can always be replaced and the server will be back to normal. However, if the drive(s) fails, data is usually lost. What should the administrator do to minimize the risk of data loss? Choose the best answer.**

   A. Set up a cluster server.

   B. Implement RAID 0.

   C. Implement RAID 1.

   D. Implement a monthly backup of the OS.

   E. Add more disk space.

7. **Brad wants to ensure that his disk drive in his file server is protected from data loss. His server has 512MB of RAM, a single 300MHz processor, and a 9GB disk drive. What should he do to ensure that downtime for his users is kept to a minimum? Choose the best answer.**

   A. Configure his drive for RAID 0.

   B. Configure his drive for RAID 1.

C. Configure his drive for RAID 5.

D. Set up a daily full backup of the drive.

E. Implement a disk-defragmenting program.

8. **Mike is new in network administration and has become somewhat confused by the term** *client/server application.* **Choose the statement that does** *not* **apply to a client/server application.**

    A. The client runs part of the application locally.

    B. The server maintains all the data for the application.

    C. Everything is run at the server.

    D. Some of the data is downloaded to the client computer.

    E. The server does most of the processing.

9. **Anne wants to set up a file server for the users in her office. There are 24 people in marketing, 15 people in development, 8 people in accounting, and 35 people in support. These people work with all kinds of applications, including spreadsheets, word processors, databases, and their own custom development software. The old system quickly became outdated and was very slow for uploading and downloading files from and to the desktop systems. To make this server operate as quickly as possible, Anne should pay attention to the most troublesome resource. Which resource is most likely to become a major bottleneck? All components are important, but which is the best answer for a file server?**

    A. Disk access speed

    B. Memory

    C. Processor

    D. Disk size

    E. Network card

10. **Adam wants to implement a new application at his site and is trying to decide whether he should get the network version of the application or install standalone versions at each of the desktops. What is one advantage to installing the network version of the application?**

    A. No additional licenses must be purchased.

    B. It's simple to upgrade.

    C. The manufacturer offers better support.

    D. More uptime is guaranteed.

    E. The cost is lower.

11. **Carol is looking to implement a new application at her site and is trying to decide whether she should get the network version of the application or install standalone versions at each of the desktops. What is an advantage to installing the standalone version of the application at each of the desktops?**

    A. No additional licenses must be purchased.

    B. It's simple to upgrade.

    C. The manufacturer offers better support.

    D. More uptime is guaranteed.

    E. The cost is lower.

ANSWER KEY

1. A	5. A	9. A
2. E	6. C	10. B
3. E	7. D	11. D
4. D	8. C	

COMPARING FILE AND PRINTER SERVERS WITH APPLICATION SERVERS

1. Joan is working in a peer-to-peer network and wishes to grant the other people in her network access to some files on her computer. She is running Windows NT Workstation 4 on her computer and has created user accounts for everyone in her network on her computer. After creating the accounts, she then assigns the appropriate permissions for these accounts to the files on her computer. Will these measures grant everyone on the network access to the files as she wishes? Select the most correct answer.

   A. Everyone on the network will have the appropriate access.

1. CORRECT ANSWER: A

Because this is a peer-to-peer network, no central user account database exists. Therefore, for Joan to allow each of the users in her office access to resources on her computer with the correct permissions, she had to create accounts on her computer for each of them. After their accounts were created, she could then assign permissions to each of those accounts. If she hadn't created individual accounts, her only other option would have been to assign permissions to the "everyone" group. In that case, everyone would end up with the same permissions for each resource.

In a peer-to-peer network using Windows NT Workstations, accounts must be created on each computer if different permissions are to be assigned for resources.

2. Peter has a computer that he wants to use as a file and printer server, but he isn't sure of all the hardware requirements he will need. His computer currently has a single 266MHz processor with 128MB of RAM and a RAID 5 disk array with 20GB of disk space. The network is Ethernet at 10Mbps. Does this setup meet the requirements for a file and printer server? Choose the best answer.

   E. Nothing should be done to this file and printer server.

2. CORRECT ANSWER: E

Given the amount of information that you have, this computer should be sufficient in most cases. A file and printer server does not normally need a fast processor unless it must handle a lot of PostScript print jobs. The amount of memory is not huge, but it will suffice for smaller networks. The drive space provides fault tolerance and has a fairly good volume. So, with the information given in the question, the best answer is that this size of computer would be fine in most cases.

3. **You have been talking to some software vendors about a possible solution for an application you want to set up on a web server. What kind of client would be best for accessing this application on the web server? Choose the best answer.**

   E. Thin client

It doesn't really matter what your operating system is, as long as you run the proper client. In the case of running an application from a web server, you want to minimize the amount of traffic passing between your computer and the server. To accomplish this, you should use a thin client because all the processing takes place on the server, and only the appropriate screen display is sent back to the client. That way, if you are running the application across a slow WAN link or a dial-up line, the screen refresh rate will be acceptable.

4. **You have been given the task of selecting a server that will act as your print server. This box will serve a color laser, two color inkjets, and a printer pool consisting of four monochrome laser printers. Approximately 100 users will access these print queues, and both PostScript and PCL documents will be sent to the queues. Which of the following options is the best bet, given these circumstances?**

   D. A server with 2GB of free disk space on the spool partition that is not in the default partition, 256MB of RAM, and two Pentium II 266MHz processors

Print servers generally do not need a lot of processing power; the most important resources are memory and free disk space. Print jobs are spooled in memory until no physical memory is available. At that point in time, the jobs are then spooled to the disk drive. The default location for spooling print jobs lies on the same partition as the operating system. To relieve some of the pressure on drives to access the system partition, it is a good idea to put the print spooling on a different partition. This can help balance the load on the drive. Better yet, place the spool folder on a different physical drive with its own disk controller.

Printing PCL files takes very little processing, as the controlling of the print job is handled by the uni-drivers and the mini-drivers. However, in the case of PostScript files, all the information for formatting the printed document is held within the print job. Therefore, the processor plays a much bigger role when printing PostScript documents. With two fast processors, the PostScript jobs will also be handled in a timely manner.

5. Paul has had numerous complaints about file access being slow on the file server. Part of the problem is that 42 new people have been hired in the last three months to work in the company's new graphics department. What should Paul do to fix the file access speed? Choose the best answer.

   A. Change the disk drives.

When access to a server becomes slow, you should examine a number of components, including memory, the network card, the processor, and the disk drive(s). In this particular case, people have been complaining that accessing their files from the server is slow, but there is no mention of other network activity being slow. Therefore, you can probably rule out the problem that the network is not fast enough. Because accessing files on a server takes very little processing power, you can also discount that this is a processor problem. That leaves two options: memory and disk drive(s). Generally, the single most important attribute that a file server should possess is drives with low access times. Because a number of people have been hired to work with very large files, the faster the drive, the better. Before these people came on board, file size was probably quite small in comparison. Therefore, it is a good idea to use Performance Monitor to see whether a problem exists with file access at the disk drive(s).

EXAM TIP

If you are planning to monitor your disk drives using Performance Monitor, remember to activate the disk drive counters using the **diskperf –y** command. By default, these counters are not activated; if you choose these objects in Performance Monitor, you will not get any readings. The Windows NT server will have to be rebooted after the **diskperf** command has been executed to activate the counters. The command **diskperf –ye** is used to turn on the counters for the individual drives if they are a part of a RAID configuration, and **diskperf –n** is used to disable the counters.

6. Disk failure is probably the single most feared occurrence that an administrator faces. If the processor or network card fails, they can always be replaced and the server will be back to normal. However, if the drive(s) fails, data is usually lost. What should the administrator do to minimize the risk of data loss? Choose the best answer.

   C. Implement RAID 1.

An administrator has a number of options for ensuring that the data on a server is safe from data loss. Of the options provided, the best is to provide some sort of fault tolerance for the data. The best choice would be to implement RAID 1, in which two drives are mirrored. As data is written to one drive, it is actually written to both drives. If one of the drives suffers a hardware failure, the second drive can then be used. Of course, using only one backup plan is not always the best option. No matter what type of fault-tolerant system you choose, it is always best to also back up the data daily. This could be done by backing up the data to tape, CD-ROM, or another disk. Table 1.1 describes the differences between RAID 0, RAID 1, and RAID 5.

TABLE 1.1   RAID 0, RAID 1, AND RAID 5 DIFFER FROM ONE ANOTHER IN FUNDAMENTAL WAYS

RAID Level	Description
RAID 0	Two or more physical drives (up to 32) are set up in a "stripe" set. This means that data is written across each drive in equal amounts and ensures that all drives are accessed the same amount. If one drive fails, all data is lost.
RAID 1	Two physical drives act as one, where data is written to both at the same time. If one fails, no data is lost because the second drive contains the exact same data. This is also referred to as "mirroring." If a separate disk controller is used for each disk drive, it is then referred to as "duplexing."
RAID 5	Three or more disk drives (up to 32) are configured in a "stripe set with parity." This means that data is written equally across all drives as in RAID 0, except that stripe parity information is written on one of the drives. If one drive fails, an algorithm is used to generate the lost information. All the drives contain parity information.

7. Brad wants to ensure that his disk drive in his file server is protected from data loss. His server has 512MB of RAM, a single 300MHz processor, and a 9GB disk drive. What should he do to ensure that downtime for his users is kept to a minimum? Choose the best answer.

　D. Set up a daily full backup of the drive.

7. CORRECT ANSWER: D

Because Brad's computer contains only a single drive, he cannot implement RAID 1 or RAID 5 without buying additional disk drives. By implementing RAID 1 or RAID 5, Brad would be protecting his data from possible disk failure. However, not all data loss occurs because of the hardware failure of a disk drive. Probably more data is lost from users deleting files than from any other cause. If a good backup schedule is maintained, data that was created and deleted in error often can be recovered completely—or at least in part. By undergoing a full daily backup, the most data that can be lost is that which is done in one day.

8. Mike is new in network administration and has become somewhat confused by the term *client/server application*. Choose the statement that does *not* apply to a client/server application.

    C. Everything is run at the server.

8. CORRECT ANSWER: C

Hopefully, you read this question carefully. Client/server applications are run at both the server and the client, hence the name. The client initiates the command to run the application on the server. However, some of the information is downloaded to the client system for processing as well. The majority of the work is done at the server, but a portion is carried out at the client as well. In the case of a thinnet client, everything is carried out at the server, and only the screen images are sent back to the client.

9. Anne wants to set up a file server for the users in her office. There are 24 people in marketing, 15 people in development, 8 people in accounting, and 35 people in support. These people work with all kinds of applications, including spreadsheets, word processors, databases, and their own custom development software. The old system quickly became outdated and was very slow for uploading and downloading files from and to the desktop systems. To make this server operate as quickly as possible, Anne should pay attention to the most troublesome resource. Which resource is most likely to become a major bottleneck? All components are important, but which is the best answer for a file server?

    A. Disk access speed

9. CORRECT ANSWER: A

As mentioned in a previous answer, the single most important component for a file server is the disk access speed. If the disk drive is slow, it doesn't matter how much memory you have, how fast the processor is, or how fast the network card is; the bottleneck will still be the disk drive. The only way to improve the speed would be to change the drive(s) to faster ones or possibly add more disk controllers if you are using multiple drives. By using multiple controllers, you could potentially access two disks at the same time.

10. Adam wants to implement a new application at his site and is trying to decide whether he should get the network version of the application or install standalone versions at each of the desktops. What is one advantage to installing the network version of the application?

    B. It's simple to upgrade.

10. CORRECT ANSWER: B

By using a network version of an application, the administrator would only have to install the upgrade of the application at the server. If 100 workstations and the standalone version of the application were installed, the upgrade would have to be performed at each of the 100 workstations. Some exceptions to this exist, however.

With some applications, even if the network version is installed, a substantial amount of software still is installed at the workstations. If an upgrade were installed, it would still have to be installed at each of the workstations as well. Normally though, the amount of software changes that would have to be made at the workstation would be minimal.

11. Carol is looking to implement a new application at her site and is trying to decide whether she should get the network version of the application or install standalone versions at each of the desktops. What is one advantage to installing the standalone version of the application at each of the desktops?

   D. More uptime is guaranteed.

11. CORRECT ANSWER: D

Although using the network version of an application makes it easy for upgrading the software, you face one disadvantage. If the server is down, or if communication between the workstations and the server is broken, the application can still be run if it is a standalone unit. The emphasis, of course, is to ensure that the server is up and available 100 percent of the time. However, some networks are less stable than others. In these situations, it may be advisable to have some applications installed locally.

COMPARING USER-LEVEL SECURITY WITH ACCESS PERMISSIONS

1. Windows 95 and Windows 98 systems can participate in both a peer-to-peer network and a domain. Which level of security is used in a peer-to-peer network using these types of operating systems?

   A. File-level security.

   B. Directory-level security.

   C. Share-level security.

   D. User-level security.

   E. No security exists in a peer-to-peer network.

2. You are setting up a share on your Windows NT Workstation computer to grant your coworkers access to a spreadsheet you have created. When you are setting up the permissions on the share, what kind of security can you apply?

   A. File-level security.

   B. Directory-level security.

   C. Share level-security.

   D. User level-security.

   E. No security exists in a peer-to-peer network.

3. Alex is using a Windows 98 system and will apply share-level permissions to a share he is setting up. What types of permission can he select? Choose all that apply.

   A. Full control

   B. List

   C. Change

   D. Read

   E. Format

4. Stella is using a Windows 95 system and will apply user-level permissions to a share she is setting up. From the list below, what permissions will be available for her to select? Choose all that apply.

   A. Full control

   B. List

   C. Change

   D. Read

   E. Format

5. Gord is setting up a share on his Windows NT Workstation. At what point can you assign a password to the share?

   A. Passwords can't be assigned in Windows NT.

   B. After the share has been established.

   C. After a name has been assigned to the share.

   D. After user names have been assigned to the share.

   E. Passwords can be assigned only on a Windows NT server.

6. Your small company has implemented a peer-to-peer network using Windows NT Workstations. Windows NT was chosen because it is supposed to have more security than Windows 95 or Windows 98. Each computer will have resources that each of the workers must access, but not everyone is to have the same level of control at each of the resources. If eight computers and 10 workers are present in the office, how many accounts should be created at any one computer?

    A. 8

    B. 10

    C. 1

    D. None

    E. 18

7. You had been running a peer-to-peer network using a mix of Windows 95 and Windows 98 systems, but since the company hired eight new employees, the network is now large enough to justify switching over to a domain model. Although most files to be shared will exist on the server, some people still running Windows 95/98 will want to share folders on their local drives. What kind of security will each computer have? Choose the correct answer(s).

    A. There is no security in Windows 95 or Windows 98.

    B. User-level security.

    C. Share-level security.

    D. Both user-level and share-level security.

    E. NTFS security.

8. As you are explaining to your co-op students how your Windows NT network is set up, a question arises as to how a share can tell whether you are allowed to access the resource. Which of the following is the proper explanation?

    A. The password you have provided is compared to a password list on the domain controller, and that determines your access.

    B. The access ticket is compared to the access control list on your workstation. The memberships you have are listed in the access control list, and each is designated a level of permission.

    C. The password you have provided is compared to a password list on the computer with the share, and that determines your access.

    D. The access control entries in your access token are compared to the access control list on the share. Each entry in the access control list is assigned a level of permission, and from that your level of permission is determined.

    E. The share views the access control entries of your token and requests that permission levels be assigned by the domain controller.

9. When share-level security is used, what three access permissions can the password provide?

    A. Read-only access

    B. No access

   C. Full control access

   D. Change access

   E. Read, write, and format access

10. **Many reasons exist for using share-level security, and many reasons exist for using user-level security. From the options below, select a reason for using user-level security.**

   A. It is the default level of security for Windows 95 and Windows 98 systems.

   B. Access can be assigned with a single password.

   C. More options exist as to the level of access each user is given.

   D. The passwords are case-sensitive.

   E. The user accounts can then access other computers on the network with the same permissions.

ANSWER KEY

1. C	5. A	9. A-B-C
2. D	6. B	10. C
3. A-D	7. B-C	
4. A-C-D	8. D	

COMPARING USER-LEVEL SECURITY WITH ACCESS PERMISSIONS

1. Windows 95 and Windows 98 systems can participate in both a peer-to-peer network and a domain. Which level of security is used in a peer-to-peer network using these types of operating systems?

   C. Share-level security.

1. CORRECT ANSWER: C

Windows 95 and Windows 98 can use either share-level security or user-level security if they are being used in a domain model network. If they are being used in a peer-to-peer network, no account database is used. Therefore, they can use only share-level security when setting up a share.

2. You are setting up a share on your Windows NT Workstation computer to grant your coworkers access to a spreadsheet you have created. When you are setting up the permissions on the share, what kind of security can you apply?

   D. User-level security.

2. CORRECT ANSWER: D

Windows NT always uses an account database. If the system is operating in a domain, it can use the central account database or its own local account database. If the system is operating in a peer-to-peer network, it uses the local account database when setting up the security of the share. The default group that is given permission on a share is the "everyone" group. This means that virtually anyone in the world could have full control of the contents of the share if they connected to the computer through its share.

3. Alex is using a Windows 98 system and will apply share-level permissions to a share he is setting up. What types of permission can he select? Choose all that apply.

   A. Full control
   D. Read

3. CORRECT ANSWERS: A-D

When applying permissions to a share using share-level security, the permissions that can be applied are full control, read only. In the dialog box, you can either not set a password (which grants everyone full control), or you can assign a password for one or both options.

4. Stella is using a Windows 95 system and will apply user-level permissions to a share she is setting up. What types of permission can she select? Choose all that apply.

A. Full control

C. Change

D. Read

When shares are set up using user-level security, a few extra options can be used. For one thing, more choices exist as to what permission will be assigned. The users can be given full control, change, read, or no access. Although this does not differ that much from share-level security, the bigger difference is that you can specifically assign permissions to users or groups of users with user-lever security. With share-level security, a single password is assigned either full control or read-only permission. That password is then given to those people who are to have access to the share. Passwords can be forgotten or accidentally passed on to others. With user-level security, the user logs on to the domain and is validated by the domain controller. When that user then tries to access the share, the account and group membership is compared to the access control list, and the appropriate permissions are granted to the user.

5. Gord is setting up a share on his Windows NT Workstation. At what point can you assign a password to the share?

A. Passwords can't be assigned in Windows NT.

Depending on the network configuration and the option chosen for a Windows 95 or Windows 98 system, either share-level or user-level security can be used. However, Windows NT is much more secure and, therefore, does not offer the option of using share-level security. Another part of Windows NT security is its capability to audit what takes place on each of the servers and workstations. If auditing is enabled, you could track who gains access to the different shares on a computer. That way, if files were lost or corrupted, a record would exist as to who was accessing the share. Share-level security has no audit capabilities because only a password is provided, not a username or group membership.

6. **Your small company has implemented a peer-to-peer network using Windows NT Workstations. Windows NT was chosen because it is supposed to have more security than Windows 95 or Windows 98. Each computer will have resources that each of the workers must access, but not everyone is to have the same level of control at each of the resources. If eight computers and 10 workers are present in the office, how many accounts should be created at any one computer?**

   B. 10

6. CORRECT ANSWER: B

The number of computers has nothing to do with the number of accounts that must be created for this question. Because 10 users potentially need access to the shares on any one computer, 10 accounts must be created on each computer that is to share data. Remember that the 10 accounts will have to be the same (username and password) on each of the computers; otherwise, access will be denied. So, the number of unique passwords that must be created is 10, but if each computer is to share data, the number of accounts that must be created in total is 80 (8 computers × 10 users).

7. **You had been running a peer-to-peer network using a mix of Windows 95 and Windows 98 systems, but since the company hired eight new employees, the network is now large enough to justify switching over to a domain model. Although most files to be shared will exist on the server, some people still running Windows 95/98 will want to share folders on their local drives. What kind of security will each computer have? Choose the correct answer(s).**

   B. User-level security.

   C. Share-level security.

7. CORRECT ANSWERS: B-C

Windows 95 and Windows 98 do not have the same level of security as Windows NT. One thing they can do, however, is use the account database of the domain for assigning permissions to shares. The default security for these operating systems is share-level, but after participating in a domain, the user has the option of using either share-level or user-level security. Remember, if you switch from one security level to the other, all existing shares are removed and must be re-created after the switch. This applies whether you switch from share-level to user-level, or vice versa.

8. **As you are explaining to your co-op students how your network is set up, a question arises as to how a share can tell whether you are allowed to access the resource. Which of the following is the proper explanation?**

   D. The access control entries in your access token are compared to the access control list on the share. Each entry in the access control list is assigned a level of permission, and your level of permission is determined from that.

8. CORRECT ANSWER: D

When a user logs on to a domain, the validating domain controller creates an access token for the user that contains the username and its security identification (SID). Along with this information, the controller also contains the group memberships of which this user is a member.

When the user makes a request to access a share (as in selecting a share name while browsing in Network Neighborhood or mapping a drive), the share compares the username and group memberships in the access token to the entries in its Access Control list. The Access Control list is basically a list of users and groups with corresponding access permissions. If the user's name or one of its groups is allowed to access the share, you are shown the contents of the share. If you are not in the list, you will not be granted access. One exception arises: Even if a user's name exists in the list, he could be refused entry if one of the groups is listed as "Denied Access." This permission overrides all other permissions and is positioned at the top of the list.

9. When share-level security is used, what three access permissions can the password provide?

   A. Read-only access

   B. No access

   C. Full control access

9. CORRECT ANSWERS: A-B-C

This is a bit of a trick question. Share-level security can grant permissions using only two passwords: one for read access and the other for full control. The third level of permission is that of no access. If you do not provide a correct password, you will not gain access to the share.

10. Many reasons exist for using share-level security, and many reasons exist for using user-level security. From the options below, select one reason for using user-level security.

   C. More options exist as to what level of access each user is given.

10. CORRECT ANSWER: C

By using user-level security, you gain more control over what permissions are granted to a user or group of users. In addition, by using user-level security, you can guarantee that only people who are a part of your domain gain access through the share. By using user-level security, you are also using the built-in security features of Windows NT.

COMPARING CLIENT/SERVER AND PEER-TO-PEER NETWORKS

1. Harris was working at one of the few companies left without a network. In an effort to prompt management to network the office, he put together a document stating the benefits of a network. Which of the following are such benefits? Choose all appropriate statements.

   A. A network will cost less.

   B. A network improves the speed at which an application runs on the workstation.

   C. Standalone computers are less stable than ones that are networked.

   D. Less paper is used.

   E. Communication could be improved.

2. Ed has an office of 10 people, and most users are very knowledgeable about how their computers operate and feel at ease installing their own software. At this point in time, they do not have a network but want to install one to ensure against lost data and increase security for confidential data. What type of network should Ed install?

   A. A client/server network

   B. A local area network

   C. A peer-to-peer network

   D. An Ethernet network

   E. A Token-Ring network

3. Trisha has been planning to implement a network in her office of 20 private contractors. Although each one works on his projects, the group decided to lease office space together to cut costs. Each person runs Windows NT Workstation and uses NTFS to ensure that files are secure. In addition to using Windows NT, each person has his own large-capacity external disk drive. What kind of network should Trisha implement?

   A. A client/server network

   B. A local area network

   C. A peer-to-peer network

   D. An Ethernet network

   E. A Token-Ring network

4. Janet is preparing a report on network security in a peer-to-peer network for the vice president. Her summarizing statement should state which of the following?

   A. Security is weak and is the responsibility of each user.

   B. Security is weak and is managed centrally.

   C. Security is strong and is the responsibility of each user.

   D. Security is strong and is managed centrally.

   E. Using a peer-to-peer network in a domain provides the most security.

5. **Your manager has asked you to provide reasons for moving from a peer-to-peer network to a client/server network. Although many good reasons might exist, choose the best answer from the list.**

   A. File size on Windows NT Server is larger than on Windows NT Workstation.

   B. Data backup is much simpler.

   C. Network traffic is decreased.

   D. Network traffic is increased.

   E. A central administrator will not be needed.

6. **Sharon's company has a small peer-to-peer network. A number of salespeople must be able to dial in from out-of-town locations on a regular basis. Sharon has been put in charge of determining the needs for a RAS (remote access service) server for the network. Choose the best option for her company.**

   A. Convert the network to a client/server network, and install the RAS software on the primary domain controller.

   B. Set up a Windows NT workstation as the RAS server on the current network.

   C. Convert the network to a client/server network, and install the RAS software on a Windows NT workstation.

   D. Convert the network to a client/server network, and install the RAS software on a Windows NT server.

   E. Set up a Windows NT server as the RAS server on the current network.

7. **The security for a Windows 95 or Windows 98 peer-to-peer network differs slightly from a Windows NT peer-to-peer network. How does the security differ? Choose the correct answer(s).**

   A. When share-level security is used in Windows 95 and 98, two passwords can be set, whereas in Windows NT three passwords can be set.

   B. Passwords cannot be assigned to shares in Windows NT.

   C. Users must log on to both Windows 95/98 and Windows NT computers in a peer-to-peer network to gain access to the network.

   D. Users must log on to both Windows 95/98 and Windows NT computers in a peer-to-peer network to gain access to the computer.

   E. No difference exists in the security between Windows 95/98 and Windows NT.

8. **Albert is preparing a report on network security in a client/server network for the vice president. His summarizing statement should support which of the following?**

   A. Security is weak and is the responsibility of each user.

   B. Security is weak and is managed centrally.

   C. Security is strong and is the responsibility of each user.

   D. Security is strong and is managed centrally.

   E. Using a peer-to-peer network in a domain provides the most security.

9. Share-level and user-level securities are forms of security that can be applied to shares. Choose the appropriate operating systems that can use share-level security.

    A. Windows NT Server

    B. Windows NT Workstation

    C. Windows 95

    D. Windows 98

    E. All of the above

10. Share-level and user-level securities are forms of security that can be applied to shares. Choose the appropriate operating systems that can use user-level security.

    A. Windows NT Server

    B. Windows NT Workstation

    C. Windows 95

    D. Windows 98

    E. All of the above

ANSWER KEY

1. A-D-E	5. B	9. C-D
2. A	6. E	10. E
3. C	7. B-C	
4. A	8. D	

ANSWERS & EXPLANATIONS

COMPARING CLIENT/SERVER AND PEER-TO-PEER NETWORKS

1. Harris was working at one of the few companies left without a network. In an effort to get management to network the office, he put together a document stating the benefits of a network. Which of the following are such benefits? Choose all the appropriate statements.

   A. A network will cost less.

   D. Less paper is used.

   E. Communication could be improved.

1. CORRECT ANSWERS: A-D-E

When a network is thoroughly planned and implemented, it should provide a cost savings. Of course, there is the initial start-up cost for network cards, cabling, and a server (if it is to be a client/server network), but once the network is installed, better productivity should arise for those that are on the network.

In the case of a local area network, data may be shared without having to put the information on disk and carry it between computers. Instead of needing multiple printers or one printer with a manual switch box, one printer can be connected to the network and can handle all the print jobs. Messages can be sent to one another, and meetings and appointments can be scheduled. Because messages can be sent to one another, this not only saves time and hopefully improves inter-office communication, but it also saves paper.

With a network, both intra- and inter-office messaging can be implemented, which would enable the employees to communicate among themselves and with other businesses more efficiently. Therefore, the cost of setting up the network should be recovered in a very short time by the increase in productivity.

2. Ed has an office of 10 people, and most users are very knowledgeable about how their computers operate and feel at ease installing their own software. At this point in time, they do not have a network but want to install one to ensure against lost data and increase security for confidential data. What type of network should Ed install?

   A. A client/server network

2. CORRECT ANSWER: A

A peer-to-peer network is designed for small networks without a central administrator. In this example, it appears that both of these conditions are met.

The users are comfortable with installing software and configuring their computers. However, the point made in this question is that the users want to improve security and prevent loss of data. A client/server network is more secure than a peer-to-peer network. In addition to being more secure, tape backups of a central server can be simpler to perform than ensuring that each user is performing his own backups. For this simple reason, it would be better to set up a client/server network.

3. Trisha has been planning to implement a network in her office of 20 private contractors. Although each one works on his own projects, the group decided to lease office space together to cut costs. Each person runs Windows NT Workstation and uses NTFS to ensure that files are secure. In addition to using Windows NT, each person has his own large-capacity external disk drive. What kind of network should Trisha implement?

C. A peer-to-peer network

3. CORRECT ANSWER: C

This network could be either a client/server or a peer-to-peer network, but it is probably simpler to set it up as a peer-to-peer network. This involves a group of people with unrelated tasks and data. Therefore, it would be difficult to determine a good directory structure that would meet all their needs.

The network will enable the users to send messages and schedule meetings and appointments if necessary, but they don't really need a central repository. The difference between this question and the previous one is that each person has his own large-capacity external drive, which could be used for backing up his own data.

Furthermore, the users are all running Windows NT on their computers, so they should be able to maintain a high degree of security.

4. Janet is preparing a report on network security in a peer-to-peer network for the vice president. Her summarizing statement should state which of the following?

A. Security is weak and is the responsibility of each user.

4. CORRECT ANSWER: A

A peer-to-peer network provides connectivity between computers but does not provide any kind of security or central administration. The users of a peer-to-peer network must/should be knowledgeable on how to secure their data and how to configure their computers.

Because no central administration exists, software installation, computer configuration, and general maintenance of each computer will often fall on each user. This type of network fails and can really cause a lot of difficulty if a few weak users continually have problems with their computers.

When Windows 95/98 are used in a peer-to-peer network, very little security can occur. If someone came up to a computer and did not log on to the network, he could still access the local disk drives. Additionally, because no file or folder security exists on these operating systems, everything is wide open to whomever sits in front of the computer. At least Windows NT systems force users to log on to the computer. If a proper username and password are not provided, the person is denied access.

Still, without a central file server, you face the problem of backing up data. If each computer is provided with a tape backup unit or large-capacity external drive, there is at least the possibility that each user may back up data.

5. Your manager has asked you to provide reasons for moving from a peer-to-peer network to a client/server network. Although many good reasons might exist, choose the best answer from the list.

    B. Data backup is much simpler.

5. CORRECT ANSWER: B

As mentioned in the last question, a peer-to-peer network depends on each of the users to ensure that his own data is secure and backed up. In a client/server network, a tape backup unit can be set up on the file server, and regular daily backups can be scheduled. In this case, as long as the users store their files on the server, their data will be backed up.

6. Sharon's company has a small peer-to-peer network. A number of salespeople must be able to dial in from out-of-town locations on a regular basis. Sharon has been put in charge of determining the needs for a RAS (remote access service) server for the network. Choose the best option for her company.

    E. Set up a Windows NT server as the RAS server on the current network.

6. CORRECT ANSWER: E

Most operating systems can be set up as dial-in servers, so the big question is which would be the best choice. First of all, you want to be using Windows NT as your dial-in server because it provides more security than Windows 95 or Windows 98. Secondly, you will probably want to use Windows NT Server for the dial-in server rather than Windows NT Workstation. This is because Windows NT Server offers a maximum of 256 concurrent dial-in lines, whereas Windows NT Workstation can accommodate only one dial-in line at any one time.

Because a number of sales staff may need to dial in at different times, you will probably want to be able to set up more than one dial-in line.

7. The security for a Windows 95 or Windows 98 peer-to-peer network differs slightly from a Windows NT peer-to-peer network. How does the security differ? Choose the correct answer(s).

B. Passwords cannot be assigned to shares in Windows NT.

C. Users must log on to both Windows 95/98 and Windows NT computers in a peer-to-peer network to gain access to the network.

7. CORRECT ANSWERS: B-C

Although both Windows 95 and Windows 98 can use either share-level security or user-level security, Windows NT can use only user-level security. This is due to the higher level of security that Windows NT provides. Because share-level security is not very secure, Windows NT does not have that as an option.

Another part of Windows NT's high level of security is that the user must provide a valid username and password to gain access to the computer. This is true even if the user simply wants to access the local drive. In the case of Windows 95 and Windows 98, a username and password must be provided if the user wishes to gain access to the network.

If users just want to access the local disk drive, they could simply cancel out of the logon dialog box and then would have access to everything on the local drives. Exceptions to this exist when the network administrator has "locked down" the computers: In this case, *locked down* infers that the administrator has configured the user's computers so that only administrators can make changes to such things as screen resolution, install software, format disks, and so on. In this case, the user would have to know what the administrator did to bypass the security.

8. Albert is preparing a report on network security in a client/server network for the vice president. His summarizing statement should support which of the following?

D. Security is strong and is managed centrally.

8. CORRECT ANSWER: D

In a client/server network, the account database is located on a central server. Therefore, if someone wants to gain access to the network and the user's data, he would have to provide a valid username and password. This would be true for any operating system.

Because the user accounts are centrally located and all the data is stored on a central file server, the accounts and data can be better managed. User accounts can be created, disabled, or deleted whenever needed. Group memberships can also be assigned according to departments or workgroups. When the directory structure is in place, the appropriate permissions can be assigned so that only those with the need to access them have the permission to do so.

After the data is in place, it can be backed up by a central backup unit. This can be scheduled to take place at a time when very little activity is taking place on the network.

9. Share-level and user-level securities are forms of security that can be applied to shares. Choose the appropriate operating systems that can use share-level security.

   C. Windows 95
   D. Windows 98

9. CORRECT ANSWERS: C-D

Windows 95 and Windows 98 are the only operating systems that can use share-level security. These systems can operate with network systems that provide a higher level of security, but by themselves, they use the less secure share-level security.

EXAM TIP

Share-level security is generally considered to be a lower level of security, but if the user follows some basic guidelines, this method can still provide decent security. For starters, give the password(s) only to those who need access to your data, do not write the password(s) on a piece of paper, remove the share when the person has finished using your data, and change the password(s) often if the share must be maintained for any length of time. This may seem like a lot of extra work, but it can protect data.

10. Share-level and user-level securities are forms of security that can be applied to shares. Choose the appropriate operating systems that can use user-level security.

   E. All of the above

10. CORRECT ANSWER: E

As mentioned earlier, Windows NT can use only user-level security to maintain its high level of security. Windows 95 and Windows 98 both default to using share-level security but may be configured to use user-level security if they are operating in a domain. As long as the system is configured to be a member of a domain, users can then access the account database for assigning permissions to shares.

EXAM TIP

If you are using Windows 95 or Windows 98 and you plan to switch from share-level security to user-level security, any existing shares will be removed. If these shares are needed, you must re-create them. This happens whether you are switching from user-level to share-level security, or vice versa.

COMPARING CONNECTION-ORIENTED AND CONNECTIONLESS COMMUNICATIONS

1. You are administering a local area network with about 55 users logged on at any one time. You are using a 16Mbps Token-Ring architecture with all the computers on one segment. Management has questioned what is meant by connection-oriented communication versus connectionless communication. Choose the best explanation.

   A. Connection-oriented communication occurs when the computers are directly connected to each other.

   B. Connectionless communication is another term for a dial-up connection between a remote computer and a RAS server.

   C. Connectionless communication refers to any kind of communication that does not use a physical link, such as infrared, satellite, and so on.

   D. Connection-oriented communication refers to guaranteed delivery of data packets.

   E. Connection-oriented communication is used only with the IPX/SPX protocol.

2. Karen is trying to improve the performance of her network. She read that connectionless communication is faster than connection-oriented communication, and

   she wants to control which method is to be used. How can she do this? Choose the best answer.

   A. Switch protocol to NetBEUI.

   B. Switch protocol to TCP/IP.

   C. Split the network into multiple subnets.

   D. She cannot determine which means of communication will be used.

   E. Switch to using Token-Ring on her network.

3. TCP/IP is not a single protocol but is actually a suite of protocols. Some of those protocols use connection-oriented communication, whereas others use connectionless communication. Select the protocol that is connection-oriented.

   A. Transport Control Protocol

   B. Network Basic Input/Output System

   C. User Datagram Protocol

   D. Internetwork Packet Exchange

   E. File Transfer Protocol

4. Jim is trying to determine how connection-oriented communication guarantees the delivery of each data packet. How is this done? Select the best answer(s).

   A. The address of the destination computer is included with each packet.

B. A 20-second delay takes place between each packet sent to allow the packet to arrive at the destination before the next packet is sent.

C. Packets are sequentially numbered before they are sent.

D. Once all the packets are received at the destination, a reply is sent to the transmitting computer.

E. Each packet is sent with a special header and trailer code that will not allow the packet to be lost.

5. **Because connection-oriented communication guarantees the delivery of data packets, why wouldn't it be used all the time?**

A. The network bandwidth would become so flooded by replies to data being sent that the network could be brought to a halt.

B. Some messages are general in nature and do not need to be guaranteed.

C. Connection-oriented communication is too fast for some applications and will cause the application to fail.

D. Connection-oriented communication is too slow for some applications and will cause the application to fail.

E. Connection-oriented communication can be used only in a Token-Ring network.

6. **Connectionless communication is a very general term. Which of the following is a common type of connectionless communication that takes place on a local area network?**

A. Named pipes

B. Remote Procedure Calls

C. Server Message Blocks

D. Broadcasts

E. Network Basic Input/Output System

7. **Connectionless communication is faster than connection-oriented communication, but some disadvantages exist. What are the drawbacks to using it? Choose the correct answer(s).**

A. Connectionless communication works best through indirect links such as infrared, satellite, and so on.

B. Connectionless communication works best with line speeds of 10Mbps or less.

C. Not all network cards can receive connectionless communication packets.

D. Special cabling is needed for connectionless communication.

E. Delivery of data is not guaranteed.

8. **Mark has read and discovered first-hand that connection-oriented communication is slower than connectionless communication, but he doesn't know why. Choose the best answer as to why connection-oriented communication is slower.**

A. The connection-oriented protocols travel across the wire slower than connectionless protocols.

B. The computers must perform a handshake to complete a communication session.

C. The connection-oriented data packets contain more information, and therefore, take longer to process than a connectionless data packet.

D. The connectionless communication data packet contains the handshake information. Therefore, fewer packets have to be sent back and forth.

E. Connection-oriented packets must go up the entire protocol stack to the recipient computer, whereas the connectionless packet must travel only to the physical layer.

9. **Chuck has often heard of the term *data streaming* used in conjunction with data communication. Choose the most correct definition for the term *data streaming*.**

A. Streaming refers to the direction in which data is traveling. Once streaming has started, data cannot travel in the other direction until the stream stops.

B. Data streaming occurs when the data bits are sent across the wire at a speed in excess of 16Mbps.

C. A data stream occurs when sequential packets of data are sent out onto the wire.

D. A data stream occurs when a group of data packets is sent out onto the wire and a reply must be received before the next group of packets is sent.

E. Streaming occurs when the Transport Control Protocol sends data packets directly to the recipient.

10. **Martha understands the difference in speed between connection-oriented communication and connectionless communication, but she feels there must be other differences between the two as well. What might these differences be? Select the correct statement(s).**

A. Although the packets are assembled differently, both forms of communication guarantee the delivery of each data packet.

B. Connectionless communication provides error-checking at the end of each data stream.

C. Connection-oriented communication provides error-checking, whereas connectionless communication does not.

D. The TCP/IP protocol suite contains protocols for both connection-oriented communication and connectionless communication.

E. A wide area network uses only connectionless communication.

ANSWER KEY

1. D	5. B	9. C
2. D	6. D	10. C-D
3. A	7. E	
4. A	8. B	

COMPARING CONNECTION-ORIENTED AND CONNECTIONLESS COMMUNICATIONS

1. You are administering a local area network with about 55 users logged on at any one time. You are using a 16Mbps Token-Ring architecture with all the computers on one segment. Management has questioned what is meant by connection-oriented communication versus connectionless communication. Choose the best explanation.

   D. Connection-oriented communication refers to guaranteed delivery of data packets.

1. CORRECT ANSWER: D

Connection-oriented communication uses a process to guarantee that each recipient receives all the data that was transmitted. If the transmitting computer does not receive an acknowledgment of the data being received within a certain period of time, it re-sends the packet(s) and doubles the amount of time that it should take to be received. By doing so, communication becomes slower but is guaranteed. This process takes place no matter what type of links are used or how far the distance is.

2. Karen is trying to improve the performance of her network. She read that connectionless communication is faster than connection-oriented communication, and she wants to control which method is to be used. How can she do this? Choose the best answer.

   D. She cannot determine which means of communication will be used.

2. CORRECT ANSWER: D

For the most part, there is no control over which method of communication is being used. In most cases, the application is written to use one type of protocol. When the user carries out a command in the application, it is the application that makes the request for which type of communication will be used. However, some (very few) applications may enable the user to switch from one type of communication to another.

3. TCP/IP is not a single protocol but is actually a suite of protocols. Some of those protocols use connection-oriented communication, whereas others use connectionless communication. Select the protocol that is connection-oriented.

   A. Transport Control Protocol

3. CORRECT ANSWER: A

As its name implies the Transport Control Protocol (TCP) controls the communication and guarantees the transmission of the packets. Its alter-ego is User Datagram Protocol (UDP), a connectionless protocol that is a part of the TCP/IP suite. This protocol is much faster, but does not guarantee that the recipient(s) will receive the data.

4. Jim is trying to determine how connection-oriented communication guarantees the delivery of each data packet. How is this done? Select the best answer(s).

    A. The address of the destination computer is included with each packet.

4. CORRECT ANSWER: A

Each packet contains the address of the recipient computer. Even if the packets get out of sequence by traveling different routes to reach the same destination, all packets should end up at the destination. As the packets are received, the destination computer sends acknowledgments back to the transmitting computer. After a sequence of acknowledgments has been received, the transmitting computer then sends the next group of packets. If acknowledgments are not received after a certain period of time, the packets are re-sent and the waiting period is doubled. This takes place a number of times until finally a message is sent to the sender that the data cannot be delivered.

5. Because connection-oriented communication guarantees the delivery of data packets, why wouldn't it be used all of the time?

    B. Some messages are general in nature and do not need to be guaranteed.

5. CORRECT ANSWER: B

Not all messages have to be received by all computers. When logging on to the network, it is important that the validating server receives your request to log on. However, if you have a monitoring application running on one server and its sole function is to verify that the server is running, it will not matter if one or two polling cycles is missed.

6. Connectionless communication is a very general term. Which of the following is a common type of connectionless communication that takes place on a local area network?

    D. Broadcasts

6. CORRECT ANSWER: D

If you look at a local area network, both connection-oriented communication and connectionless communication occur. An example of connection-oriented communication takes place when you make a request to send a print job to a printer on the network. The request is sent directly to the print server. A response is then sent back to the requesting computer to acknowledge the request.

A broadcast message is a good example of connectionless communication. When a master browser must be determined, all computers that are capable of acting as a master browser broadcast a message to all other computers stating their criteria. It does not matter whether all the computers receive the message because the election takes place with the ones that did receive the message.

7. Connectionless communication is faster than connection-oriented communication, but some disadvantages exist. What are the drawbacks to using it? Choose the correct answer(s).

    E. Delivery of data is not guaranteed.

7. CORRECT ANSWER: E

Because connectionless communication does not have to wait for a response from the recipient computer(s), the time it takes to send a message is much less. In addition, the size of the packets is also smaller because this type of communication does not require as much header and trailer information.

8. Mark has read and discovered first-hand that connection-oriented communication is slower than connectionless communication, but he doesn't know why. Choose the best answer as to why connection-oriented communication is slower.

    B. The computers must perform a handshake to complete a communication session.

8. CORRECT ANSWER: B

The handshake that takes place between computers is the process in which a computer sends a message and the recipient computer sends an acknowledgment that a session is being established. The sending computer then starts to send the message and continues to wait for acknowledgments after each group of packets is sent.

9. Chuck has often heard of the term *data streaming* used in conjunction with data communication. Choose the most correct definition for the term *data streaming*.

    C. A data stream occurs when sequential packets of data are sent out onto the wire.

9. CORRECT ANSWER: C

Connectionless communication can take advantage of data streaming because it does not have to wait for an acknowledgment before it can continue to send packets out onto the wire.

10. Martha understands the difference in speed between connection-oriented communication and connectionless communication, but she feels there must be other differences between the two as well. What might these differences be? Select the correct statement(s).

    C. Connection-oriented communication provides error-checking, whereas connectionless communication does not.

    D. The TCP/IP protocol suite contains protocols for both connection-oriented communication and connectionless communication.

10. CORRECT ANSWERS: C-D

Although connectionless communication is faster than connection-oriented communication, it does not guarantee the delivery of the packets. Therefore, connectionless communication also does not have any means for checking the integrity of the data. Even if the data does arrive at the destination, it may not be in a form that can be read. In the case of a computer trying to resolve a computer name using UDP, it broadcasts to the network by default and waits a period of time for a positive response. If no response is received, it broadcasts two more times before giving up on the name resolution.

Although both TCP and UDP are part of the TCP/IP protocol suite, that does not mean they are the same protocol. They are very different in the way they operate but are grouped together because they use the same addressing scheme as the rest of the TCP/IP suite.

DISTINGUISHING BETWEEN SLIP AND PPP

1. **Your computer has remote access dial-up utilizing TCP/IP. However, you must input your IP address manually. What dial-up protocol are you using?**

   A. TCP/IP

   B. UDP/IP

   C. SLIP

   D. PPP

   E. ICMP

2. **Mary has heard of and used both SLIP and PPP but is not certain where PPTP (Point-to-Point Transport Protocol) fits in. Select the correct answer to her quandary.**

   A. PPTP is a higher-speed version of PPP.

   B. PPTP is a tunneling protocol that uses PPP to establish a secure link to a remote LAN over the Internet.

   C. PPTP is an Internet protocol that uses PPP for secured transactions such as banking and credit card usage.

   D. PPTP is a version of PPP that can employ multiple phone lines for a higher-speed connection.

   E. PPTP is a new member of the TCP/IP protocol that is being positioned to replace the older Transport Control Protocol.

3. **Karl is in the process of having his three offices connected via 56KB ISDN lines. Which serial-link protocol should he use?**

   A. PPP

   B. CSLIP

   C. SLIP

   D. HDLC

   E. TCP/IP

4. **Two main serial link protocols exist: SLIP and PPP. However, another protocol, called CSLIP, is a hybrid form of SLIP. What advantage does CSLIP have over SLIP?**

   A. CSLIP is a new form of SLIP to support faster modems.

   B. CSLIP is a version of SLIP with data correction built-in to maintain data integrity.

   C. CSLIP is a new form of SLIP to support features in PPP.

   D. CSLIP is a version of SLIP with compression.

   E. CSLIP is a version of SLIP with a carrier-detect bit attached to the end of each data packet.

5. **Windows NT is capable of using a feature called *multi-link* to improve communication with other systems. How is multi-link implemented?**

   A. SLIP connections utilizing multiple communications links in parallel

   B. PPP connections utilizing multiple communications links in parallel

C. Multiple Internet protocols running across the same communications link

D. Multiple communication links to a number of different systems at the same time

E. Multiple protocols used over the single communication link

6. **DHCP is a service that enables a server to automatically assign IP addresses to client computers. Paul wants to ensure that all the clients dialing in use DHCP to have their addresses assigned to them. Which dial-in protocol should he make sure that the clients are *not* using?**

   A. SLIP

   B. PPP

   C. HDLC

   D. TCP/IP

   E. UDP/IP

7. **A number of clients want to be able to dial in and gain access to the NetWare Server on the network. Which dial-in protocol should the clients *not* be using if they wish to access the NetWare Server?**

   A. PPTP

   B. PPP

   C. SDLC

   D. TCP/IP

   E. SLIP

8. **Darryl wants to improve the speed of the dial-in connection to her Internet Service Provider. She is currently using a 56KB internal modem in her Windows 95**

computer, **which is the same type of modem that her provider is using. What are valid options for Darryl to consider?**

   A. Install a 126KB external modem.

   B. Install a second 56KB modem and set up multi-link with her ISP.

   C. Add more memory to the modem.

   D. Install an ISDN line between her home and her Internet Service Provider.

   E. Switch to the PPTP protocol.

9. **Barry wants to connect to the office network, which uses AppleTalk as the protocol. The Remote Access Server also acts as the file server for this small network. Which dial-in protocols should Barry use to access his files?**

   A. Ethertalk

   B. PPP

   C. SLIP

   D. CSLIP

   E. PPTP

10. **Depending on the dial-in protocol used, the user may or may not have to input the IP address manually. If the address does have to be input manually, how could this be automated?**

   A. The IP address is automatically entered regardless of the protocol; it just depends on the Internet Service Provider.

   B. This could be automated by installing DHCP on your dial-in computer.

C. A script file can be created that automatically enters the IP address.

D. The web browser application that you run after you are connected can provide the IP address.

E. Windows 95, Windows 98, and Windows NT all have a pool of addresses to which they default if they are not provided with one after they have established a connection.

ANSWER KEY

1. C	5. B	9. B-C-D-E
2. B	6. A	10. C
3. A	7. E	
4. D	8. D	

ANSWERS & EXPLANATIONS

DISTINGUISHING BETWEEN SLIP AND PPP

1. Your computer has remote access dial-up utilizing TCP/IP. However, you must input your IP address manually. What dial-up protocol are you using?

    C. SLIP

1. CORRECT ANSWER: C

Of the items listed, only two are truly dial-up protocols: SLIP and PPP. SLIP is the older protocol and has been the industry standard for many years. When it was first developed, the computers that were being used at the time did not have a means to automatically assign IP addresses to dial-in computers. Therefore, the dial-in user would be provided with an IP address.

When the users dialed in, they would have to manually enter the IP address to be able to communicate with the dial-in server. Of course, at that time there weren't as many people trying to use wide area networks or access the Internet. Because of the relatively few people needing IP addresses, it was not difficult to assign IP addresses to individuals. With so many computers all trying to access the Internet now, the IP addresses must be rotated among users.

PPP enables the server to automatically assign an IP address to a computer when it dials in. When users finish their session, they break their connection to the server, and the IP address can then be assigned to the next user who dials in. This ensures better use of the existing IP addresses, and the users do not have to be concerned with entering the IP address correctly (it is automatically done for them).

2. Mary has heard of and used both SLIP and PPP but is not certain where PPTP (Point-to-Point Transport Protocol) fits in. Select the correct answer to her quandary.

    B. PPTP is a tunneling protocol that uses PPP to establish a secure link to a remote LAN over the Internet.

2. CORRECT ANSWER: B

PPP is a dial-in protocol that was developed to improve the current standard of SLIP. As more companies were connecting to the Internet, a number realized that they could cut costs by using the existing telephone lines to connect their wide area network if they could do their network business via their Internet connection. Because such a company was already paying a monthly bill to have a high-speed Internet connection

(ISDN, T1, or T3), it thought that surely there should be a way to use the existing line for connecting its distributed network.

The protocol that was developed is called PPTP, or Point-to-Point Transport Protocol. PPTP uses the PPP protocol to establish a connection to the Internet Service Provider and, in turn, to the other segments of your network while providing security through *tunneling*. PPTP uses encrypted PPP packets, which are then sent over the TCP/IP-based Internet to remote sites. Because PPP is protocol-independent, just about any network can use the Internet to connect remote sites. Because the packets are securely encrypted and encapsulated before being sent to the desired computers, this creates a tunnel or virtual private network (VPN).

3. **Karl is in the process of having his three offices connected via 56KB ISDN lines. Which serial-link protocol should he use?**

   A. PPP

3. CORRECT ANSWER: A

PPP is really the only choice unless the dial-in server he is using accepts only SLIP connections. Otherwise, the choice would always be to use the newer and more user-friendly PPP. SLIP is the old industry standard that PPP was designed to replace. For example, Windows NT can operate as a PPP RAS server that accepts SLIP clients. However, this server cannot act as a SLIP server. PPP is also more secure than SLIP in that SLIP sends passwords as clear text, and PPP can encrypt them.

4. **Two main serial link protocols exist: SLIP and PPP. However, another protocol, called CSLIP, is a hybrid form of SLIP. What advantage does CSLIP have over SLIP?**

   D. CSLIP is a version of SLIP with compression.

4. CORRECT ANSWER: D

Although it is not commonly used, CSLIP is another available version of SLIP. CSLIP was developed to make the transfer of data across the dial-in line more efficient and quicker. This was to be accomplished by compressing the packets that were to be sent across the wire. PPP became more popular because it provides more features that enhance its operation.

5. Windows NT is capable of using a feature called *multi-link* to improve communication with other systems. How is multi-link implemented?

   B. PPP connections utilizing multiple communications links in parallel

---

5. CORRECT ANSWER: B

With Windows NT 4.0 and higher versions, dial-in lines can be run in parallel. If the multi-link option is selected and two modems of equal speed are installed at both the client and server, communication speed can be increased by 200 percent. Of course, two separate telephone lines must also be available.

---

6. DHCP is a service that enables a server to automatically assign IP addresses to client computers. Paul wants to ensure that all the clients dialing in will use DHCP to have their addresses assigned to them. Which dial-in protocol should he make sure that the clients are *not* using?

   A. SLIP

---

6. CORRECT ANSWER: A

PPP is a newer dial-in protocol that enables the server to automatically assign IP addresses to client computers. The protocol that PPP has replaced as the industry standard is SLIP. This protocol does not have the capability to be automatically configured. The only thing a user can do is create a script that configures the client with the assigned IP address during dial-up.

---

7. A number of clients want to be able to dial in and gain access to the NetWare Server on the network. Which dial-in protocol should the clients *not* be using if they wish to access the NetWare Server?

   E. SLIP

---

7. CORRECT ANSWER: E

This question does not provide a great deal of information, but if read carefully, it contains sufficient information to suggest the correct answer. Normally, when a client dials in from a PPP client to a Windows NT RAS server, it doesn't matter what protocol is being used on the network.

This is because the RAS server can enable the dial-in client to use whatever protocol is needed. However, when SLIP is used, protocol translation is not provided. So in the question, a large number of NetWare servers operate with the IPX/SPX protocol and, therefore, the client would not be able to access it.

---

8. Darryl wants to improve the speed of the dial-in connection to her Internet Service Provider. She is currently using a 56KB internal modem in her Windows 95 computer, which is the same type of modem that her provider is using. What are valid options for Darryl to consider?

   D. Install an ISDN line between her home and her Internet Service Provider.

---

8. CORRECT ANSWER: D

In this situation, not many options exist. Adding memory will not make much difference to your communication speed. Your service provider may set up multi-link so that you can try running in parallel to it, but most providers do not use Windows NT Server as dial-in systems. Therefore, the only realistic option would be to have a high-speed line installed between your home and your provider. This may be cost-prohibitive depending on your needs, but it is the only real option for increasing your Internet access speed.

9. Barry wants to connect to the office network, which uses AppleTalk as the protocol. The Remote Access Server also acts as the file server for this small network. Which dial-in protocol(s) should Barry use to access his files?

   B. PPP

   C. SLIP

   D. CSLIP

   E. PPTP

10. Depending on the dial-in protocol used, the user may or may not have to input the IP address manually. If the address does have to be input manually, how could this be automated?

   C. A script file can be created that automatically enters the IP address.

9. CORRECT ANSWERS: B-C-D-E

Because the file server is the dial-in server, the clients have to connect only to that server, not the rest of the network. Because the dial-in clients do not need to access any other computers on the network, they do not need to have the protocol used on the network. Whether IPX/SPX, AppleTalk, or any other protocol is being used, it will not make a difference to the dial-in clients.

10. CORRECT ANSWER: C

Because SLIP does not have the capability to automatically receive IP addresses from the server, the user must configure the computer at the time of dial-in. To automate this process, the user can create a script that configures the client computer each time it dials into the server.

DEFINING THE COMMUNICATION DEVICES OF THE OSI MODEL

1. Joe has been studying the OSI model and learning what each layer does from the bottom up. He is now at the Presentation layer and is trying to remember what takes place at this layer. What does the Presentation layer do?

   A. It presents data to the user.

   B. It presents data to the application.

   C. It prepares the data for the applications.

   D. It presents a uniform data format to the Application layer.

   E. It does all of the above.

2. Stan is trying to troubleshoot a problem he is having with his server losing data on the network. After analyzing the network traffic using Network Monitor, he has discovered that very large packets are seemingly being sent out onto the wire. Which layer of the OSI is responsible for breaking large messages into smaller, more manageable packets?

   A. Network

   B. Physical

   C. Data Link

   D. Session

   E. Transport

3. As you are working through which physical components communicate at each layer of the OSI model, you have finally come to the Application layer. So far, you have dealt with cables, routers, bridges, network cards, and the like. Now that you are at the Application layer, you are trying to determine what physical device is being used when you run an application on a Microsoft Terminal Server. Select the appropriate device.

   A. Hub

   B. Router

   C. Network card

   D. Gateway

   E. Computer

4. Most layers of the OSI model recognize and work with frames of data that are transmitted between the computers. Which layer of the OSI does not recognize data frames?

   A. Physical

   B. Data Link

   C. Media Access Control

   D. Logical Link Control

   E. Network

5. Before any data can be transmitted from one computer to another, computer names and security must be established. This process of establishing a connection between the two computers takes place at which layer?

   A. Network

   B. Session

   C. Transport

   D. Application

   E. Presentation

6. Alice is having a problem with data not being sent to the proper destinations from her computer. After analyzing the data that is output from her computer, she has determined that the packets are not being addressed correctly. Which layer is responsible for addressing messages and translating names and logical addresses into physical addresses?

   A. Physical

   B. Transport

   C. Network

   D. Data Link

   E. Session

7. The redirector is sometimes also called the workstation service of a networked computer. This device makes requests for access to folders and files on other computers on the network. In which layer of the OSI is the redirector found?

   A. Network

   B. Data Link

   C. Session

   D. Presentation

   E. Transport

8. As the name implies, the Application layer would seem to be the layer that is directly available to the applications on the computer. However, what exactly does the Application layer expose to the applications?

   A. Network APIs

   B. Transport protocols

   C. Application protocols

   D. An interface to the computers that already have sessions established

   E. A data path through the Presentation layer

9. The OSI model is designed so that each layer operates as if it were communicating directly with the same layer on the other computer. Which is the only layer that can actually send information directly to its corresponding layer on another computer?

   A. No layer can send information directly to the other computer.

   B. The Network layer.

   C. The Physical layer.

   D. The Data Link layer.

   E. The Session layer.

10. As the frames are passed from one layer to the next, information is added to the frame to control where the frame is to be sent, where it came from, and so on. A cyclical redundancy check (CRC) is also

added to the frame to ensure that the frame is received properly at the destination computer. Which layer provides the cyclical redundancy check to prevent data errors?

A. The Data Link layer

B. The Network layer

C. The Physical layer

D. The Transport layer

E. The Session layer

11. The IEEE 802 project enhanced the then-current OSI model. Instead of adding an eighth layer to the seven-layer model, IEEE 802 simply added two sublayers to one of the existing layers. Which layer had the Media Access Control and Logical Link Control sublayers added to it?

A. The Physical Layer

B. The Data Link layer

C. The Network layer

D. The Transport layer

E. The Session layer

12. Most devices are capable of using only one layer of the OSI model. One device, however, is capable of using all seven layers of the OSI model. Select the device that can use all seven layers of the OSI model.

A. Brouter

B. Modem

C. Bridge

D. Router

E. Gateway

ANSWER KEY

1. D	6. C	11. B
2. E	7. D	12. E
3. E	8. A	
4. A	9. C	
5. B	10. A	

DEFINING THE COMMUNICATION DEVICES OF THE OSI MODEL

1. Joe has been studying the OSI model and learning what each layer does from the bottom up. He is now at the Presentation layer and is trying to remember what takes place at this layer. What does the Presentation layer do?

   D. It presents a uniform data format to the Application layer.

1. CORRECT ANSWER: D

As the packets come up the stack, the Presentation layer translates the intermediary format that was used for transporting the packet back into a format that the Application layer can use. This layer also encrypts data, converts character sets, expands graphic commands, and manages data compression.

2. Stan is trying to troubleshoot a problem he is having with his server losing data on the network. After analyzing the network traffic using Network Monitor, he has discovered that very large packets are seemingly being sent out onto the wire. Which layer of the OSI is responsible for breaking large messages into smaller, more manageable packets?

   E. Transport

2. CORRECT ANSWER: E

The Transport layer ensures that packets are sent error-free, and it also repackages messages. If the package is too large, this layer divides the message into a number of smaller packages before it is sent. The receiving computer gathers these packages and reassembles them. After the packages are reassembled, the Transport layer typically sends an acknowledgment of receipt.

3. As you are working through which physical components communicate at each layer of the OSI model, you have finally come to the Application layer. So far you have dealt with cables, routers, bridges, network cards, and the like. Now that you are at the Application layer, you are trying to determine what physical device is being used when you run an application on a Microsoft Terminal Server. Select the appropriate device.

   E. Computer

3. CORRECT ANSWER: E

The Application layer provides a set of network APIs to the application on the computer. The only device used to run an application is the computer itself.

4. Most layers of the OSI model recognize and work with frames of data that are transmitted between the computers. Which layer of the OSI does not recognize data frames?

   A. Physical

4. CORRECT ANSWER: A

The Physical layer of the OSI model does not recognize data frames because it deals with the bits sent across the wire. After the data passes up from the Physical layer, the frames are reassembled.

5. Before any data can be transmitted from one computer to another, computer names and security must be established. This process of establishing a connection between the two computers takes place at which layer?

   B. Session

5. CORRECT ANSWER: B

As the name of the layer implies, the Session layer is the one that tries to establish a session between the two computers. Security and name recognition are performed at this layer before data is actually transmitted back and forth.

As the data is transmitted, this layer inserts checkpoints to indicate where receipt of data has been acknowledged. If connection is lost between the two computers, only data following the last checkpoint must be re-sent.

6. Alice is having a problem with data not being sent to the proper destinations from her computer. After analyzing the data that is output from her computer, she has determined that the packets are not being addressed correctly. Which layer is responsible for addressing messages and translating names and logical addresses into physical addresses?

   C. Network

6. CORRECT ANSWER: C

The Network layer is responsible for translating a logical address on the transmitting computer into the physical address of the destination computer. At the destination computer, the Network layer translates the physical address into a logical address.

7. The redirector is sometimes also called the workstation service of a networked computer. This device makes requests for access to folders and files on other computers on the network. In which layer of the OSI is the redirector found?

   D. Presentation

7. CORRECT ANSWER: D

When an application makes a request to access the files on another computer, a request must be directed to the file system on the other computer. It is the Presentation layer that redirects requests of this sort from the computer's own file system to that of another computer.

8. As the name implies, the Application layer would seem to be the layer that is directly available to the applications on the computer. However, what exactly does the Application layer expose to the applications?

A. Network APIs

The application carries out the commands required of it, as directed by the user. When the user makes a request that requires accessing the network, the Application layer presents a set of network APIs (Application Program Interfaces) from which it can choose. In general, this layer handles error recovery and network access.

9. The OSI model is designed so that each layer operates as if it were communicating directly with the same layer on the other computer. Which is the only layer that can actually send information directly to its corresponding layer on another computer?

C. The Physical layer.

The Physical layer lies at the very bottom of the OSI model. After the packets leave the Physical layer of one computer, they move to the Physical layer of the destination computer. All other layers of the OSI must send their packages down through the layers to the Physical layer to be sent to the other computer(s).

10. As the frames are passed from one layer to the next, information is added to the frame to control where the frame is to be sent, where it came from, and so on. A cyclical redundancy check (CRC) is also added to the frame to ensure that the frame is received properly at the destination computer. Which layer provides the cyclical redundancy check to prevent data errors?

A. The Data Link layer

The Data Link layer adds the CRC code to the end of the data frame to provide error-correction and verification information. This is provided to ensure that the data frames are received properly.

11. The IEEE 802 project enhanced the then-current OSI model. Instead of adding an eighth layer to the seven-layer model, IEEE 802 simply added two sublayers to one of the existing layers. Which layer had the Media Access Control and Logical Link Control sublayers added to it?

B. The Data Link layer

The Data Link layer needed a better definition, so rather than adding an additional layer, two sublayers were added: Media Access Control and Logical Link Control.

The Logical Link Control sublayer is the upper portion of the Data Link layer that is responsible for managing the data link communication and defining the use of logical interface points (service access points). These points are, in turn, used by computers to transfer information from the Logical Link Control sublayer to the upper OSI layers.

The Media Access Control sublayer talks directly to the network adapter card and is responsible for delivering error-free data between two computers on the network.

12. **Most devices are capable of using only one layer of the OSI model. One device, however, is capable of using all seven layers of the OSI model. Select the device that can use all seven layers of the OSI model.**

E. Gateway

12. CORRECT ANSWER: E

Most devices operate within a single level of the OSI model. For example, the cable lies at the Physical layer and the computer itself at the Application layer. However, the one device that can operate at all the layers of the OSI is the gateway. Figure 1.3 illustrates the seven layers of the OSI model and compares it to the Microsoft Windows networking architecture.

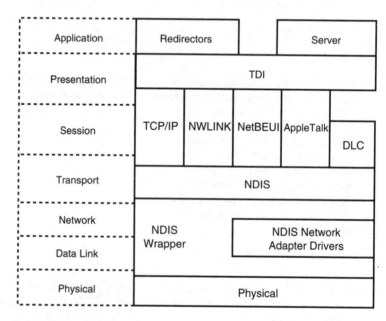

FIGURE 1.3
The seven layers of the OSI model on the left are compared to the Microsoft Windows networking architecture.

DESCRIBING THE MEDIA USED IN IEEE STANDARDS

1. The IEEE 802 project of the 1980s involved further defining the lower two layers of the OSI model. A number of standards were agreed upon during that time. Which of the following is the standard for Ethernet?

   A. 802.2

   B. 802.3

   C. 802.4

   D. 802.5

   E. 802.6

2. Thorough planning must take place when setting up an 802.3 network. A maximum number of segments can separate any two nodes on the network. What is the maximum number of segments allowed between two nodes?

   A. Five

   B. Two

   C. Four

   D. Six

   E. Three

3. Repeaters are often used on an 802.3 network to help strengthen the signals being transmitted. As with the length of segments and the number of segments, a limit exists as to how many repeaters can be used between any two nodes. What is the maximum number of repeaters that can be used?

   A. Five

   B. Two

   C. Four

   D. Six

   E. Three

4. The MAC (Media Access Control) address of the network card is used in both Ethernet and Token-Ring networks and is essential for communication. What does MAC provide?

   A. A logical address that identifies the workstation

   B. A physical address that is randomly assigned each time the computer is started

   C. A physical address that is assigned by the manufacturer

   D. The logical domain address for the workstation

   E. An alias for the computer name

5. The 802.5 standard implements a way for preventing collisions on the network. How are collisions prevented when using this standard?

   A. CSMA/CD

   B. Token passing

   C. Collision detection

   D. Time sharing

   E. Switched repeaters

6. Networks that follow the 802.5 standard appear to be in a star topology but are actually operating in what type of topology?

    A. Linear bus

    B. Modified star

    C. Modified ring

    D. Ring

    E. Hybrid hub

7. The Token-Ring architecture was developed for a more efficient way to determine who should be transmitting at any one time. With Ethernet, collisions may take place, causing the transmitting computers to have to retransmit their data. The use of token guarantees that only one computer can transmit at a time. What happens as the network increases in size? Choose the best answer.

    A. An additional token is added for every 1,000 nodes.

    B. The speed of the Token-Ring network must be 16Mbps if the number of nodes is greater than 500.

    C. The network becomes less efficient.

    D. After the number of nodes exceeds 550, the Multistation Access Unit must be replaced by the more powerful Hyperstation Unified Bandwidth device.

    E. The network becomes more efficient.

8. Ethernet networks can be cabled in a number of topologies, depending on what works best in each environment. As more nodes are added, the efficiency of Ethernet decreases. Select the best answer as to why Ethernet becomes less efficient as size increases.

    A. Network collisions occur.

    B. Repeaters cannot increase the signal strength sufficiently.

    C. Cable terminators do not reflect the signal properly.

    D. Cable terminators do not absorb the signal properly.

    E. "Line echo" occurs due to the impedance of the cable.

9. It is widely agreed that the two most popular types of network are Ethernet and Token-Ring, with Ethernet being the most popular overall. A number of reasons exist as to why these are more popular than the rest, but why is Ethernet more popular than Token-Ring? Choose all that apply.

    A. Cabling for Ethernet is less expensive than Token-Ring.

    B. Ethernet was developed after Token-Ring as an improvement.

    C. Token-Ring is limited to a maximum of 16 MAUs connected in a single segment.

    D. Ethernet was developed by a group of companies, and Token-Ring was developed by a single company.

    E. Ethernet cards are less expensive.

10. **The research and development department at your office has been experimenting with different technologies to help
improve the performance of the network.
One group has been examining the use of
a broadband network versus a baseband
network. Select the correct statement
about broadband and baseband.**

    A. Broadband networks carry several
    channels on a single cable, whereas in
    a baseband network, several cables
    carry one channel.

    B. Baseband networks carry a single
    channel on a single cable, whereas

broadband networks carry several
channels on a single cable.

C. Baseband refers to local area networks,
and broadband refers to wide area networks.

D. Baseband operates at a standard bit
rate, whereas broadband may operate
at different rates as needed.

E. Broadband and baseband refer to the
different frequencies at which infrared
operates when transmitting signals in
certain conditions.

ANSWER KEY

1. B	5. B	9. D-E
2. A	6. D	10. B
3. C	7. E	
4. C	8. A	

DESCRIBING THE MEDIA USED IN IEEE STANDARDS

1. The IEEE 802 project of the 1980s involved further defining the lower two layers of the OSI model. A number of standards were agreed upon during that time. Which of the following is the standard for Ethernet?

B. 802.3

1.   CORRECT ANSWER: B

The 802.3 standard defines how Ethernet operates and is also referred to as CSMA/CD (Carrier Sense Multiple Access with Collision Detection). This describes how each computer will listen to the wire and then, when there is no traffic, try to send its package of information. If two computers on the network send at the same time, a collision takes place and the packages must be re-sent after a variable period of time.

2. Thorough planning must take place when setting up an 802.3 network. A maximum number of segments can separate any two nodes on the network. What is the maximum number of segments allowed between two nodes?

A. Five

2.   CORRECT ANSWER: A

An Ethernet network can have a maximum of five segments between any two nodes (computers). If this number is exceeded, communication between the two computers is not possible. This is due to the increased amount of impedance as the distance becomes greater, as well as the increased chance of collisions.

3. Repeaters are often used on an 802.3 network to help strengthen the signals being transmitted. As with the length of segments and the number of segments, a limit exists as to how many repeaters can be used between any two nodes. What is the maximum number of repeaters that can be used?

C. Four

3.   CORRECT ANSWER: C

Because the maximum number of segments that can exist between any two nodes is five, it only stands to reason that the maximum number of repeaters is four.

4. The MAC (Media Access Control) address of the network card is used in both Ethernet and Token-Ring networks and is essential for communication. What does MAC provide?

C. A physical address that is assigned by the manufacturer

4.   CORRECT ANSWER: C

Although every computer is given a name that the software uses, the Physical layer does not recognize that. Therefore, for messages to be sent to the proper computer, the Physical layer must have an address to recognize; this is the MAC address. Every network card has a unique MAC address so that no confusion arises as to where the data is to be sent.

5. The 802.5 standard implements a way for preventing collisions on the network. How are collisions prevented when using this standard?

B. Token passing

A Token-Ring network avoids collisions by using a token. The only computer that can transmit packets is the one that has the token. When the computer is finished sending, the token is then passed to the next computer.

6. Networks that follow the 802.5 standard appear to be in a star topology but are actually operating in what type of topology?

D. Ring

In a Token-Ring network, all the computers are connected to the MAU, a device that appears to be similar to a hub. Internally, however, the MAU operates like a ring. As one computer finishes with the token, that token is sent from the computer into the MAU and on to the next computer. So, if the MAU was drawn in an exploded view, it would appear to be a ring topology.

7. The Token-Ring architecture was developed for a more efficient way to determine who should be transmitting at any one time. With Ethernet, collisions may take place, causing the transmitting computers to have to retransmit their data. The use of token guarantees that only one computer can transmit at a time. What happens as the network increases in size? Choose the best answer.

E. The network becomes more efficient.

In a small network, the passing of a token seems to present a lot of overhead. With a small number of computers located within close vicinity of each other, very few collisions would occur in an Ethernet network. However, as a network grows, Token-Ring becomes more efficient because the process of sending packets is very controlled.

8. Ethernet networks can be cabled in a number of topologies, depending on what works best in each environment. As more nodes are added, the efficiency of Ethernet decreases. Select the best answer as to why Ethernet becomes less efficient as size increases.

A. Network collisions occur.

As an Ethernet grows with more computers and larger distances for bits to travel, a greater occurrence of collisions arises. For this very reason, very strict rules govern the number of segments and repeaters, as well as the length of the cables. If these rules or guidelines are not followed, a lot of errors could arise on the network. For a discussion on the rules governing the number of repeaters and segments that can be implemented in an Ethernet network, see the section "Selecting the Appropriate Topology," in Chapter 2, "Planning."

9. It is widely agreed that the two most popular types of network are Ethernet and Token-Ring, with Ethernet being the most popular overall. A number of reasons exist as to why these are more popular than the rest, but why is Ethernet more popular than Token-Ring? Choose all that apply.

D. Ethernet was developed by a group of companies, and Token-Ring was developed by a single company.

E. Ethernet cards are less expensive.

9. CORRECT ANSWERS: D-E

Anytime a group of major companies get together to agree on a standard, it is more likely to be accepted than when a single company creates its own standard. Another aspect is that the more acceptance that arises, the more development will occur. With acceptance also comes a smaller cost. Because Token-Ring was not immediately accepted by the rest of the industry, its network cards are more expensive.

10. The research and development department at your office has been experimenting with different technologies to help improve the performance of the network. One group has been examining the use of a broadband network versus a baseband network. Select the correct statement about broadband and baseband.

B. Baseband networks carry a single channel on a single cable, whereas broadband networks carry several channels on a single cable.

10. CORRECT ANSWER: B

The telephone lines are set up as broadband networks to accommodate multiple signals sent across a single wire. However, this is not very efficient with electricity. This fact has created a big boost in the fiber-optic field. Because light can be sent at different frequencies without one signal interfering with another, much less cable must be laid. With electricity, the electrical signals start to interfere with each other, so more cabling is needed to accomplish the same capacity as fiber.

Broadband transmissions use analog signals and can range in frequency. The signals travel along the medium in the form of bidirectional electromagnetic or optical waves. If the bandwidth is large enough, multiple analog transmissions, such as network transmissions and cable television, can be supported on the same cable. Each transmission system is allocated a part of the total bandwidth and must be tuned to operate at its own specific frequency range. Amplifiers are used to restore the signal to its original strength.

Baseband systems use digital signaling over a single frequency. The signals travel in one direction in the form of a pulse of light or electricity. The digital signal uses the entire bandwidth of the cable and constitutes a single channel. As with broadband transmissions, baseband signals also must be strengthened if they are traveling a long distance. Repeaters are used to regenerate the signal of a baseband signal.

EXPLAINING THE PURPOSE OF NDIS AND NOVELL ODI STANDARDS

1. **A lot of developments took place in 1989, one of which was the Open Data-Link Interface, developed to enhance network performance. What exactly does the Open Data-Link Interface do to help network performance?**

   A. The Open Data-Link Interface helps bypass the Network, Transport, and Session layers of the OSI model.

   B. The Open Data-Link Interface is a seamless connection between the Physical layer and the Transport layer of the OSI.

   C. The Open Data-Link Interface provides a means for support of multiple protocols on a single network card.

   D. The Open Data-Link Interface modifies the IPX protocol to perform more like TCP.

   E. The Open Data-Link Interface replaces the Data Link layer of the OSI model.

2. **The development of ODI and NDIS involved some very specific goals. Each was created in a slightly different manner. Which of the following were *not* goals for their development?**

   A. To support multiple protocols on a single network adapter card

   B. To define specific interfaces for each protocol

   C. To define a common set of lower-level protocols that Novell and Microsoft could together develop and support on their networks

   D. To define a common interface to make the development of drivers easier

   E. To define a common set of lower-level protocols

3. **At the same time that ODI was being developed, Microsoft was working with 3COM to develop a similar standard. What is the name of that standard that Microsoft helped to develop?**

   A. MSDIS

   B. Network Device Interface Specification

   C. Media Access Control Specification

   D. Network Interface Device Specification

   E. MS-COM

4. **The standard (mentioned in question 3) that Microsoft helped to develop actually had two goals. One was to develop a standard that allowed multiple protocols to bind to a single network card. What was the other goal?**

   A. To improve the speed by reducing the overhead to convert between logical and physical addresses

   B. To standardize the interface so that more network cards would be compatible

C. To increase the compatibility with more protocols

D. To allow a single protocol to bind with multiple network cards

E. To allow a single message to be sent out on multiple protocols

5. **The NDIS standard allows Microsoft products to use multiple protocols with multiple network cards without any special configurations. What limitations did users have if they wanted to use multiple protocols prior to the NDIS standard?**

A. Users had to install a separate network card for each protocol.

B. Only one protocol could be used on a computer.

C. Only one network card could be installed in a computer.

D. OEM versions of Microsoft operating systems were developed to handle multiple protocols.

E. Processor upgrades were needed to allow multiple protocols.

6. **Operating systems other than Windows NT that implement NDIS use a *manager* to bind the protocols to the Media Access Control layer. This manager routes the incoming packets from the Media Access Control layer to the proper protocol stack. What is the name of this manager?**

A. System Manager

B. STACKMAN

C. PROTMAN

D. P-MAN

E. PROTMON

7. **Windows NT does not use the manager that other operating systems require to route the packets. What does Microsoft Windows NT use to accomplish the same process?**

A. The Registry and some code are used.

B. The Registry is used.

C. Nothing is needed, as it is included in the protocol stack.

D. The code for routing is built into the Media Access Control layer.

E. The Protocol Routing Service must be started.

8. **Unlike NDIS, ODI is made up of three main components. These components work together for a seamless integration between the Data Link layer and the Transport layer of the protocol stack. What components make up ODI?**

A. Media Access Control

B. Link Support layer

C. Protocol stacks

D. Multiple link interface drivers

E. Multiple protocol stacks

9. **In any discussion of sending and receiving information between computers, mention of the *protocol stack* inevitably arises. What is the protocol stack?**

A. The protocol stack is the interface between the Transport layer and the Network layer.

B. The protocol stack is contained within the Network layer.

C. The protocol stack is contained within the Transport layer.

D. The protocol stack is made up of the Transport layer and the Network layer.

E. The protocol stack works in parallel with the Media Access Control layer.

10. **In the ODI standard, the LSL is instrumental in ensuring that multiple protocols can operate with a single network card. What exactly does the LSL do?**

A. The LSL helps transfer the packets from one level of the protocol stack to the next.

B. The LSL is like the "glue" that keeps each of the layers operating dependently upon each other.

C. The LSL (Logical Session Link) creates a virtual link from the Network layer up to the Session layer.

D. The LSL (Link Support layer) provides a common interface for the protocols.

E. The Link Support layer routes packets.

ANSWER KEY

1. C	5. A	9. D
2. B-C-E	6. C	10. E
3. B	7. A	
4. D	8. B-C-D	

EXPLAINING THE PURPOSE OF NDIS AND NOVELL ODI STANDARDS

1. A lot of developments took place in 1989, one of which was the Open Data-Link Interface, developed to enhance network performance. What exactly does the Open Data-Link Interface do to help network performance?

   C. The Open Data-Link Interface provides a means for support of multiple protocols on a single network card.

1. CORRECT ANSWER: C

Prior to the developments of 1989, only one protocol could be bound to a network adapter card; it did not matter what type of network was being used or what topology. This became a significant restriction as local area networks became increasingly popular, and a need arose to be able to get the different networks to operate together.

2. The development of ODI and NDIS involved some very specific goals. Each was created in a slightly different manner. Which of the following were *not* goals for their development?

   B. To define specific interfaces for each protocol

   C. To define a common set of lower-level protocols that Novell and Microsoft together could develop and support on their networks

   E. To define a common set of lower-level protocols.

2. CORRECT ANSWERS: B-C-E

The goals focused on making things simpler for everyone. This meant trying to agree upon standard interfaces so that it did not matter what make of network card was being used or which protocol was to be bound; they all operated in the same manner.

3. At the same time that ODI was being developed, Microsoft was working with 3COM to develop a similar standard. What is the name of that standard that Microsoft helped to develop?

   B. Network Device Interface Specification

3. CORRECT ANSWER: B

Network Device Interface Specification, or NDIS, is the standard that Microsoft and 3COM developed. As the name implies, it is a specification that standardizes the interface between the network cards and the protocols.

NDIS has gone through a number of levels of development, and different operating systems use different versions of it. For example, Windows 95 uses NDIS 3.x, Windows NT 4.0 uses NDIS 4.0, and Windows 2000 (when it arrives) will use NDIS 5.0. Each of these versions of NDIS vary slightly in the way they handle protocols, network adapters, and their bindings.

4. The standard (mentioned in question 3) that Microsoft helped to develop actually had two goals. One was to develop a standard that allowed multiple protocols to bind to a single network card. What was the other goal?

    D. To allow a single protocol to bind with multiple network cards

This opens a lot of opportunities for the basic personal computer. Now, a single computer can use any number of protocols with a single network card to communicate with a number of other computers. Multiple network cards also can be placed into a single computer, and it can act as a router to connect multiple segments of a network.

5. The NDIS standard allows Microsoft products to use multiple protocols with multiple network cards without any special configurations. What limitations did users have if they wanted to use multiple protocols prior to the NDIS standard?

    A. Users had to install a separate network card for each protocol.

With a network card being capable only of binding to a single protocol, multiple network cards would need to be installed if more that one protocol was to be used.

6. Operating systems other than Windows NT that implement NDIS use a *manager* to bind the protocols to the Media Access Control layer. This manager routes the incoming packets from the Media Access Control layer to the proper protocol stack. What is the name of this manager?

    C. PROTMAN

PROTMAN (or Protocol Manager) is used to bind the protocols to the Media Access Control layer in systems other than Windows NT.

7. Windows NT does not use the manager that other operating systems require to route the packets. What does Microsoft Windows NT use to accomplish the same process?

    A. The Registry and some code are used.

In the case of Windows NT, the Registry provides some of the control for binding the protocols to the Media Access Control layer, but another small piece, referred to as the NDIS wrapper, surrounds the NDIS code and makes it generic to all network cards and protocols.

8. Unlike NDIS, ODI is made up of three main components. These components work together for a seamless integration between the Data Link layer and the Transport layer of the protocol stack. What components make up ODI?

   B. Link Support layer

   C. Protocol stacks

   D. Multiple link interface drivers

ODI is made up of three components: the Link Support layer, the protocol stacks, and the multiple link interface drivers. Together, these components carry out the same basic function as NDIS: to enable multiple protocols to bind to a single network card.

The Link Support layer is the router that directs the packets to the correct protocol. The protocol stacks are just as they were described in the OSI model; they are the Transport and Network layers and provide the network functionality by routing the packets to the proper destination.

The multiple link interface drivers (MLID) have two functions. One is to attach and strip media headers from packets; the other is to send and receive packets at the Physical layer.

9. In any discussion of sending and receiving information between computers, mention of the *protocol stack* inevitably arises. What is the protocol stack?

   D. The protocol stack is made up of the Transport layer and the Network layer.

The Network and Transport layers provide network functionality to packets that have been assembled in the layers above (the Application and Presentation layers). These two layers then reassemble the packages and route them to the proper destinations.

10. In the ODI standard, the LSL is instrumental in ensuring that multiple protocols can operate with a single network card. What exactly does the LSL do?

   E. The Link Support layer routes packets.

The Link Support layer seems to be similar to the protocol stack, but it is different. The LSL routes the packets to the appropriate protocol before it is passed on to the network card.

Different versions of NDIS are used with different operating systems. Windows 95 uses NDIS 3.x, while Windows NT 4.0 uses NDIS 4.0 and Windows NT 5 uses NDIS 5.0. NDIS 3.0 offers the following features:

- High-level protocol components can be independent of the network adapter card.

- The NDIS 3.0 wrapper (a small piece of NDIS 3.0 code) provides a uniform interface and controls the communications between all protocols and network adapter cards.

- It controls the communications between the network adapter card drivers and the network interface cards. This enables third-party developers to take advantage of the Window resources.

- It accommodates an unlimited number of network adapter cards in a computer, and it also provides for an unlimited number of protocols that can be bound to a single network adapter card.

NDIS 4.0 offers the following features:

- It is a communication link between network adapter cards and associated drivers.

- It enables protocol drivers and network adapter card drivers to remain independent of each other.

- It accommodates an unlimited number of network adapters.

- It provides for an unlimited number of protocols to be bound to a single adapter card.

- One or more protocols can be bound, independently, to one or more network adapter cards.

- Network adapter cards and their drivers are independent of the system protocols. Therefore, changing protocols does not require a reconfiguration of adapter cards.

SUMMARY

The main things to remember about this chapter are as follows:

- Remember the terms used for LANs and WANs. These definitely will be used throughout the exam.

- Questions on file and printer servers will not always be specific to Windows NT, but questions on them will appear.

- Make sure that you understand user security in regard to accessing a shared directory on servers. Although a lot of questions won't be asked on this subject, it can be confusing if you don't understand how it works.

- Understand the concepts and implications of using both peer-to-peer networks and client/server networks. Pros and cons exist for both of them.

- Although a lot of emphasis is placed on knowing that TCP/IP can use both connection-oriented and connectionless communication, all protocols can use both. Make sure you understand what each term means, and put extra emphasis on knowing which protocols in the TCP/IP suite use each method of communication.

- As the Internet becomes more popular, there is a great emphasis on how it can be used as a solution for business. Therefore, it is very important to understand how Microsoft Windows NT can implement access to the Internet. Learn and understand SLIP, PPP, and PPTP.

- Whether you are working with Windows 95, Windows NT, or any other networking software, it is imperative that you understand the layers of the OSI model. With it, you can work through and resolve many problems.

- Almost as important as the OSI model are the IEEE standards for network architectures. It is not necessary to know all the 802.x standards, but do know the basics for Token-Ring and Ethernet. Just in case, it would not hurt to review the other 802.x standards.

- Everyone should know the basis for developing NDIS and ODI. If you don't, you will have a very difficult time working on network problems. These are a must to know and understand.

This first chapter covers a lot of information, and some of you may be feeling that you will have to get into a lot of detail as to how Windows NT operates and is configured. Yes, the exam asks questions on Windows NT, but generally it does not get too detailed. The questions you encounter in the exam usually require more general knowledge when it comes to Windows NT.

The purpose of the Planning section of the Networking Essentials exam is to ensure that you understand the importance of determining what you need prior to actually implementing the network. The main topics include the media to be used, the protocols to be used, the necessary connectivity devices, and the requirements for WAN connections.

If you plan properly before building a network, the need for troubleshooting becomes negligible.

Planning

OBJECTIVES

Microsoft identifies the following test objectives for the Planning portion of the exam:

Select the appropriate media for various situations. Media choices include twisted-pair cable, coaxial cable, fiber-optic cable, and wireless. Situational elements include cost, distance limitations, and number of nodes. (Practice questions start on page 75.)

▶ This chapter focuses on one exam objective and the many issues that stem from it. This is due to the amount and complexity of the material associated with the topic of Transmission Media. It is just as important to know the advantages and disadvantages of different transmission media, and in what situations to use them, as it is to simply understand the characteristics of each transmission medium.

Select the appropriate topology for various Token-Ring and Ethernet networks. (Practice questions start on page 84.)

▶ This objective is necessary because Token-Ring or Ethernet networks can utilize different physical and logical topologies. This exam objective

continues

points out the need for you to be able to identify which topology should be used by a Token-Ring or Ethernet network given different circumstances or environmental conditions.

Select the appropriate network and transport protocol or protocols for various Token-Ring and Ethernet networks. Protocol choices include DLC, AppleTalk, IPC, TCP/IP, NFS, and SMB. (Practice questions start on page 92.)

▶ When devices communicate over the network, they must utilize some form of transport protocol or set of rules to move data from one device to another. This exam objective reflects the need for you to know the transport protocols that are used most often with Windows 95 and Windows NT.

Select the appropriate connectivity devices for various Token-Ring and Ethernet networks. Connectivity devices include repeaters, bridges, routers, brouters, and gateways. (Practice questions start on page 101.)

▶ In this section, a more in-depth analysis is done on the different devices that are used on various Token-Ring and Ethernet networks. In this chapter, besides simply addressing the role of each connectivity device, emphasis is placed on comparing and contrasting the devices in terms of when one would be used versus another.

List the characteristics, requirements, and appropriate situations for WAN connection services. WAN connection services include X.25, ISDN, frame relay, and ATM. (Practice questions start on page 108.)

▶ This is an important topic, because it not only applies to the theories learned in this book, but also when you face some form of WAN connectivity need or problem, one or more of these options will more than likely be your solution.

SELECTING THE APPROPRIATE MEDIA

1. **This question is based on the following scenario. Review the scenario first, followed by the objectives and the proposed solution. Then evaluate the proposed solution by choosing the best answer.**

Scenario:
Your company is moving into a new building and has asked you to plan for building the network. The building's dimensions are 100 meters by 200 meters. It is a single-story building, and the server will be located at one side of the building. The company currently has 150 employees and might add another 25 employees next spring.

Required Result:
All client computers will be able to connect to the server.

Optional Results:
The network can be connected to the Internet.

The network will be able to accommodate the 25 additional people that may be hired next year.

Proposed Solution:
You will use a Token-Ring topology, Cat 5 cabling, and the TCP/IP protocol, and you will run the network at 16Mbps.

Evaluation of Proposed Solution:
Which of the following statements is true? (Choose the best answer.)

A. All of the results are met.

B. The required result is met, but the optional results are not met.

C. The required result and one of the optional results are met.

D. The required result is not met, but the optional results are met.

E. None of the results are met.

2. **John has read that UTP cable is the simplest and cheapest cable to use. What is the maximum transmission speed that UTP is capable of in a Token-Ring network?**

A. 4Mbps

B. 8Mbps

C. 10Mbps

D. 16Mbps

E. 100Mbps

3. **A discount store has hired you to plan a network for its operation. The store measures 200 meters by 200 meters. The offices and server room are located in the back of the store. The office area has 10 computers that need to be connected to the network, in addition to the four cash registers at the front of the store. The cabling must pass overhead in the ceiling from the back of the store to the desktops and the cash registers. What type of cable would you recommend?**

A. UTP

B. STP

C. Fiber-optic

D. Thinnet

E. Thicknet

4. **All types of cable suffer from attenuation of data signals. However, each type of cable is affected differently by attenuation. What is *attenuation*?**

   A. Degradation of the signal due to interference from outside signals.

   B. Bad data that can result from cables being placed too close together and interfering with one another.

   C. Another name for *crosstalk*.

   D. Weakening of the signal due to interference from outside signals.

   E. Weakening of the signal due to the impedance of the cable.

5. **Fiber-optic cable is different from other types of cable because it does not use wire to carry signals. Instead of wire, it uses either glass or plastic. Which of the following are advantages of using fiber-optic cabling over wire cabling?**

   A. It is not affected by EMI.

   B. It is flexible.

   C. It has a lower cost-per-network transaction than does standard cabling.

   D. Signals do not suffer from attenuation.

   E. Signals travel very fast.

6. **The local university has asked your consulting company to come up with a solution for its network problem. The goal is to connect each of the buildings on campus for the network. The campus covers a number of acres, the greatest distance between two buildings being about two miles (3,200 meters). You have decided to use thicknet cables within each of the buildings and fiber-optic cable to connect the buildings. What is the cable length limit for fiber-optic (glass) cable?**

   A. 35,000 meters (21.875 miles)

   B. 300 meters (330 yards)

   C. 1,000 meters (1100 yards)

   D. 500 meters (550 yards)

   E. 25,000 meters (15.625 miles)

7. **Janice is trying to decide which type of cable she should use to wire her network, which is going to cover a distance of about 400 meters. She has narrowed her choices to either thicknet or fiber-optic cable. Why shouldn't she use fiber-optic?**

   A. Fiber-optic cable does not function well at short distances.

   B. It is not very flexible.

   C. Fiber-optic cable costs too much.

   D. It is difficult to work with.

   E. Fiber-optic cable should always be used.

8. **Paul has a restaurant with an outdoor patio for summertime dining. He thought that using infrared to connect the cash registers to the office network**

would be easier than trying to run cables through the eating area. Paul has one cash register inside the restaurant and one on the patio. The operation hours are from 11:30 a.m. to 11:00 p.m. Why might infrared not be a good choice for Paul's restaurant?

    A. Infrared cannot travel that far.

    B. Cash registers need a faster link.

    C. Infrared does not work outside.

    D. The infrared may interfere with traffic lights.

    E. Infrared can be used only as a backbone for connecting two or more local area networks.

9. Alex has just finished networking his home. He has three computers in his lab in the basement, one in his bedroom, and another in the den. To help keep costs down, he implemented an Ethernet network in a linear bus configuration. While working in his lab, however, he seemed to get a lot of bad data. By monitoring the network, Alex has found a lot of data passing back on the network. What could be the problem?

    A. He did not use twisted-pair cable.

    B. He did not use terminators.

    C. The cable lengths are too long.

    D. The cable lengths are too short.

    E. He did not use coaxial cable.

10. Julia is planning to run the network wiring for a company that has just taken over an office. The previous tenant used a Token-Ring network running at 16Mbps.

The computers that are being brought in do not yet have network cards, and the new company is trying to establish the network for the least possible cost, while still allowing for expansion. What should Julia recommend?

    A. A Token-Ring network with the same configuration the previous tenant used

    B. A Token-Ring network using Thicknet cabling

    C. An Ethernet network in a star topology

    D. An Ethernet network in a ring topology

    E. An Ethernet network in a linear bus topology

11. This question is based on the following scenario. Review the scenario first, followed by the objectives and the proposed solution. Then, evaluate the proposed solution by choosing the best answer. (Note that question 12 is also based on this scenario.)

Scenario:
Jerry has an office area that measures 500 feet by 250 feet. He needs to run cabling for a network that is going to be installed next month. The network will consist of 100 computers, all of which will be running client/server applications. Four servers will be located in a central server room, and five printers will be placed individually throughout the office. No cabling has been run up to this point, and all new cable will be run in the ceiling. All computers already have 16Mbps Token-Ring network adapter cards.

Required Result:
The cost of cabling should be kept to a minimum.

Optional Results:
All computers will be able to connect to the LAN.

All users will be able to access the network printers.

Proposed Solution:
Jerry decides to use Cat 3 cable to connect the network.

Evaluation of Proposed Solution:
Does this solution meet Jerry's needs? Select the best answer.

A. All of the results are met.

B. The required result is met, but the optional results are not met.

C. The required result and one of the optional results are met.

D. The required result is not met, but the optional results are met.

E. None of the results are met.

12. This question is based on the scenario described in question 11. If necessary, review the scenario and the objectives again. Then, read this proposed solution and evaluate it by choosing the best answer.

Proposed Solution:
Jerry will use thinnet cable in the office area for the new network.

Evaluation of Proposed Solution:
Does this solution meet Jerry's needs? Select the best answer.

A. All of the results are met.

B. The required result is met, but the optional results are not met.

C. The required result and one of the optional results are met.

D. The required result is not met, but the optional results are met.

E. None of the results are met.

ANSWER KEY

1. A	6. A	11. E
2. D	7. B-C-D	12. E
3. E	8. C	
4. E	9. B	
5. A-D	10. C	

SELECTING THE APPROPRIATE MEDIA

1. *Proposed Solution:* **You will use a Token-Ring topology, Cat 5 cabling, and the TCP/IP protocol, and you will run the network at 16Mbps.**

   A. All of the results are met.

1. CORRECT ANSWER: A

Token-Ring is a common industry-standard network architecture that allows workstations to access the Internet, providing that the proper protocol is used and there is a method for the clients on the network to connect to the Internet. To connect the network to the Internet, a service such as ISDN or T1 must be connected to the network through specific hardware such as a router or switch.

Token-Ring is also very simple to expand. Most *Multistation Access Units* (MAUs) available today have 16 ports. To allow for expansion of the ring, each MAU has a ring-in and a ring-out port that can be attached to other MAUs. If long enough cables are used, the ring can become quite large.

2. **John has read that UTP cable is the simplest and cheapest cable to use. What is the maximum transmission speed that UTP is capable of in a Token-Ring network?**

   D. 16Mbps

2. CORRECT ANSWER: D

The maximum transmission speed for unshielded twisted-pair (UTP) cable is determined by the cable's category rating—from Category 1 to Category 5. Depending on the number of wires, the number of twists, and the type of wire used, UTP is rated up to 100Mbps.

Token-Ring is currently available commercially in only two configurations: 4Mbps and 16Mbps. Therefore, the maximum transfer rate for UTP on a Token-Ring network is 16Mbps. If this were an Ethernet network and the proper hardware was being used, the maximum rate would be 100Mbps.

3. A discount store has hired you to plan a network for its operation. The store measures 200 meters by 200 meters. The offices and server room are located in the back of the store. The office area has 10 computers that need to be connected to the network, in addition to the four cash registers at the front of the store. The cabling must pass overhead in the ceiling from the back of the store to the desktops and the cash registers. What type of cable would you recommend?

  E. Thicknet

---

3. CORRECT ANSWER: E

A 10BASE-5 network (thicknet) can have a backbone of up to 500 meters in length. This length is more than ample to allow the cash registers to be connected to the rest of the network located on the other side of the store. The other concern that has to be taken into account is the fluorescent lighting that the cable will have to pass by. Fluorescent lighting can emit a large amount of electrical interference. Other cabling, such as thinnet and STP, would be sufficiently protected from the interference, but they cannot be used for the required distance. Other options, such as fiber-optic cable, are available, but most are too expensive and would just be overkill.

As a professional, it is your job to consider what components will work, but it is just as important—if not more so—to find the most cost-effective solution. In this case, a fiber-optic link would work very well, and the users would not have any problems with network connectivity or errors on the line. However, the company would incur a great expense purchasing the media, as well as having it installed.

---

4. All types of cable suffer from attenuation of data signals. However, each type of cable is affected differently by attenuation. What is *attenuation*?

  E. Weakening of the signal due to the impedance of the cable.

---

4. CORRECT ANSWER: E

A number of factors can increase the impedance in a cable. As an example, although copper is a good conductor of electricity, it is not perfect: The electrical signal becomes weaker the farther it travels. In addition, sharp bends in the wire will also impede the signals that are traveling along the cable and can prevent signals from traveling very far.

In the case of fiber-optic cable, there are very few imperfections, so the signal can travel much farther. If you compare glass fibers to plastic fibers, glass is much "cleaner" than plastic and, therefore, allows signals to travel much farther.

However, because of the characteristics of light and the fiber cable, there can be no sharp bends. Because of this restriction, special skills and equipment are needed to install fiber-optic cable properly. This is why installing fiber-optic cable can be so expensive.

5. Fiber-optic cable is different from other types of cable because it does not use wire to carry signals. Instead of wire, it uses either glass or plastic. Which of the following are advantages of using fiber-optic cabling over wire cabling?

A. It is not affected by EMI.

D. Signals do not suffer from attenuation.

5. CORRECT ANSWERS: A-D

Fiber-optic cable carries light signals instead of electrical signals. Because no electricity is being transferred, outside electrical signals will not affect the transmission. In addition, because the media is much "cleaner" than metal wire, the signal can travel much farther than an electrical signal. The published maximum length for a segment of 10BASE-FL is 2,000 meters. Theoretically then, a signal could travel several kilometers.

6. The local university has asked your consulting company to come up with a solution for its network problem. The goal is to connect each of the buildings on campus for the network. The campus covers a number of acres, the greatest distance between two buildings being about two miles (3,200 meters). You have decided to use thicknet cables within each of the buildings and fiber-optic cable to connect the buildings. What is the cable length limit for fiber-optic (glass) cable?

A. 35,000 meters (21.875 miles)

6. CORRECT ANSWER: A

Fiber-optic cable can be used to connect LANs over very large distances. In fact, this is exactly the type of configuration that is commonly deployed when LAN segments must be connected.

A single fiber-optic cable could be installed that runs from one LAN segment to the other. Each individual segment would be cabled using whatever cable is best suited to that particular environment, and then each segment would be connected to the fiber-optic cable. This keeps the cable cost to a minimum, yet provides a fast LAN equivalent link between the segments.

7. Janice is trying to decide which type of cable she should use to wire her network, which is going to cover a distance of about 400 meters. She has narrowed her choices to either thicknet or fiber-optic cable. Why shouldn't she use fiber-optic?

B. It is not very flexible.

C. Fiber-optic cable costs too much.

D. It is difficult to work with.

7. CORRECT ANSWERS: B-C-D

Every type of cable has its purpose, and that includes fiber-optic. Fiber-optic cable would definitely work in her network that measures 400 meters in length. However, thicknet would also meet her needs and is much less expensive to install than fiber-optic cable is.

Fiber strands can be bent, but only in slow arching curves. If the strand is bent at too sharp an angle, the light will not be able to pass the bend, and no signals will be transmitted.

Because of the limitations on how sharply the fiber-optic cable can be bent, it is difficult to work with, and that drives up the cost of installation. Once the cable is in place, it will function very well and will not require any other attention unless there is a need to move the cable or add additional connections.

8. Paul has a restaurant with an outdoor patio for summertime dining. He thought that using infrared to connect the cash registers to the office network would be easier than trying to run cables through the eating area. Paul has one cash register inside the restaurant and one on the patio. The operation hours are from 11:30 a.m. to 11:00 p.m. Why might infrared not be a good choice for Paul's restaurant?

   C. Infrared does not work outside.

8. CORRECT ANSWER: C

Like most transmission media, infrared is susceptible to outside interference. Infrared works best in an office that does not have outside windows or bright lights. If the infrared signal is not strong, it becomes quite susceptible to interference from outside light sources. In addition to interference from lights, a restaurant may incur other difficulties because the serving staff is constantly walking among the tables. Most infrared systems use a line-of-site method of transmitting and receiving data. If people are constantly walking between nodes that are transmitting and receiving infrared signals, the communication link will constantly be interrupted.

9. Alex has just finished networking his home. He has three computers in his lab in the basement, one in his bedroom, and another in the den. To help keep costs down, he implemented an Ethernet network in a linear bus configuration. While working in his lab, however, he seemed to get a lot of bad data. By monitoring the network, Alex has found a lot of data passing back on the network. What could be the problem?

   B. He did not use terminators.

9. CORRECT ANSWER: B

Without being able to see Alex's actual network or the data he gathered by monitoring the network, the first problem you might suspect is that the terminators are missing from the ends of the bus. Without terminators, when signals reach the end of the bus, they bounce back along the cable. The terminator has a lot more impedance than the cable does, and it is designed to absorb signals when they reach the end of the cable.

If Alex did install terminators, he should check to make sure that they are functioning properly and determine whether the signal is actually reaching the cable. A physical break or cut in the cable before the terminator would also cause the signal to bounce.

10. Julia is planning to run the network wiring for a company that has just taken over an ofice. The previous tenant used a Token-Ring network running at 16Mbps. The computers that are being brought in do not yet have network cards, and the new company is trying to establish the network for the least possible cost, while still allowing for expansion. What should Julia recommend?

   C. An Ethernet network in a star topology

10. CORRECT ANSWER: C

In most cases, Token-Ring network adapter cards cost anywhere from two to three times as much as Ethernet network adapter cards. So, if 50 computers are to be installed, and the price difference between a Token-Ring network adapter card and an Ethernet network adapter card is $100, the company can save itself $5,000 by installing Ethernet.

Although Token-Ring operates on the idea of a ring topology, the ring is actually located within the MAU itself. Therefore, after a Token-Ring network is cabled, it actually looks like a star topology.

Finally, Token-Ring and Ethernet 10BASE-T both use UTP (or STP) cable. The cabling would not have to be changed if the company used network adapter cards with RJ-45 connectors.

11. *Proposed Solution:* **Jerry decides to use Cat 3 cable to connect the network.**

    E. **None of the results are met.**

11. CORRECT ANSWER: E

Cat 4 cable is rated to be able to carry signals at up to 16Mbps. Cat 5 cable is rated to carry data signals at up to 100Mbps. However, Cat 3 cable is rated only for networks up to 10Mbps. Therefore, the transmission of data on the network would be suspect. Because it cannot be guaranteed that the data being transmitted will be error-free, Cat 3 cable would not be a good solution for this network. The cable would have to be changed to operate properly, which would make it an expensive solution (although the cable itself is inexpensive). In addition, people would not be able to use the printers, and in essence, no one would really be connected to the LAN.

12. *Proposed Solution:* **Jerry will use thinnet cable in the office area for the new network.**

    E. **None of the results are met.**

12. CORRECT ANSWER: E

Either UTP or STP cable must be used in a Token-Ring network. Whereas thinnet could certainly meet the needs for this office space, it would have to be implemented in an Ethernet network. Because there is no BNC connector on a Token-Ring network adapter card, a thinnet cable could not be connected to it.

SELECTING THE APPROPRIATE TOPOLOGY

1. The *topology* of a network refers to how the wiring of the workstations and servers is laid out. There are a number of different topologies, and each works well in certain circumstances. A Token-Ring network can use which of the following topologies?

   A. Star

   B. Linear bus

   C. Ring

   D. Star bus

   E. Star ring

2. Ethernet is the most common architecture deployed today. Unlike Token-Ring, it uses *contention* to determine which computer can transmit on the network. Ethernet can be configured in which of the following topologies?

   A. Star

   B. Linear bus

   C. Ring

   D. Star bus

   E. Star ring

3. When you're designing a network, one of the most important decisions you'll make is which topology to use. Which of the following factors do you need to consider when choosing a topology?

   A. Cost restrictions

   B. Type of cable to be used

   C. Size of the server

   D. The building

   E. Number of computers

4. Brad recently set up a Token-Ring network for his office of 275 users. To prevent interference from the electrical wiring in the ceiling, he used STP cable, and he distributed the 17 16-port MAUs throughout the office to ensure that none of the cable lengths would be too long. First, he brought up the three servers, and then he brought up the workstations in groups of 25. When all of the systems were online, the network experienced communication problems. What is the likely cause?

   A. All MAUs must be within eight feet of each other.

   B. There are too many computers.

   C. Only 10 workstations should be brought online at a time.

   D. UTP cable should be used in a Token-Ring network.

   E. No more than 15 MAUs can be connected in a single ring.

5. Murray is setting up a small network in his home. He has five computers running Windows 98 and one computer running Windows NT Server. A local computer store was clearing out old equipment, and he was able to purchase six Token-Ring adapter cards and an 8-port MAU for next to nothing. Murray made up cables and verified the wiring. But even after he verified the cabling, the network did not function properly. What three things should Murray check first?

   A. Make sure that the MAU and the Token-Ring cards are from the same manufacturer.

   B. Check the speed of the network cards.

   C. Initialize the ports on the MAU.

   D. Initialize the ports on the network cards.

   E. Check the length of the patch cables.

6. Your company has just moved into an office that is already wired for an Ethernet network using STP cable in a star configuration. Most of the cable lengths for the workstations are between 50 and 100 feet. What changes would you need to make in order to convert to a Token-Ring network?

   A. Change the cable to UTP.

   B. Run a bus, and connect each of the workstation cables to the bus.

   C. Replace the cable with thicknet cabling.

   D. Keep the cable and connect it to an MAU.

   E. Remove all the cabling and switch to a ring topology.

7. Carol has a small office with seven computers that need to be connected. The distance between any two computers is no more than 50 feet. What type of network will be least expensive to install?

   A. Ethernet using 100BASE-TX

   B. Ethernet using 10BASE-5

   C. Token-Ring using UTP

   D. Ethernet using 10BASE-2

   E. Ethernet using 10BASE-T

8. Your consulting firm has been called in to help a client resolve a networking problem. The client is using a thinnet Ethernet network, but not everyone is able to connect to the network. They have five segments to the network, with four repeaters connecting the segments. You have checked to make sure that no segment measures more than 250 feet and that the total length of the network is not more than 1,000 feet. What could be the problem? Select the best answer.

   A. Thicknet cabling should have been used.

   B. UTP cabling should have been used.

   C. There are too many computers on the network.

   D. Hubs should be used instead of repeaters.

   E. There are computers on more than three segments.

9. Your company has won the bid to design and implement the network for a power company that is just completing construction of a hydro-electric dam in Alaska. It needs two networks in the dam itself—one at each end—and a third network at the off-site operations office. The dam is three-fourths of a mile across, and the operations office is located in a small town five miles away. How would you link the three networks? Select the best answer.

   A. Install ISDN routers at each network and connect them using dedicated telephone lines.

   B. Install fiber-optic links between the three networks.

   C. Install a fiber-optic link between the two networks in the dam and a microwave link between the dam and the operations office.

   D. Install infrared links between the three networks.

   E. Install infrared links between the two networks at the dam and a microwave link between the office and the dam.

10. Your office has been in a state of constant change for the last seven months. People are forced to move their computers from location to location on a regular basis to accommodate renovations and expansion. Which type of Ethernet best suits this environment?

   A. 10BASE-2

   B. 10BASE-5

   C. 10BASE-F

   D. 10BASE-T

   E. 10BASE-100

11. Bill is working with a 10BASE-2 Ethernet network in an old warehouse. The building was recently refurbished and the electrical power upgraded. The network is broken into four segments, measuring approximately 100 meters (330 feet) each. Bill has also purchased 10 printers that are to be connected to the network. What is the maximum number of computers Bill can connect to this network?

   A. 90

   B. 120

   C. 110

   D. 80

   E. 100

ANSWER KEY

1. E	5. B-C-E	9. C
2. A-B-C-D-E	6. D	10. D
3. A-B-D-E	7. D	11. D
4. B	8. E	

SELECTING THE APPROPRIATE TOPOLOGY

1. The *topology* of a network refers to how the wiring of the workstations and servers is laid out. There are a number of different topologies, and each works well in certain circumstances. A Token-Ring network can use which of the following topologies?

   E. Star ring

1. CORRECT ANSWER: E

Although Token-Ring architecture functions on the basis of a ring, the actual topology is that of a star. The ring itself is located within the MAU. Most MAUs have 16 ports available for computers to connect to. If more ports are needed, MAUs can be linked together by their ring-in and ring-out ports. When multiple MAUs are connected, the topology takes on the form of a *star ring*. The MAUs can be very far apart and be connected in a *ring*, yet have many computers connected to each of them.

2. Ethernet is the most common architecture deployed today. Unlike Token-Ring, it uses *contention* to determine which computer can transmit on the network. Ethernet can be configured in which of the following topologies?

   A. Star

   B. Linear bus

   C. Ring

   D. Star bus

   E. Star ring

2. CORRECT ANSWERS: A-B-C-D-E

One of the reasons Ethernet is so popular is because it is so flexible. Ethernet can be cabled in any of these topologies, plus several combinations of topologies. So, Ethernet is an option for almost every networking solution; you just have to decide which topology best suits the environment.

3. When you're designing a network, one of the most important decisions you'll make is which topology to use. Which of the following factors do you need to consider when choosing a topology?

   A. Cost restrictions

   B. Type of cable to be used

   D. The building

   E. Number of computers

3. CORRECT ANSWERS: A-B-D-E

You must consider many factors when designing a network; some of those include the cable type, the topology, the network architecture, the number of computers to be deployed, the layout of the building, and the list goes on. About the only thing that doesn't really affect the network is the size of the server(s) or workstations.

4. Brad recently set up a Token-Ring network for his office of 275 users. To prevent interference from the electrical
wiring in the ceiling, he used STP
cable, and he distributed the 17 16-
port MAUs throughout the office to
ensure that none of the cable lengths
would be too long. First, he brought up
the three servers, and then he brought
up the workstations in groups of 25.
When all of the systems were online,
the network experienced communication problems. What is the likely
cause?

B. There are too many computers.

5. Murray is setting up a small network in
his home. He has five computers running Windows 98 and one computer
running Windows NT Server. A local
computer store was clearing out old
equipment, and he was able to purchase six Token-Ring adapter cards
and an 8-port MAU for next to nothing.
Murray made up cables and verified the
wiring. But even after he verified the
cabling, the network did not function
properly. What three things should
Murray check first?

B. Check the speed of the network
cards.

C. Initialize the ports on the MAU.

E. Check the length of the patch cables.

4. CORRECT ANSWER: B

One drawback of Token-Ring is that it is limited to 260 computers per network when using STP cable (or 72 computers
per concentrator when using UTP). If the network were broken into segments by a router, Brad would not have this problem of too many computers on the network; but because all
the computers are on one segment, errors will occur on the
network.

5. CORRECT ANSWERS: B-C-E

Because you cannot see Murray's network, you must use basic
troubleshooting skills and remember some specifics about
Token-Ring.

First of all, Token-Ring can operate at two different speeds:
4Mbps and 16Mbps. The speed is determined by the capability of the network adapter card and which option the installer
has chosen. Most Token-Ring adapters are shipped at 4Mbps
even if they are capable of operating at 16Mbps. This often
causes problems because people forget to set the speed before
they put computers on the network. Token-Ring can operate
at either of the speeds, but it cannot operate on a network that
combines the two. If both speeds are used on a single network,
beaconing occurs, and the network comes to a screeching halt.

▼ **NOTE**

Beaconing occurs when a fault is detected by a computer on a Token-
Ring network. The computer that detects the fault sends the beacon
on to the network continuously until it notices that the *upstream
computer* (the computer it receives tokens from) is sending bea-
cons. This process continues until the computer that is directly *downstream* of the failure begins beaconing. When the computer that
started the beaconing receives its own beacon, it regenerates a
token and passes it on to the network.

Second, old 8-port MAUs did not have built-in power supplies; they depended on the signals from the network adapters of each of the computers. Because of this, any static or residual electricity at the ports interfered with communication. Therefore, the old 8-port MAUs usually came equipped with a port initializer. This device (which is battery operated) would reset the port to a state in which it would accept signals.

Finally, although the wiring may be alright, the cables may be too long. Because this network is in his home, it is unlikely that Murray would have made the cables too long. But it is a possibility, and one that is worth checking into if nothing else rectifies the problem. The maximum cable length for UTP cable in a Token-Ring ring network is 45 meters (150 feet), and the minimum cable length is about 2.5 meters (8 feet).

6. Your company has just moved into an office that is already wired for an Ethernet network using STP cable in a star configuration. Most of the cable lengths for the workstations are between 50 and 100 feet. What changes would you need to make in order to convert to a Token-Ring network?

    D. Keep the cable and connect it to an MAU.

6. CORRECT ANSWER: D

No changes to the cable are necessary, provided that the cables are still in good condition. Because most Token-Ring networks are wired in a star configuration, the cabling does not need to be changed. The only thing you would need to do is replace the hub(s) with MAU(s).

7. Carol has a small office with seven computers that need to be connected. The distance between any two computers is no more than 50 feet. What type of network will be least expensive to install?

    D. Ethernet using 10BASE-2

7. CORRECT ANSWER: D

The least expensive network would be a 10BASE-2 network using thinnet cabling in a linear bus topology. Very little cable is needed, no additional hardware is needed (except for the two terminators), and running the cable would be simple.

8. Your consulting firm has been called in to help a client resolve a networking problem. The client is using a Thinnet Ethernet network, but not everyone is able to connect to the network. They have five segments to the network, with four repeaters connecting the segments. You have checked to make sure that no segment measures more than 250 feet and that the total length of the network is not more than 1,000 feet. What could be the problem? Select the best answer.

   E. There are computers on more than three segments.

One thing to remember about Ethernet is that, although you can have multiple segments to a network (which allows you to increase the length of the network), there are limitations. Ethernet must adhere to the *5-4-3 rule*. This rule states that a network can have five segments, separated by four repeaters, with nodes on no more than three segments. From the description in the question, you know that the network does not exceed the number of segments and repeaters, but you do not know how many computers there are or which segments they are located on. The first thing to do is see if there are computers on four or five of the segments. If so, some of the computers will have to be repositioned.

9. Your company has won the bid to design and implement the network for a power company that is just completing construction of a hydro-electric dam in Alaska. It needs two networks in the dam itself—one at each end—and a third network at the off-site operations office. The dam is three-fourths of a mile across, and the operations office is located in a small town five miles away. How would you link the three networks? Select the best answer.

   C. Install a fiber-optic link between the two networks in the dam and a microwave link between the dam and the operations office.

Running the link within the dam is quite simple. The only potential problem you would have to contend with is the sheer distance. To connect these two networks, it would be best to use fiber-optic cabling. Connecting the dam to the operations office is another matter, however. Generally speaking, hydro dams are often located in areas of rugged terrain. To run cable between the locations would probably be difficult, plus who knows what stresses may be placed on it from the environment (snow, ice, shifting ground, animals, and so on). Therefore, it may be advantageous to use a form of wireless communication to connect the two sites. Microwave is both fast and reliable and would, therefore, be a good choice. Table 2.1 describes the types of wireless communication available for networking.

TABLE 2.1   TYPES OF WIRELESS COMMUNICATION

Transmission Type	Description
Infrared	An infrared light beam is used to carry the signal from one computer to another. These signals need to be very strong because they are highly susceptible to interference from interior lighting and windows. Rates tend to be high because of infrared's high bandwidth, but infrared cannot operate at distances greater than 100 feet.
Laser	Laser is similar to infrared, except that its light is much more intense, which means the signals can travel much farther. Still, like infrared, laser is susceptible to interference from other light sources.

Transmission Type	Description
Narrow-band radio	This is similar to a radio station broadcast. Both the transmitter and the receiver must be tuned to a certain frequency. This type of transmission does not require a line-of-site (as do infrared and laser), but because it operates at a high frequency, the transmission cannot pass through steel or load-bearing walls. Narrow-band radio works well over long distances, but is relatively slow at about 4.8Mbps.
Spread-spectrum radio	As the name implies, this signal is transmitted over a range of frequencies.

10. **Your office has been in a state of constant change for the last seven months. People are forced to move their computers from location to location on a regular basis to accommodate renovations and expansion. Which type of Ethernet best suits this environment?**

    D. **10BASE-T**

10. CORRECT ANSWER: D

The biggest factor to be considered here is that computers have to be moved all the time. 10BASE-T cable (UTP and STP) is light, flexible, and easy to work with. Therefore, moving these cables is not a problem. Also, because 10BASE-T tends to be used in a star topology, moving computers around is even simpler because only one cable connects each computer to the central hub. Therefore, to move a computer in a star topology, you have to move only one cable. To move a computer in a ring or bus topology, you have to move both the cable coming from the upstream computer and the cable going to the downstream computer.

11. **Bill is working with a 10BASE-2 Ethernet network in an old warehouse. The building was recently refurbished and the electrical power upgraded. The network is broken into four segments, measuring approximately 100 meters (330 feet) each. Bill has also purchased 10 printers that are to be connected to the network. What is the maximum number of computers Bill can connect to this network?**

    D. **80**

11. CORRECT ANSWER: D

A thinnet network (10BASE-2) is subject to specific limitations regarding the number of segments, the number of repeaters, and the number of computers per segment. This is referred to as the "5-4-3 rule." This rule states that a network cannot have more than five segments, it cannot have more than four repeaters to separate the segments, and only three of the segments can have attached nodes.

In this case, the network has four segments, but only three segments can have nodes attached. Also, thinnet is restricted to having a maximum of 30 nodes per 185 meters (610 feet). Three segments of 30 nodes adds up to a total of 90 nodes. However, because the network will have 10 printers connected to it, only 80 nodes are available for computers.

SELECTING NETWORK AND TRANSPORT PROTOCOLS

1. A new network is being planned for your company, which has 25 locations across North and Central America and 16 sites throughout Europe. The expected number of users in Europe is 23,000, and the number in North and Central America will be 30,000–35,000. The new network must work in both LAN and WAN environments. Which protocol is best suited for this network?

   A. IPX/SPX

   B. AppleTalk

   C. DLC

   D. TCP/IP

   E. NFS

2. You currently have a Microsoft Windows NT network in your office of software developers. You have to make plans for a new group of graphic artists that are to be developing graphics for marketing your products. The new people are all Macintosh users. You are already running NWLink. Do you need to run any other protocol? If so, which one?

   A. TCP/IP.

   B. No other protocol is needed.

   C. DLC.

   D. AppleTalk.

   E. IPX/SPX.

3. Your network is made up of a Windows NT domain connected to a UNIX server. Connected to the network are three printers, which are controlled by the Windows NT server, and one fax server. In most UNIX environments, what TCP/IP protocol does the UNIX server use to allow file sharing?

   A. IP

   B. SMB

   C. NFS

   D. ICMP

   E. SNMP

4. Your file and printer server has not been working correctly since a power outage on Sunday evening. Users are having difficulty connecting to the server, and you suspect that one or more of the protocols may be corrupt. Which protocol does Windows NT use for sharing files?

   A. IP

   B. SMB

   C. NFS

   D. ICMP

   E. SNMP

5. Your network is made up of a Windows NT domain that is connected to a UNIX server. Connected to the network are three printers, which are used by both

the Microsoft network clients and the UNIX clients. Which protocol makes the printers available to all clients? The printers are connected directly to the network with HP JetDirect cards.

   A. DLC

   B. TCP/IP

   C. AppleTalk

   D. HPLINK

   E. IPX

6. **ARP is a part of the TCP/IP suite of protocols. It operates at the lower end of the OSI model and plays a key role in directing messages to the proper computers. What exactly does the ARP protocol do?**

   A. ARP is responsible for applying sequence numbers to the header of each package that is sent.

   B. ARP checks the CRC of each package that is received to ensure that the package is not corrupt.

   C. ARP is responsible for setting the TTL clock when sending packets to the destination computer.

   D. ARP is responsible for matching the IP address to the MAC address of a network device.

   E. ARP is responsible for matching the IP address to the segment number of the destination computer.

7. **The marketing domain has three printers that it wants to make available to everyone on the network. Also on the network is a NetWare server that is still used for** specific applications. The protocol that is in use on the network is IPX/SPX, so the users can access either the NetWare server or the NT servers without any problem. The printers are to be controlled by one of the NT servers, and they are going to be set up with TCP/IP. What will need to be done to the client computers to enable users to access the printers? Select the best answer.

   A. Nothing; the NT server will access the printers for them.

   B. TCP/IP must be installed on each of the client computers.

   C. TCP/IP must be installed on each of the client computers, and IPX/SPX must be removed.

   D. TCP/IP won't work; instead, the DLC protocol should be used.

   E. Nothing; the printers should be set up with IPX/SPX.

8. **This question is based on the following scenario. Review the scenario first, followed by the objectives and the proposed solution. Then, evaluate the proposed solution by choosing the best answer.**

Scenario:
Erik has been administering a Windows NT network for the past year and has found that the users experience a lot of problems printing documents reliably. Currently, the four printers are connected directly to individual workstations in the office. The problem is that those people often turn off or reboot their computers. This causes very long print queues on the other computers with printers. Sometimes it takes hours to get a job printed.

Required Result:
Erik wants to use the protocol that is simplest to set up and configure for the printers.

Optional Results:
Erik wants to reduce the size of the print queues so users do not have to wait so long for their print jobs.

All printers must be available to the users all the time.

Proposed Solution:
Erik decides to connect the printers directly to the network using HP JetDirect cards. He is going to use the TCP/IP protocol for the printers and set them up in a printer pool.

Evaluation of Proposed Solution:
Select the correct answer.

   A. The required result is met, but the optional results are not met.

   B. The required result and one of the optional results are met.

   C. The required result is not met, but the two optional results are met.

   D. The required result is not met, but one of the optional results is met.

   E. None of the results are met.

9. Jack wants to be able to access an application on an application server that is on the other side of a firewall. When he asked his network manager how he could gain access, the manager asked which ports the application used. Jack did not know there were different ports and asked what the ports were used for. What are port numbers used for?

   A. To identify the protocol that is being used.

   B. To establish the priorities of the message requests.

   C. To assign the TTL data (Time To Live) for packets that are being sent.

   D. To identify which virtual circuit the data belongs to.

   E. They are identification numbers that are assigned by the IEEE to monitor the use of each application.

10. Generally, when a client accesses files on a server, a single protocol is used. When a client accesses a web site, which three protocols are used?

   A. TCP, DLC, and OSPF

   B. UDP, NWLink, and ARP

   C. TCP, RIP, and OSPF

   D. SNMP, ICMP, and ARP

   E. TCP, ARP, and IP

11. An office has multiple segments (one on each floor) that are connected with routers. Communication within a segment is quite fast, but communication between segments is quite slow. It seems that the routers are not responding fast enough. What protocol change could speed up the routers?

   A. Changing OSPF to RIP

   B. Changing RIP to OSPF

   C. Changing TCP/IP to NWLink

   D. Changing TCP/IP to SMB

   E. Changing NWLink to TCP/IP

12. Jana needs to download some files from a server that can be accessed through a web site. The files are relatively large, and Jana needs to download them before her meeting, which starts in an hour. Which protocol should she use to download the files?

    A. FTP

    B. TCP

    C. UDP

    D. SNMP

    E. OSPF

ANSWER KEY

1. D	6. D	11. B
2. D	7. A	12. A
3. C	8. C	
4. B	9. D	
5. B	10. E	

ANSWERS & EXPLANATIONS

SELECTING NETWORK AND TRANSPORT PROTOCOLS

1. A new network is being planned for your company, which has 25 locations across North and Central America and 16 sites throughout Europe. The expected number of users in Europe is 23,000, and the number in North and Central America will be 30,000–35,000. The new network must work in both LAN and WAN environments. Which protocol is best suited for this network?

   D. TCP/IP

1. CORRECT ANSWER: D

TCP/IP has become the protocol of choice for most local area networks as well as for large-scale networks (WANs). This suite of protocols allows users to work locally, connect to remote network segments, and communicate on the Internet. It can use a combination of connection-oriented communication and connectionless communication to transfer data to other computers. Although its configuration is more complex than other protocols, its networks can be expanded as necessary.

2. You currently have a Microsoft Windows NT network in your office of software developers. You have to make plans for a new group of graphic artists that are to be developing graphics for marketing your products. The new people are all Macintosh users. You are already running NWLink. Do you need to run any other protocol? If so, which one?

   D. AppleTalk.

2. CORRECT ANSWER: D

The Macintosh computers are probably all running the AppleTalk protocol, and it is unlikely that they are using any form of IPX/SPX. Therefore, it would probably be easier to install the additional AppleTalk protocol on the server than to convert all the Macintosh computers.

3. Your network is made up of a Windows NT domain connected to a UNIX server. Connected to the network are three printers, which are controlled by the Windows NT server, and one fax server. In most UNIX environments, what TCP/IP protocol does the UNIX server use to allow file sharing?

   C. NFS

3. CORRECT ANSWER: C

The UNIX server uses the protocol NFS (Network File Service) to allow client computers to access files on the server and send print jobs to the network printer. The NFS Network service uses the Remote Procedure Call (RPC) facility to connect to UNIX machines. Windows NT does not natively support NFS. Therefore, another package must be obtained that enables the Windows NT system to mount an NFS volume on it. Many third-party packages allow this; which you should use depends on your requirements.

4. Your file and printer server has not been working correctly since a power outage on Sunday evening. Users are having difficulty connecting to the server, and you suspect that one or more of the protocols may be corrupt. Which protocol does Windows NT use for sharing files?

B. SMB

4. CORRECT ANSWER: B

Windows NT uses a protocol similar to that of the UNIX server that is called SMB (Server Message Block). This protocol was developed by a number of PC industry leaders in an effort to create a uniform set of commands for passing data across a network.

SMB makes use of both the Server and Workstation services. These services enable a computer to either act as a server and provide resources to other computers or act as a client and access other computers' resources across the network. Both functions are accomplished through connection-oriented sessions using low-level protocols such as TCP/IP.

To request a file from another computer, the Workstation service creates a series of SMB packets that are used to establish a connection with the remote computer. The SMB packets also request the file from that computer.

5. Your network is made up of a Windows NT domain that is connected to a UNIX server. Connected to the network are three printers, which are used by both the Microsoft network clients and the UNIX clients. Which protocol makes the printers available to all clients? The printers are connected directly to the network with HP JetDirect cards.

B. TCP/IP

5. CORRECT ANSWER: B

Both Windows NT and UNIX are capable of using the TCP/IP protocol suite. If the printers are configured using TCP/IP, both Windows NT clients and UNIX clients can send print jobs to the network printers.

6. ARP is a part of the TCP/IP suite of protocols. It operates at the lower end of the OSI model and plays a key role in directing messages to the proper computers. What exactly does the ARP protocol do?

D. ARP is responsible for matching the IP address to the MAC address of a network device.

6. CORRECT ANSWER: D

Most applications operate at a high level, using NetBIOS names to indicate which computer they want to communicate with. However, for communication to take place, that name has to be resolved to a network address, and then the network address has to be resolved to the hardware address of the network adapter card.

ARP is the protocol that resolves the network address (the IP address) to a hardware (MAC) address. After the address has been resolved, it is stored in cache for a period of time before it is flushed. Static entries may be made for computers that are accessed on a regular basis; these addresses are not flushed from the cache.

7. The marketing domain has three printers that it wants to make available to everyone on the network. Also on the network is a NetWare server that is still used for specific applications. The protocol that is in use on the network is IPX/SPX, so the users can access either the NetWare server or the NT servers without any problem. The printers are to be controlled by one of the NT servers, and they are going to be set up with TCP/IP. What will need to be done to the client computers to enable users to access the printers? Select the best answer.

A. Nothing; the NT server will access the printers for them.

7. CORRECT ANSWER: A

No changes to the client computers are necessary as far as protocols are concerned. The Windows NT server is the computer that actually communicates directly with the printers. When a client sends a job to be printed, the workstation spools the print job, and then it is sent to the server. The server spools the print job again, and then it makes the request to the printer. Because the print job goes through the server, only the server has to be running the TCP/IP protocol.

8. *Proposed Solution:* Erik decides to connect the printers directly to the network using HP JetDirect cards. He is going to use the TCP/IP protocol for the printers and set them up in a printer pool.

C. The required result is not met, but the two optional results are met.

8. CORRECT ANSWER: C

By connecting the printers to the network and configuring them in a printer pool, you solve a lot of the printer problems. If the server is rarely rebooted, the printers are going to be available to the users all the time. By configuring them in a printer pool, the queues will be much more consistent from printer to printer. The four printers will appear to be one entity to the user, and the server will send each print job to the first available printer.

The required result was not met because TCP/IP is not the simplest protocol to configure. It has to be configured at both the printer and the server. The simplest protocol would have been DLC, which allows the printer to be set up on the server in a matter of seconds and does not require any configuration at the printer. The only problem with using DLC is that it does not provide a fully functional protocol stack, which means it does not support connectivity between Windows 95 and Windows NT computers.

DLC is used only for connectivity with some mainframe computers and for setting up network printers. If DLC was used for printing, another protocol would be needed to enable communication between the computers. When you are trying to optimize a network, you want to use the fewest possible protocols.

9. Jack wants to be able to access an application on an application server that is on the other side of a firewall. When he asked his network manager how he could gain access, the manager asked which ports the application used. Jack did not know there were different ports and asked what the ports were used for. What are port numbers used for?

D. To identify which virtual circuit the data belongs to.

9. CORRECT ANSWER: D

Ports are used to identify a virtual circuit or thread that a particular application uses to communicate. Some applications can share a port, whereas some applications need their own. For a high degree of control over which applications can be accessed in a secure network, firewalls are often configured to allow only specific computers across the firewall through certain ports.

As an example, if Jack's computer was on one side of the firewall and an application server was on the other side, the firewall would have to be configured specifically to allow him to run his application on the server. Once the firewall was configured as such, he would have access to that application. If Jack then tried to run a different application, however, he would probably be denied because the port the second application uses is probably not the same as that of the first application and would not be open to him.

10. Generally, when a client accesses files on a server, a single protocol is used. When a client accesses a web site, which three protocols are used?

E. TCP, ARP, and IP

10. CORRECT ANSWER: E

TCP is needed to access the Internet. ARP is needed to resolve an IP address to a hardware address before communication can be established between two computers or between a computer and a router. And finally, the IP protocol is used for routing. It sends packets using a computer's IP address. Every computer on the network (the Internet is actually one very large network) must have a unique IP address.

11. An office has multiple segments (one on each floor) that are connected with routers. Communication within a segment is quite fast, but communication between segments is quite slow. It seems that the routers are not responding fast enough. What protocol change could speed up the routers?

    B. Changing RIP to OSPF

11. CORRECT ANSWER: B

Routing Information Protocol (RIP) uses a distance-vector algorithm to determine routes. Before communication between segments can take place, the RIP must calculate which path or route to take. Open Shortest Path First (OSPF) is a link-state algorithm that uses more processing power than RIP but allows more control and responds to changes faster than RIP does.

The distance in RIP is the number of routers a packet must cross to reach a destination. Each of these routers is referred to as a *hop*. The maximum number of hops allowed in RIP is 15. A destination is considered unreachable if the hop count is greater than 15. Routers use the hop count to determine the best route to use for a given packet at a given time.

The OSPF (link-state) protocol creates a graph abstracting the topology of the network. It then computes the shortest path according to weights on the arcs of the graph. This graphing and weighting of the paths uses more processor power, but it generally responds to path changes more quickly than RIP does.

12. Jana needs to download some files from a server that can be accessed through a web site. The files are relatively large, and Jana needs to download them before her meeting, which starts in an hour. Which protocol should she use to download the files?

    A. FTP

12. CORRECT ANSWER: A

File Transfer Protocol (FTP) is a member of the TCP/IP protocol suite that is designed specifically for transferring files between a server and a client. This protocol allows bidirectional transfer of binary and ACII files between computers.

SELECTING APPROPRIATE CONNECTIVITY DEVICES

1. At his training center, Paul is setting up two classrooms for technical courses that are to take place next week. Ethernet is usually used in the classrooms, but one class needs to be configured using Token-Ring. If Paul wants both classrooms to be able to use the same download server, what type of device can he use to connect the segments?

   A. Switch

   B. Bridge

   C. Router

   D. Gateway

   E. Repeater

2. Shelley is setting up a 10BASE-T network and needs to connect two computers that are 180 meters apart. Because she works for a nonprofit organization, she must use the least expensive connection device possible. The device that she chooses must be able to extend the network without introducing any packet filtering. What device should Shelley choose?

   A. Gateway

   B. Switch

   C. Router

   D. Hub

   E. Repeater

3. In question 2, remember that Shelley was trying to find the least expensive device to connect two computers 180 meters apart. Suppose some local businesses get together and donate funds for her network. Now that cost is not a factor, Shelley wants to use the fastest possible device. Which device is the fastest?

   A. Gateway

   B. Switch

   C. Router

   D. Hub

   E. Repeater

4. The LMN Corporation provides vital information for a number of industries. The links between its network and its clients are of paramount importance. To ensure connectivity, redundant components have been set in place. To make use of the redundant paths, what components must be used?

   A. Bridges

   B. Routers

   C. Switches

   D. Repeaters

   E. Gateways

5. Your company has expanded its office space, but the Ethernet network cannot be extended because it already has the

maximum number of repeaters allowed. What device could be used to extend the network without causing errors?

A. Bridge

B. Active hub

C. Multiport repeater

D. Gateway

E. Passive hub

6. Your consulting firm has been asked to help a seasonal charity group with some network problems. It is using an Ethernet network with 135 computers connected to it. NetBEUI is being used, and network traffic is becoming a problem. Because it is only in operation for another two months, it wants to treat its problems with a minimum of changes. What device could it use?

A. Router

B. Bridge

C. Repeater

D. Gateway

E. Hub

7. The business manager for your firm has requested that you find a solution to enable the research group and the marketing group to share information. Until now, sharing has not been possible because each group has had its own network, one of which is using the IPX/SPX protocol and the other of which is using the NetBEUI protocol. Your job is to enable them to communicate, yet make as few configuration changes as possible. What device could you use?

A. Repeater

B. Router

C. Gateway

D. Switch

E. Brouter

8. Karl has a network of 500 users who recently started reporting that they were experiencing *broadcast storms* at different times during the day. They are using the TCP/IP protocol suite, and a DHCP server is used to configure each of the workstations. What could be done to reduce the network traffic problem?

A. Switch from TCP/IP to the NetBEUI protocol.

B. Remove the DHCP server and statically assign IP addresses to each of the workstations.

C. Create segments using a router.

D. Separate the servers from the rest of the network using a gateway.

E. Set up separate scope IDs for each 100 computers.

9. Jane is trying to troubleshoot a problem on the network. It appears that devices are not forwarding the data packets properly. The devices are supposed to be forwarding the packets according to the hardware address in the frame, but this is not happening. What type of device is supposed to forward packets according to the hardware address in the frame?

A. Repeater

B. Router

   C. Gateway

   D. Bridge

   E. Hub

10. **The previous network administrator configured your network's servers, workstations, printers, and routers. Everything was working fine when you took over the position, but last week when a segment went down, the traffic was not rerouted. What could be wrong with the configuration?**

   A. The routers are configured for Open Shortest Path First, and they always try to use the first path they learned.

   B. The routers are configured to use Routing Information Protocol, which is a distance vector protocol.

   C. The routers are configured with static routes.

   D. Switches should have been used instead of routers.

   E. Gateways can switch routes automatically, whereas routers must be reconfigured manually.

11. **Your firm recommends that a client should not allow its Internet firewall to learn routes dynamically. This is a basic security measure intended to reduce the** risk of someone hacking into your network. What can the client use instead of allowing the firewall to learn routes?

   A. Proxy

   B. Network Address Translation

   C. Firewall

   D. Gateway

   E. Static routes

12. **Shelley needs to connect two remote networks, but she is having difficulty deciding what to do. The client has two offices that have 46 and 63 computers, respectively, all of which are running Ethernet. She would have used routers to connect the two sites, but both are using NetBEUI as the only protocol, and neither wants to change. What can Shelley do to appease her clients?**

   A. Install routers and configure them to forward broadcasts.

   B. Install brouters.

   C. Add TCP/IP to each of the computers so that they run two protocols.

   D. Run a direct fiber-optic link between the two sites.

   E. Find a new site large enough for both offices.

ANSWER KEY

1. C	5. A	9. D
2. E	6. B	10. C
3. E	7. C	11. E
4. B	8. C	12. B

SELECTING APPROPRIATE CONNECTIVITY DEVICES

1. **At his training center, Paul is setting up two classrooms for technical courses that are to take place next week. Ethernet is usually used in the classrooms, but one class needs to be configured using Token-Ring. If Paul wants both classrooms to be able to use the same download server, what type of device can he use to connect the segments?**

   C. Router

1. CORRECT ANSWER: C

Routers can connect networks that are using two different architectures. If Paul uses a router, both classrooms will be able to connect to and communicate with the same server.

2. **Shelley is setting up a 10BASE-T network and needs to connect two computers that are 180 meters apart. Because she works for a nonprofit organization, she must use the least expensive connection device possible. The device that she chooses must be able to extend the network without introducing any packet filtering. What device should Shelley choose?**

   E. Repeater

2. CORRECT ANSWER: E

A repeater is a very simple device that regenerates weakened signals and passes them to the next segment. Repeaters do not do any translation or filtering, so they are not expensive. They are also capable of extending a network.

The repeater operates at the Physical layer of the OSI model. This is the lowest level in the model, which indicates that a repeater functions at a very low level. It simply takes the signal it receives, regenerates it, and passes it on to the next segment. Because it operates at such a low level and does not provide any kind of filtering, it could pass along bad data. In addition to passing bad data, the repeater can also contribute to network traffic by passing broadcast storms from one segment to another.

A *broadcast storm* is a time when there are so many broadcast messages on the network that the available bandwidth is nearly used up.

3. In question 2, remember that Shelley was trying to find the least expensive device to connect two computers 180 meters apart. Suppose some local businesses get together and donate funds for her network. Now that cost is not a factor, Shelley wants to use the fastest possible device. Which device is the fastest?

E. Repeater

3. CORRECT ANSWER: E

Part of the reason the repeater is inexpensive in comparison to other devices is that it does not have a lot of built-in capabilities. Because there is relatively little overhead associated with a repeater's functions, it is also one of the fastest devices.

4. The LMN Corporation provides vital information for a number of industries. The links between its network and its clients are of paramount importance. To ensure connectivity, redundant components have been set in place. To make use of the redundant paths, what components must be used?

B. Routers

4. CORRECT ANSWER: B

A router chooses a path to a remote site, provided the proper protocol is installed. Because the router is able to learn a path, connectivity is nearly guaranteed, no matter what the circumstances.

5. Your company has expanded its office space, but the Ethernet network cannot be extended because it already has the maximum number of repeaters allowed. What device could be used to extend the network without causing errors?

A. Bridge

5. CORRECT ANSWER: A

Like a repeater, a bridge can be used to extend a network. However, unlike a repeater, a bridge is capable of isolating portions of a network to reduce network traffic and eliminate bottlenecks. While the bridge listens to the network, it builds its own routing table as information becomes available. When the bridge receives a signal that needs to go to a computer that is in its routing table, it forwards the signal to the segment that has that computer. A repeater, on the other hand, passes signals on to the next segment whether the computer is on that segment or not.

6. Your consulting firm has been asked to help a seasonal charity group with some network problems. It is using an Ethernet network with 135 computers connected to it. NetBEUI is being used, and network traffic is becoming a problem. Because it is only in operation for another two months, it wants to treat its problems with a minimum of changes. What device could it use?

B. Bridge

6. CORRECT ANSWER: B

A bridge will allow the group to isolate segments of its network without having to do too much to the network itself. Routers would also be a consideration for isolating portions of the network, but because NetBEUI is not a routable protocol, another protocol would have to be installed on every computer. Bridges operate at the Data Link layer of the OSI model.

7. The business manager for your firm has requested that you find a solution to enable the research group and the marketing group to share information. Until now, sharing has not been possible because each group has had its own network, one of which is using the IPX/SPX protocol and the other of which is using the NetBEUI protocol. Your job is to enable them to communicate, yet make as few configuration changes as possible. What device could you use?

   C. Gateway

Most devices transfer signals without translating the protocols. However, the gateway is capable of filtering and translating signals. Because it can operate at a higher level (right up to the Application layer), the gateway does not require the same protocol to be used on both segments.

Because the gateway is such a specialized device, it is not commonly used to connect remote networks. It is generally used only to translate between personal computers and mainframe computers. In Windows NT, a gateway service is commonly used to enable communication between a Windows NT domain and a NetWare network. Again, the gateway converts the requests from the Microsoft network to calls that are recognized on the NetWare side.

8. Karl has a network of 500 users who recently started reporting that they were experiencing *broadcast storms* at different times during the day. They are using the TCP/IP protocol suite, and a DHCP server is used to configure each of the workstations. What could be done to reduce the network traffic problem?

   C. Create segments using a router.

A router is often used to separate segments of a network in order to reduce network traffic. However, one important point was not covered in this question: "How will the workstations be configured with the TCP/IP protocol?" Because you will not want the router(s) to pass broadcast storms from one segment to another, either the workstations will have to be configured manually, or a DHCP server will have to be set up on each segment.

9. Jane is trying to troubleshoot a problem on the network. It appears that devices are not forwarding the data packets properly. The devices are supposed to be forwarding the packets according to the hardware address in the frame, but this is not happening. What type of device is supposed to forward packets according to the hardware address in the frame?

   D. Bridge

Bridges listen to the network and build routing tables according to the hardware addresses of computers. If bridges are being used in your network, but the frames are not being passed as they should be, you might need to make a configuration change.

10. **The previous network administrator configured your network's servers, workstations, printers, and routers. Everything was working fine when you took over the position, but last week when a segment went down, the traffic was not rerouted. What could be wrong with the configuration?**

   C. **The routers are configured with static routes.**

Routers can be configured to find routes on their own. However, if they do not have the protocols installed, routes are entered manually. These are referred to as *static routes*, and they work fine as long as the routes are available. However, the router will not be able to "learn" new routes, so if the necessary route is not available, the connection will not be established.

In a nutshell, *static routes* are manually added to the routing table by an administrator. If the routes need to be changed, the administrator has to make the changes manually. *Dynamic routes* are added to a device's routing table by the device itself. They are based on either information the device gains from other routers or information the device calculates. If the routes change, the routing table automatically updates itself.

11. **Your firm recommends that a client should not allow its Internet firewall to learn routes dynamically. This is a basic security measure intended to reduce the risk of someone hacking into your network. What can the client use instead of allowing the firewall to learn routes?**

   E. **Static routes**

As in the last question, if you want to maintain a certain level of security, you can prevent your firewall from learning routes. If the firewall is only allowed to communicate with routes you establish, it is much more difficult for someone to hack in. And if someone does hack in, you have a narrow scope of where to look to find the infiltrator.

12. **Shelley needs to connect two remote networks, but she is having difficulty deciding what to do. The client has two offices that have 46 and 63 computers, respectively, all of which are running Ethernet. She would have used routers to connect the two sites, but both are using NetBEUI as the only protocol, and neither wants to change. What can Shelley do to appease her clients?**

   B. **Install brouters.**

A brouter is similar to a router in that it will route routable protocols. In addition, it can also bridge protocols that cannot be routed. Therefore, a brouter can be used to connect two remote networks that use a protocol such as NetBEUI.

Suppose you need to connect several network segments, some of which need a router, and some of which need a bridge. Using a brouter can be more cost-effective and manageable than using separate routers and bridges. Routers operate at the Network layer of the OSI model.

UNDERSTANDING THE CHARACTERISTICS, REQUIREMENTS, AND SITUATIONS FOR WAN SERVICES

1. Nancy has been negotiating with the local telecommunications company about increasing the company's "pipe" to the Internet. One option is to use a fractional T1 line that can be split into a number of channels. By using channels on a T1, the company could expand its network later. A T1 line can operate at 1.544Mbps and can be split into 24 separate channels. In a 100Mbps Ethernet network, at what speed can each of these channels operate?

   A. 64Kbps

   B. 24Kbps

   C. 100Mbps

   D. 1.544Mbps

   E. 10Mbps

2. Your company needs to establish LAN connectivity of at least 1Mbps between two sites that are almost 45 miles apart. Installing a dedicated line between the two locations would be too expensive, so you are looking at leased line options. Which would be the best option?

   A. DS-0

   B. T1

   C. T2

   D. T3

   E. T4

3. You have set up a modest-size company that is importing and exporting goods between North and South America. You established an office in Ecuador so you can stay abreast of what is taking place in the South American markets. What WAN type should you use to establish relatively fast communication between the offices?

   A. Leased T1

   B. X.25

   C. ATM

   D. Frame relay

   E. T3

4. Steve is planning a WAN that connects his office in Chicago with an office in Liverpool. Previous connections were not reliable, and his company found that it could not depend on data being delivered reliably. As a result, Steve is planning to use a reliable error-correcting service. Which service should Steve use?

   A. ATM

   B. Frame relay

   C. X.25

   D. ISDN

   E. Leased T1

5. Having set up the WAN connection between the Chicago and Liverpool offices (refer to question 4), Steve needs to establish a connection with the satellite office in Winnipeg. For this connection, he wants relatively fast communication at a minimal cost. What type of network connection should Steve use between the Chicago and Winnipeg offices?

   A. X.25

   B. Frame relay

   C. ISDN

   D. Leased T1

   E. ATM

6. Stacey has been discussing different WAN options with her telecommunications company. One option was to use a switched virtual circuit. The term *virtual circuit* has Stacey confused about whether this is really what she needs. What does the term *switched virtual circuit* mean?

   A. The circuit becomes active only when there is data to be transferred.

   B. The circuit is always active and dedicated.

   C. The circuit automatically switches to another path if a router is not active.

   D. The circuit is used over point-to-point leased lines.

   E. The circuit can switch speeds according to the requested destination.

7. Typically, WAN connections are not as fast as LAN connections because of the media over which the data is being transferred and the overhead that is included in each packet. Which WAN connection service has the greatest overhead?

   A. Leased T1

   B. ISDN

   C. ATM

   D. X.25

   E. Frame relay

8. Some WAN connection services use a lot of overhead to transfer data because they assume the media is not "clean" and that there will be a lot of errors. However, with the cleaner and faster media available now, WAN connection services with relatively little overhead can be used. Which service has the least overhead?

   A. Leased T1

   B. ISDN

   C. ATM

   D. X.25

   E. Frame relay

9. Gerry's company has a leased T1 line connecting its two offices. However, some applications must be accessed across the WAN all the time. To make a redundant connection, it has set up a dial-up line in case the T1 fails. What type of circuit is designed for WAN dial-up connectivity?

   A. Leased T1

   B. Frame relay

C. ISDN

D. ATM

E. X.25

10. Sam has an application that requires very fast communication between the client and server. The LAN at the main site is an Ethernet 100Mbps network. For the satellite offices to be able to run the application, they need a WAN connection of a similar speed. What WAN service can provide a throughput of 100Mbps?

A. Leased T1

B. ISDN

C. Frame relay

D. ATM

E. X.25

11. Salid is reviewing the expenses his company has accrued over the past six months for communications. To cut costs and combine expenses, he wants to use a connection service that will carry voice, data, and video together. Which service can meet this requirement?

A. Leased T1

B. ISDN

C. Frame relay

D. ATM

E. X.25

ANSWER KEY

1. A	5. B	9. C
2. B	6. A	10. D
3. B	7. D	11. D
4. C	8. A	

UNDERSTANDING THE CHARACTERISTICS, REQUIREMENTS, AND SITUATIONS FOR WAN SERVICES

1. Nancy has been negotiating with the local telecommunications company about increasing the company's "pipe" to the Internet. One option is to use a fractional T1 line that can be split into a number of channels. By using channels on a T1, the company could expand its network later. A T1 line can operate at 1.544Mbps and can be split into 24 separate channels. In a 100Mbps Ethernet network, at what speed can each of these channels operate?

   A. 64Kbps

1. CORRECT ANSWER: A

A T1 line can operate at approximately 1.544Mbps, which is a very common line speed for WAN connectivity. The T1 line can be split (fractional T1) into a number of channels—24 in total. This works out to be 24 channels at approximately 64Kbps. It does not matter what speed the LAN is operating at; each channel can have a throughput of approximately 64Kbps. In most cases, communication between sites does not need to be more than 64Kbps. By using a fractional T1, the company will be able to add channels as it grows.

2. Your company needs to establish LAN connectivity of at least 1Mbps between two sites that are almost 45 miles apart. Installing a dedicated line between the two locations would be too expensive, so you are looking at leased line options. Which would be the best option?

   B. T1

2. CORRECT ANSWER: B

All except DS-0 can provide line speeds of at least 1Mbps. The T1 line would operate closest to the speed of 1Mbps. Therefore, to meet the line speed needs yet keep costs down, T1 would be the best option.

Using a leased line means you're guaranteed that the line is always available to your company and that the signal will be of a higher quality (because it does not have to go through a series of switches). The leased line becomes dedicated to you and your company.

3. You have set up a modest-size company that is importing and exporting goods between North and South America. You established an office in Ecuador so you can stay abreast of what is taking place in the South American markets. What WAN type should you use to establish relatively fast communication between the offices?

   B. X.25

3. CORRECT ANSWER: B

Typically speaking, anytime you try to establish WAN connectivity from one continent to another, you should not expect quality connectivity. Because each country or continent has its own standards, you have to expect a certain degree of error to accompany each transmission over an intercontinental connection. Because X.25 was originally used on telephone lines to transmit data, it was designed with extensive error checking. Although the overhead of checking errors causes X.25 to be somewhat slower than other WAN environments, it is very reliable.

X.25 is a set of protocols combined in a packet-switching network. The network uses switches, circuits, and routes to provide the best routing at any particular time. If a circuit or route is unavailable, it automatically switches to one that is available. A PAD (packet assembler/disassembler) is needed at each end to assemble and disassemble the packets.

Although X.25 may be slower than T1 or ATM, it is faster than a dial-up connection and is more reliable for international connections.

4. Steve is planning a WAN that connects his office in Chicago with an office in Liverpool. Previous connections were not reliable, and his company found that it could not depend on data being delivered reliably. As a result, Steve is planning to use a reliable error-correcting service. Which service should Steve use?

   C. X.25

4. CORRECT ANSWER: C

As mentioned in the answer to question 3, X.25 was designed to be used over telephone lines and, therefore, has extensive error checking built into it. Although the overhead that accompanies error checking will slow down communication, users are guaranteed that bad data will not be transferred.

5. Having set up the WAN connection between the Chicago and Liverpool offices (refer to question 4), Steve needs to establish a connection with the satellite office in Winnipeg. For this connection, he wants relatively fast communication at a minimal cost. What type of network connection should Steve use between the Chicago and Winnipeg offices?

   B. Frame relay

5. CORRECT ANSWER: B

Unlike WAN connections between continents, network connectivity in North America is relatively reliable and fast. Therefore, a service such as frame relay is definitely an option in this situation. Like X.25, it uses packet switching, but without a lot of the checking functions of X.25.

Frame Relay is a point-to-point system that uses a Private Virtual Circuit to transmit variable length frames. Because the path from one end to the other is known, there is no need for fragmentation and reassembly or to provide best-path routing.

The disadvantage of frame relay is that it requires a leased line with routers that are capable of working with frame relay. The leased line must also be high quality because frame relay does not have the advanced error checking that X.25 has.

6. Stacey has been discussing different WAN options with her telecommunications company. One option was to use a switched virtual circuit. The term *virtual circuit* has Stacey confused about whether this is really what she needs. What does the term *switched virtual circuit* mean?

   A. The circuit becomes active only when there is data to be transferred.

6. CORRECT ANSWER: A

As the name *virtual circuit* implies, the user sees what looks like a constant available circuit. In truth, the connection is not established until both computers have exchanged information and agreed on communication parameters. Communication parameters establish and maintain the connection, including the message path and size. These virtual channels can be either temporary (lasting as long as the conversation) or permanent (lasting as long as the communication channel is open).

A switched virtual circuit differs from and is less expensive than a dedicated line. With virtual circuits, a number of clients could be using the same lines at different times and for varying lengths of time. With dedicated lines, only the client that purchases the dedicated line can use it.

If a person or company needs the circuit only for different periods during the day or week, they are better off to use a virtual circuit. However, if the business requires that it needs constant connectivity, it should opt for a dedicated line.

7. Typically, WAN connections are not as fast as LAN connections because of the media over which the data is being transferred and the overhead that is included in each packet. Which WAN connection service has the greatest overhead?

   D. X.25

7. CORRECT ANSWER: D

X.25 provides a great deal of accounting and error checking to ensure that data arrives at the destination with relatively few errors, which, unfortunately, causes greater overhead. X.25 was originally designed to be used over telephone lines.

8. Some WAN connection services use a lot of overhead to transfer data because they assume the media is not "clean" and that there will be a lot of errors. However, with the cleaner and faster media available now, WAN connection services with relatively little overhead can be used. Which service has the least overhead?

   A. Leased T1

8. CORRECT ANSWER: A

T1 is the industry standard digital network that can accommodate both voice and data. T1 can be very expensive because it is a point-to-point technology that uses wire pairs to transmit full-duplex signals. The maximum transfer rate of a T1 line is 1.544Mbps. Individuals and companies that cannot afford the expense of a full T1 line can lease one or more channels in 64Kbps increments. This is known as *fractional T1*. T1 service is not available in all countries. Another service that may be available is E1, which has a signaling rate of 2.048Mbps.

9. Gerry's company has a leased T1 line connecting its two offices. However, some applications must be accessed across the WAN all the time. To make a redundant connection, it has set up a dial-up line in case the T1 fails. What type of circuit is designed for WAN dial-up connectivity?

   C. ISDN

9. CORRECT ANSWER: C

Integrated Services Digital Network (ISDN) was originally designed to connect homes to businesses across copper telephone lines. This depended on the telephone circuits being converted from analog to digital, which is taking place around the world.

ISDN is the digital replacement for the public switched telephone network (PSTN) and, as such, is only a dial-up service. Unlike T1 service, ISDN is not designed to be a 24-hour service. And, unlike frame relay, it is not meant to be bandwidth-on-demand. It is designed to be a dial-up connection that is used when needed and released when communication is complete.

Given the scenario in this question, the ISDN connection is strictly for redundancy and would be used only if T1 service is not available.

10. Sam has an application that requires very fast communication between the client and server. The LAN at the main site is an Ethernet 100Mbps network. For the satellite offices to be able to run the application, they need a WAN connection of a similar speed. What WAN service can provide a throughput of 100Mbps?

    D. ATM

10. CORRECT ANSWER: D

Asynchronous Transfer Mode (ATM) is advanced packet switching that provides high-speed data transmissions over LANs or WANs. ATM can theoretically offer transfer rates of up 1.2Gbps, but most commercial hardware currently operates at 155Mbps. To reach higher speeds, ATM uses a uniform data packet size. To reach the maximum speeds, fiber media would also have to be used. ATM can be implemented with any type of media that is normally used, such as coaxial, twisted-pair, and fiber-optic cable.

The biggest disadvantage to using ATM right now is that it is still relatively new and, therefore, is much more expensive than other solutions. As the technology becomes more accepted, the cost will decrease. The ATM network also uses new devices, and the support of these devices is another problem.

11. Salid is reviewing the expenses his company has accrued over the past six months for communications. To cut costs and combine expenses, he wants to use a connection service that will carry voice, data, and video together. Which service can meet this requirement?

    D. ATM

11. CORRECT ANSWER: D

Both ATM and T1 are capable of transmitting voice, data, and video over the same lines. However, the speed of ATM is much greater than that of T1 because it does not use a dedicated line. The biggest drawback to using ATM in this situation is that the existing equipment would have to be replaced, which could be expensive depending on the size of the network. Depending on current usage, however, combining voice and data into one component could be cost-effective and convenient enough to make it worth replacing equipment.

FURTHER REVIEW

Table 2.2 shows the different line speeds available from digital leased lines. These are good things to understand and commit to memory for the exam.

TABLE 2.2   LINE SPEEDS AVAILABLE FROM DIGITAL LEASED LINES

Carrier	Number of T1 Channels	Number of Voice Channels	Data Rate (Mbps)
N/A	N/A	1	0.064
T1	1	24	1.544
T-1C	2	48	3.152
T2	4	96	6.312
T3	28	672	44.736
T4	168	4032	274.76

SUMMARY

There is no quick and easy way to come to a conclusion through logic unless you know the specifications and limitations of different pieces of hardware. When selecting the proper media in real life, you would look up the information in a table or book. But for the exam, you should at least know the specifications for the more common types of networks.

When selecting the appropriate topology, you have to look at the whole scenario first before jumping to any conclusions. The exam often throws curves at you, and you have to be ready to think through the question. What initially seems to be the correct answer might not be correct for the given situation.

Learn and know your protocols. These are always important whether it be for an exam or for day-to-day administration. Know what each one was designed for and how it can be used. Always try to use a minimum number of protocols to reduce network traffic.

The exam will include a number of questions on the different devices that can be used to connect local and remote network segments. It's important that you know these for the exam. As technology moves on, it will be important that you know what is available now, what has been available in the past, and what will become available in the future. You will see a number of questions regarding WAN connection services. If you are not sure of these services, the wording of these questions will be sure to catch you.

Implementation

To successfully install, configure, and maintain a network, you must build a plan of action well in advance. A lot of potentially good networks have failed because of poor planning. A network can be well-designed yet still fail due to an oversight regarding security or disaster recovery. The most secure network is useless without a disaster plan.

All procedures should be reviewed and documented so that they are up-to-date and so that anyone in the IS department could carry out the procedures.

Microsoft identifies the following test objectives for the Implementation portion of the exam:

Choose an administrative plan to meet specified needs, including performance management, account management, and security. (Practice questions start on page 119.)

▶ Network security can vary depending on the network operating system being used. Because of the existence of different security models, it is important to understand the different administrative models that exist. One model may be ideal for one situation but impractical for another. This chapter analyzes these issues and explains the various administrative models in order to address the issues of performance, account management, and security. To master this exam topic, pay particular attention to the differences between Workgroup and Domain administrative models. This objective is addressed throughout the entire chapter.

continues

Choose a disaster recovery plan for various situations. (Practice questions start on page 130.)

▶ This exam topic deals with proactive measures that you can take to prevent lost data and server downtime.

Given the manufacturer's documentation for the network adapter, install, configure, and resolve hardware conflicts for multiple network adapters in a Token-Ring or Ethernet network. (Practice questions start on page 139.)

▶ As a network professional, it is vital that you have the ability to not only install and configure network adapter cards, but also to resolve hardware conflicts between network adapter cards and other adapters and peripherals. If these conflicts exist and are not resolved, your network adapter card will not function, thereby preventing your device from connecting to the network.

Implement a NetBIOS naming scheme for all computers on a given network. (Practice questions start on page 148.)

▶ Microsoft networking components rely on the capability to reference other machines on the network using NetBIOS names. This exam objective makes it clear that you must have the ability to deal with NetBIOS naming rules for computers.

Select the appropriate hardware and software tools to monitor trends in the network. (Practice questions start on page 156.)

▶ One of the most important things an administrator can do is monitor the network. By monitoring the network, the administrator is able to determine the demand placed upon the system and the usage of resources. This exam objective is designed to encourage you to develop your ability to determine what tools you should use in monitoring the network for trends.

CHOOSING AN ADMINISTRATIVE PLAN

1. The main reason to implement a network is to enable users to share resources. In a Windows environment, a user accesses a resource by connecting to the resource via a UNC name. Suppose a share name of "Data" exists in the Marketing domain, which is on the E: drive of the computer named "market12." This computer also shares data with the Sales workgroup. What would be the proper syntax to connect to this share from a command prompt on a Windows NT Workstation?

   A. net use g: \\market12\data

   B. net use E: \\market12\\data

   C. map D: \\market12\data

   D. net use g: \\marketing\data

   E. net use E: \\marketing\\data

2. This question is based on the following scenario. Review the scenario first, followed by the objectives and the proposed solution. Then, evaluate the proposed solution by choosing the best answer. (Note that questions 3–6 are also based on this scenario.)

   Scenario:

Network type:	Windows NT
Protocol used:	TCP/IP
Network size:	1 Windows NT Server, 40 Windows 95 workstations

In addition to your primary duties as law clerk, you are responsible for administering the small network in your office. Although the office is small and everyone knows one another, client/attorney privilege demands that the data on the network be secure. In addition, most of the users are computer literate and can be considered "power users." A large client has just been signed, and it is imperative that the level of security on your network be improved. To meet these needs, you must develop a security plan.

Required Result:
All sensitive data must be protected.

Optional Results:
The plan must be simple and easy to administer.

Access to the sensitive data needs to be tracked and kept in a log.

Proposed Solution:
You decide to replace all Windows 95 systems with Windows NT Workstation and convert to NTFS on the workstations with auditing enabled.

Evaluation of Proposed Solution:
Which of the following statements is true? (Choose the best answer.)

   A. The required result and both of the optional results are met.

   B. The required result and one of the optional results are met.

C. The required result is met, but neither of the optional results is met.

D. The required result is not met, but both of the optional results are met.

E. None of the results are met.

3. **This question is based on the scenario described in question 2. If necessary, review the scenario and the objectives again. Then, read this proposed solution and evaluate it by choosing the best answer.**

Proposed Solution:
You implement Windows NT Workstation on all the workstation computers, and you use user-level access permissions on the sensitive network resources to protect them.

Evaluation of Proposed Solution:
Which of the following statements is true? (Choose the best answer.)

A. The required result and both of the optional results are met.

B. The required result and one of the optional results are met.

C. The required result is met, but neither of the optional results is met.

D. The required result is not met, but both of the optional results are met.

E. None of the results are met.

4. **This question is based on the scenario described in question 2. If necessary, review the scenario and the objectives again. Then, read this proposed solution and evaluate it by choosing the best answer.**

Proposed Solution:
You continue to use Windows 95 on the workstations, but you move all sensitive data to the server. You create a user account for each user, assign them into groups, and control access to network resources using the groups.

Evaluation of Proposed Solution:
Which of the following statements is true? (Choose the best answer.)

A. The required result and both of the optional results are met.

B. The required result and one of the optional results are met.

C. The required result is met, but neither of the optional results is met.

D. The required result is not met, but both of the optional results are met.

E. None of the results are met.

5. **This question is based on the scenario described in question 2. If necessary, review the scenario and the objectives again. Then, read this proposed solution and evaluate it by choosing the best answer.**

Proposed Solution:
You continue to use Windows 95 on the workstations, but you convert the Windows NT Server disk to NTFS. You enable auditing for the shared resources and place everyone in the same group to protect the sensitive data.

Evaluation of Proposed Solution:
Which of the following statements is true? (Choose the best answer.)

A. The required result and both of the optional results are met.

B. The required result and one of the optional results are met.

C. The required result is met, but neither of the optional results is met.

D. The required result is not met, but both of the optional results are met.

E. None of the results are met.

6. **This question is based on the scenario described in question 2. If necessary, review the scenario and the objectives again. Then, read this proposed solution and evaluate it by choosing the best answer.**

Proposed Solution:
You continue to use Windows 95 on the workstations, and you create a user account for each user. You convert the Windows NT Server disk to NTFS and enable file-level auditing. You then enable user-level access to control access to network resources.

Evaluation of Proposed Solution:
Which of the following statements is true? (Choose the best answer.)

A. The required result and both of the optional results are met.

B. The required result and one of the optional results are met.

C. The required result is met, but neither of the optional results is met.

D. The required result is not met, but both of the optional results are met.

E. None of the results are met.

7. **As part of your security policy, you set user accounts to be locked out after three bad attempts within a one-hour time period. The reason for this change in policy is that someone has been guessing passwords and getting into other people's files. Jan has asked you what will happen if the Administrator account becomes locked out. What explanation should you give her?**

A. You have created two extra administrator-equivalent accounts that you can use to carry out the administrative work if the original account becomes locked out.

B. In the Account Policies dialog box, you set the Administrator account to not be locked out.

C. The Administrator account cannot be locked out.

D. The Administrator account can be locked out for only one hour.

E. All accounts are locked out for only one hour.

8. **Barry is setting up a small network in his home to study for the MCSE exams and has asked for your advice on making sure it is secure. He has Internet access from his network and wants to make sure that he is not vulnerable. Which of the following options should he implement? Select all that apply.**

A. Set the minimum password length to 16 characters.

B. Make the usernames case sensitive.

C. Rename the Administrator account.

D. Use the NTFS file format on all partitions.

E. Rename the Everyone group.

9. **If you're working with more than one domain, it is important that you use groups properly. Placing people into groups when a network is first created simplifies administration work. Also, network traffic is greatly reduced by the use of groups. Which of the following statements correctly describes group structure in a Windows NT network?**

A. Users go into local groups, local groups go into global groups, and global groups are shared across domains.

B. Users are grouped together in local groups, local groups are grouped together in domain groups, and global groups are grouped together in domain groups.

C. Users go into global groups, global groups go into local groups, and local groups are assigned to resources.

D. Local groups are placed into workgroups, workgroups are placed into domain groups, domain groups are placed into global groups, and global groups go into the Everyone group, which cannot be modified.

E. Resource permissions are assigned to users, global groups are assigned rights within the domain, and local groups are assigned rights in trusted domains.

10. **Cal is a labor market analyst who needs access to a lot of the data on the network. To be able to access all the data, he has been assigned to several groups. Cal needs to access the census department's folder with last year's statistics. To accommodate him, it has added his account to the "census" group. This table shows the permissions assigned to Cal and the groups of which he is a member:**

Group	Permission
Cal	Read
Census	Full Control
Labor	No Access
Stats	Change

What permission does Cal have to the census group's folder?

A. No Access

B. Full Control

C. Change

D. Read

E. Read for the folder, but Full Control for the files

11. **A marketing office needs to implement a new network with security for data on both the servers and the workstations. It must also create a plan for disaster recovery. In addition, the users from another domain must be able to access resources on the servers of the marketing network. Which solution will best satisfy these needs?**

A. Windows NT Server is deployed for the servers, and Windows 95 is set up on the desktops. The network is set up in a workgroup, with a single tape backup unit for the three servers.

B. A Windows NT domain is set up, and RAID 5 is used on each of the servers to protect the data. The system/boot partition is formatted as FAT to allow for easier disaster recovery in case files should become corrupted.

C. Windows NT Server is used on each server, and Windows NT Workstation is installed on the desktops. The network is set up in a domain, and an auto-loader tape backup unit is connected to one of the servers. NTFS is used on all the partitions for both the servers and the workstations.

D. Windows NT Workstation is deployed on the desktops and the servers. All partitions are formatted with NTFS, and tape backup is done across the LAN for the servers and the workstations.

E. Windows NT Server is used on the servers, and Windows 95 is installed on the desktops. A separate tape backup unit is configured for each of the servers, and all partitions on the servers and desktops are formatted as NTFS. The network is set up in a domain.

12. **Kelly needs to change the administration policy for her network. Until now, the network has been relatively small; but with the addition of a new division, Kelly now has to manage another 125 extra desktops and six servers. What steps should Kelly take to manage the performance of the network?**

A. Run Network Monitor on each of the servers.

B. Create a baseline for each of the servers using data from both Performance Monitor and Network Monitor. Carry out monthly monitoring, and compare the results with the baseline.

C. Create a baseline on one of the servers, and compare it to each of the servers once a month.

D. Upgrade both hardware and software whenever new products are released to ensure that the most current hardware and software are used.

E. Run Performance Monitor and Network Monitor on a daily basis. If performance fluctuations occur, note them and troubleshoot the problem.

ANSWER KEY

1. A	5. D	9. C
2. E	6. A	10. A
3. B	7. C	11. C
4. B	8. C-D	12. B

CHOOSING AN ADMINISTRATIVE PLAN

1. The main reason to implement a network is to enable users to share resources. In a Windows environment, a user accesses a resource by connecting to the resource via a UNC name. Suppose a share name of "Data" exists in the Marketing domain, which is on the E: drive of the computer named "market12." This computer also shares data with the Sales workgroup. What would be the proper syntax to connect to this share from a command prompt on a Windows NT Workstation?

   A. `net use g: \\market12\data`

1. CORRECT ANSWER: A

Microsoft networking uses the `net use` command to establish a "mapping" to a shared resource. This shared resource could be a directory or a printer located somewhere on the network.

To specify the path, a standard called the *Universal Naming Convention* (UNC) was established. The first part of the UNC path is the double backslash (\\), which indicates that the path is on the network. This is followed by the NetBIOS (computer) name of the computer where the share is located (even printers that are connected directly to the network have a computer that performs the spooling). Another single backslash is used to separate the computer name from the share name. The share name defaults to the name of the directory where the share is created. However, a more descriptive name may be entered that can be as long as a long filename (255 characters).

If you did not want to connect to a share by "mapping a drive," you can locate the computer and share by browsing in Network Neighborhood. However, some shares (share names) cannot be seen when browsing. These are called *administrative* or *hidden shares*. Any share name with a dollar sign ($) at the end will not be displayed when browsing. Using hidden shares keeps the curious from trying to access shares to which they should not have access.

Now that you understand the standard for determining the path to the shared resource, you should look at the syntax for assigning a drive letter to the shared resource.

```
Net use [D]: \\[server name]\[share name]
```

Here [D] refers to the available drive letter that you want to assign to the shared directory.

You can also use the command

```
Net use lpt[n] \\[server name]\[share name]
```

where [n] refers to the LPT number that you want to assign to the shared printer. (For example, replace [n] with LPT1, LPT2, and so on, referring to the number of the printer.)

2. *Proposed Solution:* **You decide to replace all Windows 95 systems with Windows NT Workstation and convert to NTFS on the workstations with auditing enabled.**

    E. **None of the results are met.**

2. CORRECT ANSWER: E

Because the network does have a server, you should assume that everyone is being validated by a central account database. This provides some security on the network, and switching the workstations to Windows NT Workstation also helps. However, the proposed solution does not mention where the data is being stored. If the data is stored on the server, you do not know what security has been applied there. If the data is stored on each of the workstations, it is going to be difficult to audit the file access because the log files will be on each of the workstations. This will make monitoring difficult and possibly require additional staffing. If the files are kept on each of the workstations, each of the users must follow good security practices.

3. *Proposed Solution:* **You implement Windows NT Workstation on all the workstation computers, and you use user-level access permissions on the sensitive network resources to protect them.**

    B. **The required result and one of the optional results are met.**

3. CORRECT ANSWER: B

This solution provides for good security practices no matter where the data is stored (whether it be on the server or the workstations). Therefore, the data is protected in either case.

4. *Proposed Solution:* **You continue to use Windows 95 on the workstations, but you move all sensitive data to the server. You create a user account for each user, assign them into groups, and control access to network resources using the groups.**

    B. **The required result and one of the optional results are met.**

4. CORRECT ANSWER: B

This solution ensures that all sensitive data is stored on the server and that access to the data is carefully controlled. By using a central database for logon and assigning permissions, it is simple to control access to the files and folders.

The only issue that is not addressed in this solution is the auditing of file and folder access.

5. *Proposed Solution:* **You continue to use Windows 95 on the workstations, but you convert the Windows NT Server disk to NTFS. You enable auditing for the shared resources and place everyone in the same group to protect the sensitive data.**

   D. The required result is not met, but both of the optional results are met.

6. *Proposed Solution:* **You continue to use Windows 95 on the workstations, and you create a user account for each user. You convert the Windows NT Server disk to NTFS and enable file-level auditing. You then enable user-level access to control access to network resources.**

   A. The required result and both of the optional results are met.

7. **As part of your security policy, you set user accounts to be locked out after three bad attempts within a one-hour time period. The reason for this change in policy is that someone has been guessing passwords and getting into other people's files. Jan has asked you what will happen if the Administrator account becomes locked out. What explanation should you give her?**

   C. The Administrator account cannot be locked out.

5. CORRECT ANSWER: D

Although all sensitive data is stored in a central location and auditing is turned on, the data is not well protected. By placing each person in the same group, you give everyone access and grant everyone the exact same permissions to all the data. For those clients that expect client/attorney confidentiality, this solution fails.

6. CORRECT ANSWER: A

This solution meets all the requirements needed to protect each client's interests. The data is secure, and access to it is audited. In addition, this solution is simple to administer.

7. CORRECT ANSWER: C

Part of Microsoft Windows NT's security policy enables the administrator to configure accounts to be locked out after a selected number of bad attempts. When an account is locked out, either the person has to wait a certain period of time before the account becomes unlocked, or if the network is so configured, the user must contact the administrator and ask to have the account unlocked. Each bad attempt and account lockout is tracked in the Event Log for security purposes.

This could cause a great deal of problems if the Administrator account were to become locked out. If there is not another administrative account to unlock it, all administrative functions could come to a halt. For this reason, the original Administrator account (even if it is renamed) cannot be locked out. If additional administrator accounts are created, they can be locked out and even deleted if necessary. However, the original Administrator account cannot be locked out or deleted.

8. Barry is setting up a small network in his home to study for the MCSE exams and has asked for your advice on making sure it is secure. He has Internet access from his network and wants to make sure that he is not vulnerable. Which of the following options should he implement? Select all that apply.

C. Rename the Administrator account.

D. Use the NTFS file format on all partitions.

A good practice when creating any network is to rename the Administrator account. Everyone knows what the default administrative account name is, so to gain administrative access, a person would have to guess only the password. If you rename the account, however, a hacker would have to guess both the account name and the password.

In addition, if he uses the NTFS file system, Barry will be able to assign permissions to his files and folders to restrict the kind of access people might have to his computers if they did "hack" their way in.

To make it more difficult to guess a password, Barry should use the maximum number of characters (14), mixing case and using numbers and symbols.

9. If you're working with more than one domain, it is important that you use groups properly. Placing people into groups when a network is first created simplifies administration work. Also, network traffic is greatly reduced by the use of groups. Which of the following statements correctly describes group structure in a Windows NT network?

C. Users go into global groups, global groups go into local groups, and local groups are assigned to resources.

Although permissions may be assigned to users, global groups, and local groups, the rule of thumb is to place users into global groups, place global groups into local groups, and assign permissions to local groups. Although this may seem like a lot of additional work to start with, a well-planned directory structure can save a lot of administrative work later if the network grows.

When you work in a single-domain model, global groups are not really needed, but you can still implement them. This means additional work in the beginning, but if your network ever grows to include additional domains, the use of global groups will be very important.

Just as local groups enable you to organize users in a local domain, global groups allow you to assign users from one domain membership in a local group in another domain. The advantage of placing users into a global group before giving them membership in a local group in another domain is that it can greatly reduce the amount of network traffic that must pass between the two domains. For each user who's given access to a resource on another domain, a certain number of packets must travel across the network. However, no matter how many users are assigned membership to a global group, that global group always generates a constant amount of network traffic.

10. Cal is a labor market analyst who needs access to a lot of the data on the network. To be able to access all the data, he has been assigned to several groups. Cal needs to access the census department's folder with last year's statistics. To accommodate him, it has added his account to the "census" group. This table shows the permissions assigned to Cal and the groups of which he is a member:

Group	Permission
Cal	Read
Census	Full Control
Labor	No Access
Stats	Change

What permission does Cal have to the census group's folder?

A. No Access

10. CORRECT ANSWER: A

When a user is a member of multiple groups that have been assigned permission to a folder, the user is given the combination of all the permissions. For example, if one group was given Read access and another group was given Change access, the resulting permission is Change. However, there is always one exception. The No Access permission always overrides all other permissions. This is to prevent someone from accidentally gaining access to a resource to which he or she is not supposed to have access.

11. A marketing office needs to implement a new network with security for data on both the servers and the workstations. It must also create a plan for disaster recovery. In addition, the users from another domain must be able to access resources on the servers of the marketing network. Which solution will best satisfy these needs?

C. Windows NT Server is used on each server, and Windows NT Workstation is installed on the desktops. The network is set up in a domain, and an auto-loader tape backup unit is connected to one of the servers. NTFS is used on all the partitions for both the servers and the workstations.

11. CORRECT ANSWER: C

Windows NT is very secure for both servers and desktop computers. Unless users enter correct usernames and passwords, they will not gain access to the local computer, let alone the rest of the network. The file and folder security can also be used to secure data even if a person is able to log on to one of the computers. Altogether, this provides a great deal of security for the data.

For disaster recovery, the single tape backup unit can perform a backup of the data on the servers. It is quite normal to back up multiple servers (within reason) on one tape backup unit.

Finally, using the domain model makes it much easier to control user accounts and their permissions on the server. In a domain model, only one account is needed for each user. If a workgroup was established instead of a domain, multiple accounts would have to be created for each user, and the same username and password would have to be configured on each server and workstation to which the user was given access.

12. Kelly needs to change the administration policy for her network. Until now, the network has been relatively small; but with the addition of a new division, Kelly now has to manage another 125 extra desktops and six servers. What steps should Kelly take to manage the performance of the network?

B. Create a baseline for each of the servers using data from both Performance Monitor and Network Monitor. Carry out monthly monitoring, and compare the results with the baseline.

12. CORRECT ANSWER: B

Although multiple servers may have the same equipment and software installed, they are not likely to perform exactly the same. For that reason, it is always a good idea to create a baseline for the server.

Performance Monitor and Network Monitor are tools that come with Windows NT to help users and administrators tune their systems for optimum performance. When a large load is added to an existing network, it is a good idea to see what kind of impact it has on the existing infrastructure. Depending on how the servers and network were configured to begin with, the added workstations may have very little impact on performance. However, changes probably will have to be made, and using a baseline to show how much of an impact there was can help you determine what changes you need to make.

CHOOSING A DISASTER RECOVERY PLAN

1. This question is based on the following scenario. Review the scenario first, followed by the objectives and the proposed solution. Then, evaluate the proposed solution by choosing the best answer. (Note that questions 2–4 are also based on this scenario.)

Scenario:

Network type:	Windows NT servers, NetWare servers
Protocols:	NetBEUI, IPX/SPX
Workstations:	300 Windows NT Workstations
Servers:	Seven servers: NetWare and Windows NT

All the servers in your network contain some critical data. If the data were lost, the company would have no choice but to go out of business or, at the very least, shut down operations for eight to twelve months to rebuild the information. Traffic and network performance are operating within normal baseline parameters. The office has three locations connected via a WAN. You want to implement a backup plan.

Required Results:

The network must have no more than eight hours of downtime.

If one site goes down, the others must be able to function.

Optional Result:

Network performance should not be adversely impacted by the strategy, and the cost should be minimal.

Proposed Solution:

You decide to implement a fully redundant backup network. You use an isolated network segment and a centralized tape backup server. You also keep a spare server in reserve.

Evaluation of Proposed Solution:

Which of the following statements is true? (Choose the best answer.)

A. Both of the required results are met, and the optional result is met.

B. Both of the required results are met, but the optional result is not met.

C. One of the required results is met, and the optional result is met.

D. Neither of the required results is met, but the optional result is met.

E. None of the results are met.

2. This question is based on the scenario described in question 1. If necessary, review the scenario and the objectives again. Then, read this proposed solution and evaluate it by choosing the best answer.

Proposed Solution:
You decide to use single tape units on each server. You maintain a spare server just in case it's needed. In addition, you do daily full backups and move the tapes to each of the other locations.

Evaluation of Proposed Solution:
Which of the following statements is true? (Choose the best answer.)

A. Both of the required results are met, and the optional result is met.

B. Both of the required results are met, but the optional result is not met.

C. One of the required results is met, and the optional result is met.

D. Neither of the required results is met, but the optional result is met.

E. None of the results are met.

3. **This question is based on the scenario described in question 1. If necessary, review the scenario and the objectives again. Then, read this proposed solution and evaluate it by choosing the best answer.**

Proposed Solution:
You decide to implement a redundant-heart-beat server for each server so that if a catastrophe occurs, the new server will simply take over for the failed unit. You augment this with a tape unit on each server.

Evaluation of Proposed Solution:
Which of the following statements is true? (Choose the best answer.)

A. Both of the required results are met, and the optional result is met.

B. Both of the required results are met, but the optional result is not met.

C. One of the required results is met, and the optional result is met.

D. Neither of the required results is met, but the optional result is met.

E. None of the results are met.

4. **This question is based on the scenario described in question 1. If necessary, review the scenario and the objectives again. Then, read this proposed solution and evaluate it by choosing the best answer.**

Proposed Solution:
You implement full RAID 1 mirroring for each disk drive on your servers. You determine that by using this method, you can recover from a failure quickly, and you no longer have to rely on tapes.

Evaluation of Proposed Solution:
Which of the following statements is true? (Choose the best answer.)

A. Both of the required results are met, and the optional result is met.

B. Both of the required results are met, but the optional result is not met.

C. One of the required results is met, and the optional result is met.

D. Neither of the required results is met, but the optional result is met.

E. None of the results are met.

5. Steve is on your network admin team and has put together a proposal for setting up the backups for your network. He thinks the most economical solution for implementing backups is to use a single centralized backup server. You agree that this solution is the most economical, but you know that it has its drawbacks. Which of the following are disadvantages to using a central backup server?

A. More than one server can be backed up at once.

B. Network traffic is reduced.

C. Network traffic is increased.

D. There is a single point of failure for troubleshooting.

E. Tape backup is done centrally.

6. In addition to Steve's plan to run the backups from a central backup server, he also suggests securing the tapes and their backup sets. Which of the following procedures will help ensure security for the data and minimize downtime?

A. Keep the backup tapes close to the server in case they are needed during an emergency.

B. Secure the backup sets with passwords to prevent someone from hacking in.

C. Keep the tapes in a secure central location.

D. Schedule the backups to run during off-peak hours.

E. Keep the tapes in a secure location offsite.

7. You should keep logs of your backups to ensure that all backups have been successful and as a reference of what has been backed up. How does Microsoft recommend that administrators handle logs? (Choose the best answer.)

A. Create a duplicate so that one can be kept onsite and the other offsite.

B. Secure the log in a safe place, such as a vault.

C. Keep the log offsite, because it won't be needed unless there is a failure.

D. Keep the log on the backup server on an NTFS secured partition.

E. Keep the log on a central file server so that it can be used for reference from any workstation.

8. Although a good backup strategy is important, it is equally important that all servers be connected to their power supplies through a UPS. What function(s) can a UPS provide? Choose the correct statement(s).

A. Sends a message to a telephone pager.

B. Broadcasts a message to all connected users.

C. Runs a command file at power loss.

D. Shuts down the server gracefully.

E. Executes a backup prior to shutdown.

9. Maggie has read that RAID 0, RAID 1, and RAID 5 can be implemented through Windows NT's Disk Administrator. To make sure that all information on the server is protected by

redundancy, she has decided to implement RAID 5 for all the disk space on her file and printer server. Her server has two physical disks that have been partitioned into three partitions using FDISK. Why will Maggie have a problem getting this to work? Choose the correct statement(s).

A. Disk Administrator cannot set up a RAID 5 configuration.

B. The system partition cannot be part of a RAID 5 partition.

C. The boot partition cannot be part of a RAID 5 partition.

D. RAID configurations need at least three physical disks.

E. Disk Administrator needs at least three physical drives to implement RAID 5.

10. **Lola wants to utilize Windows NT's fault tolerance to its full capacity. She has seven 9GB drives in her server. She is planning to set up RAID 1 with two**

drives for the partition on which she installs Windows NT Server, and she will use the remaining five drives to set up RAID 5 for the data storage. Select the best statement about this plan for fault tolerance.

A. This is an excellent choice that will provide fast access to the system partition and safety for the data.

B. This choice works but is not recommended due to slow performance.

C. This is a good choice because of the fast performance on the RAID 5 partition, but the data on the system partition is not safe.

D. This is a poor choice and will not work because Windows NT Server does not support both RAID 1 and RAID 5 on the same server.

E. This is a good choice because of the fast performance of both the RAID 1 and RAID 5 partitions.

ANSWER KEY

1. E	5. C-D	9. B-C-E
2. A	6. B-D-E	10. B
3. B	7. A	
4. C	8. A-B-C-D	

ANSWERS & EXPLANATIONS

CHOOSING A DISASTER RECOVERY PLAN

1. *Proposed Solution:* You decide to implement a fully redundant backup network. You use an isolated network segment and a centralized tape backup server. You also keep a spare server in reserve.

   E. None of the results are met.

1. CORRECT ANSWER: E

A redundant backup network is commonly used because it helps reduce network traffic on the segments that handle the normal day-to-day operations. However, in a WAN, data is backed up and restored across a slow link. An alternative is to install a fiber link between each of the WAN sites, but the cost is prohibitive. In addition, backups across a WAN would take substantially longer and would probably run into prime operation time. This would affect the server's capability to respond to file and folder access requests.

If the site where the backup server is located were to go down, no backups would be performed, and the data on all servers would be in jeopardy. Therefore, this choice is simply not effective when dealing with a WAN.

2. *Proposed Solution:* You decide to use single tape units on each server. You maintain a spare server just in case it's needed. In addition, you do daily full backups and move the tapes to each of the other locations.

   A. Both of the required results are met, and the optional result is met.

2. CORRECT ANSWER: A

If tape backup units are installed on each of the servers and any one of the servers goes down, all others can continue to operate (complete with backups). To bring the failed server back online, you would have to set up the spare server, install Windows NT and the backup software, and then restore everything.

Also, because backups are performed on each of the servers, no network traffic is generated.

3. *Proposed Solution:* You decide to implement a redundant-heartbeat server for each server so that if a catastrophe occurs, the new server will simply take over for the failed unit. You augment this with a tape unit on each server.

   B. Both of the required results are met, but the optional result is not met.

3. CORRECT ANSWER: B

This solution probably has the quickest response time for resolving a disaster. However, you would incur significant hardware cost to double the number of servers that are deployed. If one server were to go down, it would not affect any other servers or increase the amount of network traffic.

The new redundant server could be operational within minutes after the original server goes down. The only reason more companies do not implement this solution is that they cannot handle the high cost associated with all the additional hardware. In most cases, the benefits would not outweigh the costs.

4. *Proposed Solution:* **You implement full RAID 1 mirroring for each disk drive on your servers. You determine that by using this method, you can recover from a failure quickly, and you no longer have to rely on tapes.**

   C. **One of the required results is met, and the optional result is met.**

4. CORRECT ANSWER: C

Disk mirroring does allow for fast recovery in the event of a disk crash. However, it does not prevent the loss of data. If someone deletes a file or a folder and all of its subfolders, there is no way to recover that data unless it has been backed up. In addition, if whatever causes the disk crash also destroys files, that same destruction also takes place on the mirroring drive.

5. **Steve is on your network admin team and has put together a proposal for setting up the backups for your network. He thinks the most economical solution for implementing backups is to use a single centralized backup server. You agree that this solution is the most economical, but you know that it has its drawbacks. Which of the following are disadvantages to using a central backup server?**

   C. **Network traffic is increased.**

   D. **There is a single point of failure for troubleshooting.**

5. CORRECT ANSWERS: C-D

This is the most economical choice because only one tape backup unit and one copy of the backup software are required. However, because the backups are performed across the network, traffic is going to increase during backups. If no one will be in the office using the network during off-peak hours, this is not a concern. But if someone does need to use the network while backups are running, he or she will see slow response times. Also, as the amount of data on the servers increases, the amount of time needed to perform the backups will also increase and potentially run into prime hours.

In addition to possible time constraints, if there is a failure at the tape unit—backup unit failure or tape failure, for example—no backups would be done. If a separate backup unit is located at each of the sites, only the servers at the failure site would not be backed up.

6. In addition to Steve's plan to run the backups from a central backup server, he also suggests securing the tapes and their backup sets. Which of the following procedures will help ensure security for the data and minimize downtime?

   B. Secure the backup sets with passwords to prevent someone from hacking in.

   D. Schedule the backups to run during off-peak hours.

   E. Keep the tapes in a secure location offsite.

A good practice is to make sure that tapes (or at least copies of the tapes) are not kept in the same location as the network. Granted, a disk failure or someone deleting files does not always cause the server to go down. Other factors such as fire or flood can cause the loss of a server, but it's unlikely that two separate locations will catch fire or be flooded at the same time.

In addition, if tapes are stored at the same site as the server, it could be quite simple for someone to restore data from the tape to a location where he or she can access the files. To prevent this unauthorized access to files, it is also a good practice to assign passwords to backup sets. Then, a person could restore data from that set only if he or she could provide the proper password.

To make the network operate as quickly as possible, it is recommended that you always run backups during off-peak hours. This enables the server to respond to requests more quickly during peak hours, and it also reduces the amount of network traffic that would take place if you were to combine backup traffic and normal peak traffic.

7. You should keep logs of your backups to ensure that all backups have been successful and as a reference of what has been backed up. How does Microsoft recommend that administrators handle logs? (Choose the best answer.)

   A. Create a duplicate so that one can be kept onsite and the other offsite.

As you do backup tapes, you should always make two copies of the logs. That way, one log can be kept onsite for use as a quick reference when necessary. The second copy of the logs should be kept at a remote site so that if something happens to the onsite logs, the duplicates remain available for use.

8. Although a good backup strategy is important, it is equally important that all servers be connected to their power supplies through a UPS. What function(s) can a UPS provide? Choose the correct statement(s).

   A. Sends a message to a telephone pager.

   B. Broadcasts a message to all connected users.

   C. Runs a command file at power loss.

   D. Shuts down the server gracefully.

8. CORRECT ANSWERS: A-B-C-D

An *uninterruptible power supply* (UPS) should be a standard piece of hardware for any network. Every server should be connected to a UPS to ensure that the server is always up or that it will remain up long enough to be shut down properly. Many UPSs come with additional software that allows the administrator to configure them to warn users and administrators of the loss of power. This could involve broadcasting messages to users, sending a page to the on-call administrator, carrying out a particular command (provided that the command does not take too long), or shutting down the server.

One feature of a UPS that is not always considered is that they help to provide a more consistent power supply to the systems connected to them. Most people know of their ability to provide power in the event of a power failure. However, they are also capable of stopping power spikes in areas that do not have a consistent power supply. Many areas—especially remote areas—have fluctuating power supplies. A spike of power can be just as damaging as a power loss.

9. Maggie has read that RAID 0, RAID 1, and RAID 5 can be implemented through Windows NT's Disk Administrator. To make sure that all information on the server is protected by redundancy, she has decided to implement RAID 5 for all the disk space on her file and printer server. Her server has two physical disks that have been partitioned into three partitions using FDISK. Why will Maggie have a problem getting this to work? Choose the correct statement(s).

   B. The system partition cannot be part of a RAID 5 partition.

   C. The boot partition cannot be part of a RAID 5 partition.

   E. Disk Administrator needs at least three physical drives to implement RAID 5.

9. CORRECT ANSWERS: B-C-E

RAID 0 refers to striping a set of physical disks to improve the disk access performance. RAID 1 is disk mirroring, in which all information is written to two disks so that if the first fails, the second disk can be used. RAID 5 is disk striping with parity, which can be implemented across 3–32 physical disks and provides fault tolerance if one of the drives fails. Windows NT can implement any of these RAID configurations. However, the system and boot partitions of a Windows NT computer cannot be part of a Windows NT–implemented RAID 0 or RAID 5 configuration. Two physical drives can be configured for striping (RAID 0), but they cannot take part in striping with parity (RAID 5) because the third drive is needed to store the parity information.

10. Lola wants to utilize Windows NT's fault tolerance to its full capacity. She has seven 9GB drives in her server. She is planning to set up RAID 1 with two drives for the partition on which she installs Windows NT Server, and she will use the remaining five drives to set up RAID 5 for the data storage. Select the best statement about this plan for fault tolerance.

   B. This choice works but is not recommended due to slow performance.

10. CORRECT ANSWER: B

If you were to read the literature on each of these implementations, you would think that using a combination of these would provide tremendous fault tolerance for your server. This configuration does protect your data and your server as expected, but all of this overhead can cause Windows NT to become extremely slow. A better solution is to implement your optional levels of RAID through a hardware solution, and then let Windows NT handle the file and folder security. Or, if necessary, let Windows NT handle one of the RAID configurations, and use a hardware solution for the other configuration. However, the best answer during the exam would be to agree that Windows NT can handle all three of the RAID implementations.

INSTALLING AND CONFIGURING MULTIPLE NETWORK ADAPTERS

1. Your company has decided to continue using Novell NetWare servers but to deploy Windows NT and Windows 9x clients. Currently, all the systems are using the IPX/SPX protocol (or its Microsoft equivalent), and they are all on the same segment. For some reason, all the machines are able to "see" the other client computers, but they cannot "see" the servers. What could be the problem? (Select the best answer.)

   A. Microsoft Windows computers cannot be used as NetWare clients.

   B. The wrong cabling has been used for NetWare servers.

   C. The client computers are using the wrong frame type.

   D. The client computers are using the NetBIOS names.

   E. The version of NetWare is not compatible with Microsoft Windows computers.

2. For this question, assume that you are administering the network described here:

   Network type: Windows NT servers using NetBEUI; NetWare servers using IPX; UNIX servers using TCP/IP

Workstations:	Windows NT workstations; UNIX workstations; Windows 95 workstations
Network interface cards:	Ethernet 10BASE-T using twisted-pair

   You have a large network with multiple routers. You limit access to certain servers by loading only those protocols necessary for communication. You then find, however, that not all of the Windows clients can connect to the Windows NT servers on other segments. What is the most likely problem?

   A. Your routers are using the frame type 802.2, but the Windows NT servers have defaulted to 802.3.

   B. The protocol has not been configured correctly.

   C. Your TCP/IP address is invalid.

   D. NetBEUI is the only protocol on the workstations.

   E. There are too many segments in the network.

3. For this question, assume that you are administering the network described here:

Network type: Windows NT servers using NetBEUI; NetWare servers using IPX; UNIX servers using TCP/IP

Workstations: Windows NT workstations; UNIX workstations; Windows 95 workstations

Network interface cards: Ethernet 10BASE-T using twisted-pair

You decide to abandon your plans to use protocols to secure the network. However, for Microsoft networking, you need to use NetBIOS. As a result, which protocol *must* you use?

A. IPX.

B. TCP/IP.

C. NetBEUI.

D. NWLink.

E. You can use any of these protocols.

4. Kyle is in the process of setting up his computer at the office. He has installed Windows NT Workstation and has installed the network card so that he can install the rest of the software from the server. When he reboots his computer after the installation, he finds that he does not have network connectivity. What should Kyle try first to find the problem?

A. Verify his username and password.

B. Verify that he is using the same type of cable as the rest of the office.

C. Make sure he is using the same protocol as the rest of the network.

D. Make sure a computer account has been created for his computer.

E. See if the protocol(s) is bound to the network card.

5. This question refers to question 4. If the network card is not bound to any protocols, how should Kyle try to rectify the problem?

A. Install the network adapter drivers that came with the network card.

B. Reinstall the network adapter drivers from the Windows NT Workstation CD.

C. Install the network adapter drivers from the Windows 98 CD.

D. Use the network adapter drivers from the network adapter manufacturer's web site.

E. Use a network adapter from a different manufacturer.

6. If the solution from question 5 does not rectify the problem, what should Kyle try next?

A. Install the network adapter drivers that came with the network card.

B. Reinstall the network adapter drivers from the Windows NT Workstation CD.

C. Install the network adapter drivers from the Windows 98 CD.

D. Use the network adapter drivers from the network adapter manufacturer's web site.

E. Use a network adapter from a different manufacturer.

7. You have been monitoring the flow of data in and out of your servers, and you think there is room for improvement. What component is responsible for preparing the data for the transmission medium, sending data, and controlling the flow of data from the computer? (Select the best answer.)

    A. The processor

    B. The network adapter

    C. Windows NT kernel

    D. The application

    E. The operating system

8. Jeff is the administrator of a network that is using a mix of NetWare and Windows NT servers. To reduce network traffic, he has decided to split the computers into two segments. One segment will have all the NetWare clients and their servers, and the other segment will have the Windows NT clients and their servers. A single Windows NT server is being set up as a file and printer server, and a router will separate the two segments. Broadcasting is not allowed past the router. IPX/SPX is used on the NetWare segment, and TCP/IP is used on the Windows NT segment. What should Jeff do to make sure that the router runs more efficiently? Choose the best answer.

    A. Disable unnecessary bindings.

    B. Remove NWLink from the server.

    C. Add NetBEUI to enable computers to communicate across the router.

    D. Install Gateway Services for NetWare on the router.

    E. Token-Ring network adapters should be used.

9. To make backups run more efficiently, your IT department has decided to install a second network adapter into each of the Windows NT servers. This way, backups can take place on one segment, while normal network traffic takes place on the other segment. What should be done prior to installing the second network adapter? Choose the best answer.

    A. Remove all protocols from each of the servers.

    B. Disable all protocols on each server.

    C. Run Windows NT Diagnostics.

    D. Install the driver for the second network adapter.

    E. Install NetBEUI to isolate the segments.

10. Vern has been supporting Windows 95 for a number of years and has recently moved into a junior support role for Windows NT systems. He suspects that one of the member servers has a hardware conflict between two devices. In Windows 95, he would open the System applet in Control Panel and select the Device Manager tab to review which devices had a conflict. Where should he check to see whether a device has a conflict in Windows NT? Select the correct answer.

A. Open the System applet in Control Panel.

B. Run Windows NT Diagnostics.

C. Open the Registry.

D. Open the Network applet in Control Panel.

E. Run Event Viewer.

11. **For this question, assume that you are administering the network described here:**

Network type: **Windows NT servers, NetWare servers, UNIX servers**

Protocols: **NetBEUI, IPX, TCP/IP**

Workstations: **Windows NT Workstation, UNIX, Windows 95**

Network interface cards: **Ethernet 10BASE-T using twisted-pair**

One client cannot access the NetWare servers, but she can access the Windows NT and UNIX servers just fine. Your troubleshooting has determined that the correct client software and protocols are loaded. What is the most likely cause of the problem?

A. An incorrect Ethernet link

B. An incorrect BNC to 9-pin media filter

C. An incorrect Token-Ring link

D. An incorrect frame type

E. An incorrect network adapter

ANSWER KEY		
1. C	5. A	9. C
2. D	6. D	10. E
3. E	7. B	11. D
4. C-D	8. A	

INSTALLING AND CONFIGURING MULTIPLE NETWORK ADAPTERS

1. Your company has decided to continue using Novell NetWare servers but to deploy Windows NT and Windows 9x clients. Currently, all the systems are using the IPX/SPX protocol (or its Microsoft equivalent), and they are all on the same segment. For some reason, all the machines are able to "see" the other client computers, but they cannot "see" the servers. What could be the problem? (Select the best answer.)

   C. The client computers are using the wrong frame type.

2. For this question, assume that you are administering the network described here:

   Network type: Windows NT servers
                        using NetBEUI;
                        NetWare servers
                        using IPX; UNIX
                        servers using
                        TCP/IP

   Workstations: Windows NT work-
                        stations; UNIX work-
                        stations; Windows
                        95 workstations

   Network   Ethernet 10BASE-T
   interface cards: using twisted-pair

   You have a large network with multiple routers. You limit access to certain servers by loading only those protocols necessary for communication. You then find, however, that not all the Windows clients can connect to the Windows NT servers on other segments. What is the most likely problem?

   D. NetBEUI is the only protocol on the workstations.

1. CORRECT ANSWER: C

There is more than one definition (standard) for a frame of data that can be used when working with the IPX/SPX protocol. Two of the more common ones are 802.2 and 802.3. To be able to communicate, the computers must be using the same frame type. If they are not using the same frame type, they may not be able to communicate.

In this example, it appears that all the client computers are using one frame type, and the servers are using another. The frame type of either the servers or the client computers will have to be changed to rectify the communication problem.

2. CORRECT ANSWER: D

A different protocol will have to be used to enable the Windows NT clients to communicate with servers on other network segments. Because NetBEUI cannot be routed, communication is limited to computers on the same segment. To enable communication between servers on different segments, you must use either TCP/IP or IPX/SPX on both the servers and the clients.

NetBEUI was originally designed for small networks and proved to be very fast. The reason for the speed of the protocol is that very little addressing information is included in the data packages. Not including additional address information keeps the packages small and transmissions quick. The drawback to the small size is that there is not enough address information in each package to pass across a router onto another segment.

3. For this question, assume that you are administering the network described here:

Network type:	Windows NT servers using NetBEUI; NetWare servers using IPX; UNIX servers using TCP/IP
Workstations:	Windows NT work-stations; UNIX work-stations; Windows 95 workstations
Network interface cards:	Ethernet 10BASE-T using twisted-pair

You decide to abandon your plans to use protocols to secure the network. However, for Microsoft networking, you need to use NetBIOS. As a result, which protocol *must* you use?

E. You can use any of these protocols.

3. CORRECT ANSWER: E

Microsoft networking always uses NetBIOS for communication between computers. This in no way has any bearing on the protocol that is used on the network. NetBIOS is a standard, much as sockets is a network standard API. Although it was originally designed for use with the NetBEUI protocol, it works with any of the protocols.

4. Kyle is in the process of setting up his computer at the office. He has installed Windows NT Workstation and has installed the network card so that he can install the rest of the software from the server. When he reboots his computer after the installation, he finds that he does not have network connectivity. What should Kyle try first to find the problem?

C. Make sure he is using the same protocol as the rest of the network.

D. Make sure a computer account has been created for his computer.

4. CORRECT ANSWERS: C-D

If you start Windows NT Workstation or Server and you do not have network connectivity, you normally have an idea that something is wrong before you ever log on. Usually, a warning dialog box appears, indicating that one of the services did not start and that the user should check the Event Viewer to see which service(s) has not started. This normally represents a problem with the network adapter, the network adapter drivers, or the cabling. Because the adapter was just installed, you should check to see whether the protocol(s) were bound properly to the adapter and make sure that they are the same as those being used on the network.

5. This question refers to question 4. If the network card is not bound to any protocols, how should Kyle try to rectify the problem?

    A. Install the network adapter drivers that came with the network card.

If the protocols are not bound to the network adapter properly, you have to assume that either the drivers were installed incorrectly, or maybe the driver that comes with the operating system CD is faulty and needs to be updated. This is quite common, and it is not unusual for the drivers that come with the network adapter to be more current than what comes with the operating system software (Windows 95 or Windows NT).

6. If the solution from question 5 does not rectify the problem, what should Kyle try next?

    D. Use the network adapter drivers from the network adapter manufacturer's web site.

Like any product that is released on floppy disk or CD, some time passes between development, publication, and arrival at the client sites. By the time software arrives at a client site, it could very well be obsolete. That is why it is important to check the manufacturer's web site whenever you have a question about hardware or software. It seems like nearly every computer product released in the last few years has had a hotfix, service release, or patch released within weeks of the product itself.

So, if you ever question how current the software for a product is, check the appropriate web sites.

7. You have been monitoring the flow of data in and out of your servers, and you think there is room for improvement. What component is responsible for preparing the data for the transmission medium, sending data, and controlling the flow of data from the computer? (Select the best answer.)

    B. The network adapter

Many components are involved in transmitting packets from one computer to another. The component that is responsible for preparing the data for the transmission medium (wire cable, fiber-optic cable, and so on), sending the data, and controlling the flow of data is the network adapter.

8. Jeff is the administrator of a network that is using a mix of NetWare and Windows NT servers. To reduce network traffic, he has decided to split the computers into two segments. One segment will have all the NetWare clients and their servers, and the other segment will have the Windows NT clients and their servers. A single Windows NT server is being set up as a file and printer server, and a router will separate the two segments. Broadcasting is not allowed past the router. IPX/SPX is used on the NetWare segment, and TCP/IP is used on the Windows NT segment. What should Jeff do to make sure that the router runs more efficiently? Choose the best answer.

   A. Disable unnecessary bindings.

9. To make backups run more efficiently, your IT department has decided to install a second network adapter into each of the Windows NT servers. This way, backups can take place on one segment, while normal network traffic takes place on the other segment. What should be done prior to installing the second network adapter? Choose the best answer.

   C. Run Windows NT Diagnostics.

10. Vern has been supporting Windows 95 for a number of years and has recently moved into a junior support role for Windows NT systems. He suspects that one of the member servers has a hardware conflict between two devices. In Windows 95, he would open the System applet in Control Panel and select the Device Manager tab to review which devices had a conflict. Where should he check to see whether a device has a conflict in Windows NT? Select the correct answer.

   E. Run Event Viewer.

8. CORRECT ANSWER: A

Because the Windows NT server is acting as a file and printer server for both the Windows NT segment and the NetWare segment, it will have to have both TCP/IP and NWLink installed on it. However, because the client computers do not need to communicate with the computers on the segments, both protocols are not needed for both network adapters.

The network adapter that is attached to the NetWare segment needs to be bound to the NWLink protocol only, and the network adapter that is connected to the Windows NT segment needs to be bound to the TCP/IP protocol only. Therefore, Jeff should open the Network applet in Control Panel and go to the Bindings tab. From that dialog box, he can disable the unnecessary bindings.

9. CORRECT ANSWER: C

All hardware devices must be assigned things such as IRQ, base memory address, and DMA channel. If any of these items is assigned to more than one device, you will have device failures. If you open Windows NT Diagnostics before installing the new hardware, you will be able to determine which settings have already been assigned, and your installation will proceed much more smoothly.

10. CORRECT ANSWER: E

The Windows NT Diagnostics dialog box will identify which resources have been assigned to which devices. However, it does not indicate which devices are involved in a hardware conflict. The best place to look for that kind of information is the Event Viewer. It indicates which services have not started and what hardware could have prevented each of the services from starting.

Often, when a number of services do not start, it is because one driver is not loaded properly. Because the driver for one device does not load, its corresponding service also will not start. Often, one or more services depend on another service to start. These relationships are known as *dependencies*, and if you can get the one service to start, the other services will also start. Therefore, it is valuable to learn which services depend on others.

If an inexperienced troubleshooter were to open the Services dialog box and see that a number of services did not start, he might start with the first service and try to solve its problem. However, an experienced troubleshooter would look at all the services and determine which service all the other services depend on. If she could resolve the problem for that one service, the other services would also probably start.

11. For this question, assume that you are administering the network described here:

Network type: Windows NT servers, NetWare servers, UNIX servers

Protocols: NetBEUI, IPX, TCP/IP

Workstations: Windows NT Workstation, UNIX, Windows 95

Network interface cards: Ethernet 10BASE-T using twisted-pair

One client cannot access the NetWare servers, but she can access the Windows NT and UNIX servers just fine. Your troubleshooting has determined that the correct client software and protocols are loaded. What is the most likely cause of the problem?

D. An incorrect frame type

The IPX/SPX (NWLink) protocol uses specific frame types. If one computer uses a different frame type than the other computers on the network do, the first computer will not be able to communicate with the others.

Some possible frame types are 802.2, 802.3, and so on. These are IEEE standards that correspond to Ethernet and Token-Ring configurations. In this case, the problem could be either of two things. The Windows clients could be using a different frame type than the NetWare servers but the same frame type as the Windows NT servers. Or, communication between the clients and the Windows NT servers and UNIX servers is established with a different protocol (possibly TCP/IP). You will have to change the frame type of either the NetWare servers or the client machines.

PRACTICE QUESTIONS

IMPLEMENTING A NETBIOS NAMING SCHEME

1. Hank was setting up a new Microsoft network for a client that has about 250 computers. To implement an automated method of installing upgrades, patches, and new software, he was also installing Systems Management Server (SMS). To simplify the use of SMS, Hank needed to establish a detailed computer naming scheme. He made the following choice: *xxxxx-yyyyy-zzz*, where *xxxxx* is the asset tag number, *yyyyy* is the department code, and *zzz* is either 95 or NT. What is wrong with Hank's naming scheme?

   A. Only one hyphen (-) can be used in a computer name.

   B. Hyphens cannot be used in a computer name.

   C. Computer names must be a minimum of 20 characters.

   D. Computer names cannot start with a number.

   E. Computer names are limited to 15 characters.

2. To make the names of the computers in the office more recognizable, Karen has documented a naming scheme that all computer names will have to follow. Her scheme involves using letters, numbers, and symbols as shown here:

   kar@market\1

The first three characters of the name represent the person who uses the computer. The @ symbol separates the person's name from the department the computer is used in. The \ symbol separates the department name from the number of the particular computer within the department. If there is a flaw in Karen's naming plan, what is it?

   A. The @ symbol cannot be used in a NetBIOS name.

   B. The \ symbol cannot be used in a NetBIOS name.

   C. Karen's naming scheme will work.

   D. This scheme will work until a department needs to have two digits.

   E. Symbols cannot be used in a NetBIOS name.

3. This question is based on the following scenario. Review the scenario first, followed by the objectives and the proposed solution. Then, evaluate the proposed solution by choosing the best answer. (Note that questions 4–6 are also based on this scenario.)

Scenario:

Network type:	Windows NT servers, multiple domains
Protocols:	NetBEUI, IPX, TCP/IP
Workstations:	30 Windows NT Workstations

You decide to implement a NetBIOS naming scheme for your network. You are currently part of a standalone network with one server, but you are scheduled to be connected to the multi-domain corporate WAN in several months. Your users have email accounts on the corporate WAN mail hub.

Required Results:
The naming scheme must contain unique names.

The naming scheme must continue to function after the WAN integration.

Optional Result:
The naming scheme should be informative about the computer's role.

Proposed Solution:
You decide to generate a unique hexadecimal number for each of the workstations. You will keep a list of all the numbers and carefully control which numbers are available. A copy of the list will be given to the main office to ensure that the names are not already being used.

Evaluation of Proposed Solution:
Which of the following statements is true? (Choose the best answer.)

A. Both of the required results are met, and the optional result is met.

B. Both of the required results are met, but the optional result is not met.

C. One of the required results is met, and the optional result is met.

D. The optional result is met, but the required results are not met.

E. None of the results are met.

4. This question is based on the scenario described in question 3. If necessary, review the scenario and the objectives again. Then, read this proposed solution and evaluate it by choosing the best answer.

Proposed Solution:
You decide to use the burned-in MAC address of the Ethernet card in each system as the NetBIOS name. Because the first several characters of the MAC address indicate the manufacturer, you feel this will help indicate the role of the PC.

Evaluation of Proposed Solution:
Which of the following statements is true? (Choose the best answer.)

A. Both of the required results are met, and the optional result is met.

B. Both of the required results are met, but the optional result is not met.

C. One of the required results is met, and the optional result is met.

D. The optional result is met, but the required results are not met.

E. None of the results are met.

5. This question is based on the scenario described in question 3. If necessary, review the scenario and the objectives again. Then, read this proposed solution and evaluate it by choosing the best answer.

Proposed Solution:
You decide to use the user's email address as the computer's NetBIOS name.

Evaluation of Proposed Solution:
Which of the following statements is true? (Choose the best answer.)

   A. Both of the required results are met, and the optional result is met.

   B. Both of the required results are met, but the optional result is not met.

   C. One of the required results is met, and the optional result is met.

   D. The optional result is met, but the required results are not met.

   E. None of the results are met.

6. This question is based on the scenario described in question 3. If necessary, review the scenario and the objectives again. Then, read this proposed solution and evaluate it by choosing the best answer.

Proposed Solution:
You create a naming convention that uses a three-character building code, followed by a four-character floor code, followed by the user's email address.

Evaluation of Proposed Solution:
Which of the following statements is true? (Choose the best answer.)

   A. Both of the required results are met, and the optional result is met.

   B. Both of the required results are met, but the optional result is not met.

   C. One of the required results is met, and the optional result is met.

   D. The optional result is met, but the required results are not met.

   E. None of the results are met.

7. Bruce has set up a share on his Windows NT Workstation so that others in his workgroup can access the fundraising statistics he has compiled. The share-point for the others to connect to is \\bruce-c\fundrais%stats. This seems to work well for the users who have Windows NT and Windows 95, but the three computers that are still running MS-DOS 6.22 with the network client cannot connect to the share. What could be the problem?

   A. The share name is too long.

   B. The computer name cannot have a hyphen in it.

   C. Machines running MS-DOS 6.22 with the network client can only connect to shares created on a Windows NT Server.

   D. Machines running MS-DOS 6.22 with the network client can only work with computer and share names that are in uppercase.

   E. The % symbol cannot be used in a share name.

8. Paul is designing a Windows NT network for a client that wants to migrate from OS/2 to a Windows network. This network will be a WAN that connects a number of cities. Each city will have its

own domain, and two-way trusts will be established between all of the domains. All servers will be Windows NT Servers, but there will be a variety of desktop systems, including DOS, Windows for Workgroups 3.11, Windows 95, Windows 98, and Windows NT Workstation 4.

Paul is developing a naming policy so that each computer name will indicate the city, the department, the domain, and the workgroup it belongs to. The name will look like

ddddaaaaWWWWDDDD

where *dddd* is a four-number department code, *aaaa* refers to the first four characters of the city's name, *WWWW* is a four-digit workgroup number, and *DDDD* is the four characters of the domain name.

Which of the following statements most accurately evaluates Paul's naming scheme?

A. This is an excellent naming scheme, and it will work with any domain.

B. This naming scheme would be good except that NetBIOS names cannot mix numeric and alphabetical characters.

C. This naming scheme would be good except that a NetBIOS name cannot start with numeric characters.

D. This naming scheme will work, but a better idea would be to have a separate naming scheme for each of the domains to improve the modularity.

E. This naming scheme will not work for all the systems.

9. Alex is working on a Windows NT network using TCP/IP that has approximately 340 computers including servers. This network is split between two office buildings located adjacent to one another. Recently, the workstations have been unable to connect to the servers and desktop computers on the other segments of the network. It is close to the end of the fiscal year, and the entire computer budget has been spent. What option(s) does Alex have to resolve this problem?

A. Install WINS on one of the existing servers.

B. Install the ARP protocol to resolve the IP addresses.

C. Install WINS on each of the workstations.

D. Create an LMHOSTS file.

E. Install DHCP on one of the servers.

ANSWER KEY		
1. E	4. B	7. A
2. B	5. B	8. E
3. B	6. B	9. D

ANSWERS & EXPLANATIONS

IMPLEMENTING A NETBIOS NAMING SCHEME

1. Hank was setting up a new Microsoft network for a client that has about 250 computers. To implement an automated method of installing upgrades, patches, and new software, he was also installing Systems Management Server (SMS). To simplify the use of SMS, Hank needed to establish a detailed computer naming scheme. He made the following choice: *xxxxxx-yyyyy-zzz*, where *xxxxxx* is the asset tag number, *yyyyy* is the department code, and *zzz* is either 95 or NT. What is wrong with Hank's naming scheme?

   E. Computer names are limited to 15 characters.

1. CORRECT ANSWER: E

Computer or NetBIOS names are limited to no more than 15 characters in size. Hank's solution would create names of 16 characters. Normally, the 16th character is one that is used internally by Microsoft networking to determine such things as the role a computer plays. Although Hank's naming scheme has a lot of merit, it is one character too long.

2. To make the names of the computers in the office more recognizable, Karen has documented a naming scheme that all computer names will have to follow. Her scheme involves using letters, numbers, and symbols as shown here:

   kar@market\1

   The first three characters of the name represent the person who uses the computer. The @ symbol separates the person's name from the department the computer is used in. The \ symbol separates the department name from the number of the particular computer within the department. If there is a flaw in Karen's naming plan, what is it?

   B. The \ symbol cannot be used in a NetBIOS name.

2. CORRECT ANSWER: B

Symbols are allowed in NetBIOS names. However, certain symbols are reserved for specific functions. For example, the \ (backslash) symbol acts as a separator between folders and files or separates computer names from share names in a designated path to a resource (such as a file, folder, or printer).

3. *Proposed Solution:* You decide to generate a unique hexadecimal number for each of the workstations. You will keep a list of all the numbers and carefully control which numbers are available. A copy of the list will be given to the main office to ensure that the names are not already being used.

    B. Both of the required results are met, but the optional result is not met.

3. CORRECT ANSWER: B

This solution will generate unique names for each of the computers, and the scheme should work in the WAN because the WAN administrators have been notified of the names. However, there is nothing to indicate the computer's role in the network. Because the number is randomly generated, you would not be able to associate any part of the name with the computer's role.

4. *Proposed Solution:* You decide to use the burned-in MAC address of the Ethernet card in each system as the NetBIOS name. Because the first several characters of the MAC address indicate the manufacturer, you feel this will help indicate the role of the PC.

    B. Both of the required results are met, but the optional result is not met.

4. CORRECT ANSWER: B

Using the MAC address of a network adapter is similar to using a randomly generated number to assign names to the computers. The name will be unique, but it will not have any meaning as to the role the computer plays. The manufacturer's name may be a part of the MAC address, but it is just another identifier that will be found on all cards supplied by that manufacturer.

5. *Proposed Solution:* You decide to use the user's email address as the computer's NetBIOS name.

    B. Both of the required results are met, but the optional result is not met.

5. CORRECT ANSWER: B

Unless the usernames reflect what roles the computers play in your organization (and they usually don't), this solution again provides unique names for each of the computers, but the name does not indicate what role the computer plays.

6. *Proposed Solution:* You create a naming convention that uses a three-character building code, followed by a four-character floor code, followed by the user's email address.

    B. Both of the required results are met, but the optional result is not met.

6. CORRECT ANSWER: B

Unless each department is located in a different part of the building, this naming convention also fails to provide a name that indicates the role of the computer.

7. Bruce has set up a share on his Windows NT Workstation so that others in his workgroup can access the fundraising statistics he has compiled. The share-point for the others to connect to is \\bruce-c\fundrais%stats. This seems to work well for the users who have Windows NT and Windows 95, but the three computers that are still running MS-DOS 6.22 with the network client cannot connect to the share. What could be the problem?

A. The share name is too long.

8. Paul is designing a Windows NT network for a client that wants to migrate from OS/2 to a Windows network. This network will be a WAN that connects a number of cities. Each city will have its own domain, and two-way trusts will be established between all of the domains. All servers will be Windows NT Servers, but there will be a variety of desktop systems, including DOS, Windows for Workgroups 3.11, Windows 95, Windows 98, and Windows NT Workstation 4.

Paul is developing a naming policy so that each computer name will indicate the city, the department, the domain, and the workgroup it belongs to. The name will look like

ddddaaaaWWWWDDDD

where *dddd* is a four-number department code, *aaaa* refers to the first four characters of the city's name, *WWWW* is a four-digit workgroup number, and *DDDD* is the four characters of the domain name.

Which of the following statements most accurately evaluates Paul's naming scheme?

E. This naming scheme will not work for all the systems.

---

7. CORRECT ANSWER: A

MS-DOS systems can work with names that are the same size as filenames: eight characters for the filename, followed by a period(.), followed by three characters for the extension. This all adds up to a total of 12 characters. Any name that is longer than 12 characters is not recognized by a machine running MS-DOS 6.22. When creating such shares, you will often be informed that some systems will not be able to work with a name that long.

8. CORRECT ANSWER: E

This naming scheme would work very well if all the systems were Windows 95 or above. However, some of the systems are DOS and Windows for Workgroups 3.11. These systems follow the old DOS naming conventions, which means they can work with NetBIOS names only up to 12 characters. If the name exceeds 12 characters, these computers will not be able to browse for the name (Windows for Workgroups) or be able to connect without using extra characters. These older systems can connect if quotation marks ("") are used around the long names when the user tries to map a drive. This requirement is not needed in Windows 95 and above because newer systems automatically work with long names.

9. Alex is working on a Windows NT network using TCP/IP that has approximately 340 computers including servers. This network is split between two office buildings located adjacent to one another. Recently, the workstations have been unable to connect to the servers and desktop computers on the other segments of the network. It is close to the end of the fiscal year, and the entire computer budget has been spent. What option(s) does Alex have to resolve this problem?

D. Create an LMHOSTS file.

9. CORRECT ANSWER: D

The reason that the computers cannot communicate with the computers in the other building is probably that they cannot resolve the NetBIOS name (computer name) to an IP address when they try to map a drive. In most cases, implementing WINS would be the obvious choice for resolving NetBIOS names to IP addresses. However, in this case, there isn't money left in the computer budget to buy the software and licenses needed to implement WINS.

The most economical solution to this problem is to create an LMHOSTS file. This static file contains a table of sorts that lists IP addresses and their corresponding NetBIOS names. The big drawback to using an LMHOSTS file is that it is static and has to be manually changed each time a computer is added, removed, or modified (when a computer is moved to a different subnet, for example).

To reduce the amount of time that Alex has to work on the LMHOSTS files on each desktop computer, he could keep a current copy of the file on each of the domain controllers. When a user logs on, the logon script could copy the newest LMHOSTS file to the user's computer. Alex would need to keep the file current and create a batch file that runs as part of the logon script.

SELECTING TOOLS TO MONITOR NETWORK TRENDS

1. You have been assigned the task of monitoring each of the five Windows NT Servers in your network. What is the first thing you should do to monitor them? Choose the best answer.

   A. Determine a monitoring schedule for each of the servers.

   B. Create a baseline for one of the servers.

   C. Decide which monitoring tools you will use.

   D. Create monitoring accounts on each of the servers.

   E. Disconnect the server from the network when it is to be monitored to prevent interference from the rest of the network.

2. Jennifer has been having problems with her network, which uses the master domain model. Three domains trust the master domain. For some time, the performance of some of the servers seems to be slow at certain times of the day. When she contacted Microsoft, it suggested that she review her baseline. Unfortunately, Jennifer is not sure what a baseline is and doesn't know how to find it. How can she get a baseline? Select the best answer.

   A. Go to the hardware manufacturer's web site and download one.

   B. Use the baseline that came with the server on the CD or disk that is supplied with each server.

   C. The baseline is included in the README.TXT file.

   D. She has to create the baseline.

   E. Baselines are needed when working with Windows NT Servers.

3. Steve has decided to use Performance Monitor to create a baseline for his Windows NT file and printer server. The baseline is going to consist of information about memory and disk access, because those items are very important for a file and printer server. After collecting data for five hours, Steve looks at the logs and finds that no disk information was collected. What is the problem? Choose the best answer.

   A. The disk counters were not enabled.

   B. The network counters were not enabled.

   C. Performance Monitor cannot collect disk information.

   D. Performance Monitor can collect data on only one resource at a time.

   E. Steve needs to purchase a separate license to use Performance Monitor on his server.

4. Will is setting up servers at his staging site and then sending them to the different remote sites for deployment. At his site, he installs the operating system, WINS, DHCP Server, and other server utilities. To make it easier for the onsite support staff to troubleshoot problems, he also creates log files with Performance Monitor and Network Monitor for four hours the day before the shipment to the site. What is wrong with Will's methodology? Select the best answer.

   A. Performance Monitor and Network Monitor should not be run at the same time.

   B. WINS and DHCP Server should not be installed on the same server.

   C. Logs should be taken during off-peak hours, not during the day.

   D. The logs should have been created before the utilities were installed.

   E. The logs should be created after the servers are connected to the network.

5. Mary has had a number of complaints about network and server performance. Until now, she has not monitored either the server or the network. What should Mary use to monitor network performance? Select the correct tools.

   A. A time-domain reflectometer

   B. Performance Monitor

   C. Network Monitor

   D. A UPS

   E. A digital volt meter

6. A number of users in the domain have recently complained to Charlie about slow access to their file server. It seems that whenever a user tries to copy files to or from the server, it takes a very long time. What tool should Charlie use and what should he monitor? Choose the best answer.

   A. Use Performance Monitor to monitor disk reads and writes per second.

   B. Use Performance Monitor to monitor physical memory.

   C. Use Network Monitor to monitor bytes per second for the protocol(s) being used.

   D. Use Network Monitor to monitor the number of retransmissions sent per minute.

   E. Use Performance Monitor to monitor the disk queue length.

7. Jake has been planning network maintenance very carefully to ensure that the network runs at peak performance as long as possible. In the past, other networks Jake has worked on were not well maintained, and they had numerous problems—and a lot of downtime because of it. He wants to make sure that he creates a baseline for future reference. When should he create the baseline? (Choose all correct answers.)

   A. When the server and utilities are first set up, when utilities are installed, and when the server is placed online.

   B. After any major software or hardware changes.

C. Once a month.

D. After the server has been set up, but before it is placed online with the rest of the network.

E. As soon as a problem occurs.

8. **Eddie works with Jake and is going to create the baseline for the servers in Jake's network. However, Jake didn't tell Eddie what tool(s) to use to create the baseline. What tool(s) should Eddie use to create the baseline?**

   A. Windows NT Diagnostics

   B. Performance Monitor

   C. TechNet

   D. Network Monitor

   E. Windows NT Resource Kit

9. **Helen wants to monitor the servers in her network to check the resource utilization for memory and processor. However, she is concerned about how the performance will be affected when she runs Performance Monitor. She needs accurate measurements so she can plan for upgrades. What should she do? Choose the best solution for Helen's problem.**

A. Run Performance Monitor during off-peak hours so that it does not impact the users.

B. Run Network Monitor instead because it does not use as many resources as Performance Monitor does.

C. Run Performance Monitor on a Windows NT Workstation to monitor each of the servers.

D. Run Performance Monitor in "stealth" mode to limit the resource usage.

E. Use the Systems Management Server version of Network Monitor to limit its impact on the servers.

10. **Eddie has found out from Jake which tools he should use to monitor the servers, but now he is not sure what to monitor. He knows that a lot of components are involved in keeping a server up and running, but he is not sure which things are supposed to be in a baseline. Which of the following items should be included in a baseline?**

   A. Disk performance

   B. Processor and memory usage

   C. Network traffic

   D. Monitor resolution

   E. Free disk space

ANSWER KEY

1. C	5. B-C	9. C
2. D	6. E	10. A-B-C
3. A	7. A-B	
4. E	8. B-D	

SELECTING TOOLS TO MONITOR NETWORK TRENDS

1. You have been assigned the task of monitoring each of the five Windows NT Servers in your network. What is the first thing you should do to monitor them? Choose the best answer.

   C. Decide which monitoring tools you will use.

1. CORRECT ANSWER: C

The first thing to do when you're planning to monitor a server and/or network is to determine what tool(s) you are going to use for the monitoring; Microsoft provides Performance Monitor and Network Monitor with Windows NT. It is very difficult to create a baseline if you have not determined which tool to use to create the baseline. Also, after you have created a baseline with one tool, you should use that tool again later when you want to compare results.

If you use different tools to perform the same function, the results may differ even if the system is running the same. This could result from the way the tools have been configured to gather data. For example, Network Monitor is often used to create a portion of a baseline. However, if you use only Network Monitor, and the next person to check server performance uses Performance Monitor, it would be difficult to compare the two sets of results. Comparing the two sets of data would be like comparing apples to oranges. All of it would be valid, but it would tell you nothing.

You usually create baselines and monitor systems while the server is online and is being used at normal, low, and high levels of usage. That way, you can get a good idea of how the system performs under different loads.

2. Jennifer has been having problems with her network, which uses the master domain model. Three domains trust the master domain. For some time, the performance of some of the servers seems to be slow at certain times of the day. When she contacted Microsoft, it suggested that she review her baseline. Unfortunately, Jennifer is not sure what a baseline is and doesn't know how to find it. How can she get a baseline? Select the best answer.

   D. She has to create the baseline.

2. CORRECT ANSWER: D

Although manufacturers can provide their clients with specifications as to how well their systems can operate, the numbers they provide will never be the same as what you have at your site. Too many options factor into the performance of a system.

Because of this, it is important that you create a baseline for each server you deploy. Even if you install two "identical" servers with the exact same software, there will be differences in how the two perform. This is partly due to the specification ranges of every component that makes up a computer. If every component could be guaranteed to be exactly the same in two computers, you could end with the same results for two computers. But because this will not happen in the near future, it is always a good practice to create a baseline for every server.

3. Steve has decided to use Performance Monitor to create a baseline for his Windows NT file and printer server. The baseline is going to consist of information about memory and disk access, because those items are very important for a file and printer server. After collecting data for five hours, Steve looks at the logs and finds that no disk information was collected. What is the problem? Choose the best answer.

A. The disk counters were not enabled.

3. CORRECT ANSWER: A

When you use Performance Monitor, you must remember that the disk counters are not activated by default. So, even though you may request that it monitor certain objects and counters from the disk, nothing will be displayed unless the disk counters are enabled. This is a legacy setting from Windows NT 3.5 and possibly earlier. At that time, Windows NT Server could be installed on a 486 machine. If the disk counters were enabled on those older systems, they took a definite performance hit. Therefore, to ensure good performance when the system was not being monitored, the disk counters were disabled.

To activate the disk counters in Performance Monitor, run this command:

```
diskperf -y
```

If the system has multiple disk drives, use the following command:

```
diskperf -ye
```

This will activate the disk counters the next time the server is rebooted. When you finish monitoring the system, you can deactivate the counters by running this command:

```
diskperf -n
```

If the server is running on a Pentium or RISC processor, leaving the counters activated all the time should not be a problem, because the performance usage is negligible.

4. Will is setting up servers at his staging site and then sending them to the different remote sites for deployment. At his site, he installs the operating system, WINS, DHCP Server, and other server utilities. To make it easier for the onsite support staff to troubleshoot problems, he also creates log files with Performance Monitor and Network Monitor for four hours the day before the shipment to the site. What is wrong with Will's methodology? Select the best answer.

   E. The logs should be created after the servers are connected to the network.

4. CORRECT ANSWER: E

It is great that Will is able to set up the servers at a staging site and then send them to the remote sites for deployment. However, when you create a baseline, the system should be running in a live situation where results can be logged during low, medium, and high load periods. This will provide you with the most accurate information.

5. Mary has had a number of complaints about network and server performance. Until now, she has not monitored either the server or the network. What should Mary use to monitor network performance? Select the correct tools.

   B. Performance Monitor
   C. Network Monitor

5. CORRECT ANSWERS: B-C

Performance Monitor and Network Monitor are tools that come with Windows NT Server and are very useful for monitoring the activity of computers and the network. The other devices that were listed are also used for testing and monitoring, but they are normally used to troubleshoot hardware problems, such as shorts, breaks, and so on.

6. A number of users in the domain have recently complained to Charlie about slow access to their file server. It seems that whenever a user tries to copy files to or from the server, it takes a very long time. What tool should Charlie use and what should he monitor? Choose the best answer.

   E. Use Performance Monitor to monitor the disk queue length.

6. CORRECT ANSWER: E

A couple of factors can greatly affect the performance of a file server. One is that the users are trying to access the server across the network. Therefore, an obvious thing to suspect is the network. However, the users are operating in a domain, and they are not complaining about logon time or anything else that involves the network. So, the next logical thing to suspect would be the disk on the file server. By checking the disk queue length on the server, you can get an idea of the difficulties the disk on the server is having. If the queue length is two or more, the disk is probably the problem, and you should look into replacing it with a faster one.

7. Jake has been planning network maintenance very carefully to ensure that the network runs at peak performance as long as possible. In the past, other networks Jake has worked on were not well maintained, and they had numerous problems—and a lot of downtime because of it. He wants to make sure that he creates a baseline for future reference. When should he create the baseline? (Choose all correct answers.)

   A. When the server and utilities are first set up, when utilities are installed, and when the server is placed online.

   B. After any major software or hardware changes.

7. CORRECT ANSWERS: A-B

A baseline is like a living thing: As changes are made to the server—hardware or software is added and removed—the baseline changes. Obviously, a server on which WINS and DHCP Server are installed will perform differently than will a server with neither of those services installed. Therefore, each time you make a major change to the server, you should create another baseline.

8. Eddie works with Jake and is going to create the baseline for the servers in Jake's network. However, Jake didn't tell Eddie what tool(s) to use to create the baseline. What tool(s) should Eddie use to create the baseline?

   B. Performance Monitor

   D. Network Monitor

8. CORRECT ANSWERS: B-D

In question 5, you were asked which tools should be used to monitor the network and servers, and the answers were Performance Monitor and Network Monitor. To create the baseline, you should use the same tool you use to monitor your servers. That way the results should be fairly accurate. If different tools were used to monitor the servers and create a baseline, different results could occur.

9. Helen wants to monitor the servers in her network to check the resource utilization for memory and processor. However, she is concerned about how the performance will be affected when she runs Performance Monitor. She needs accurate measurements so she can plan for upgrades. What should she do? Choose the best solution for Helen's problem.

   C. Run Performance Monitor on a Windows NT Workstation to monitor each of the servers.

9. CORRECT ANSWER: C

Because Helen is primarily concerned with the processor and memory, it is a good idea to monitor the servers from a separate system. This reduces the resource usage on the system that is being monitored, which provides more accurate results. Windows NT Workstation comes with the same version of Performance Monitor that Windows NT Server does, so monitoring from another system is a very simple process. The only resource that will be affected by monitoring the server from across the network is the network card and its traffic. Because this is not important to Helen at this time, it is not a factor. To be able to perform remote monitoring, the user must at least be a member of the Admins local group of the remote system.

10. Eddie has found out from Jake which tools he should use to monitor the servers, but now he is not sure what to monitor. He knows that a lot of components are involved in keeping a server up and running, but he is not sure which things are supposed to be in a baseline. Which of the following items should be included in a baseline?

A. Disk performance

B. Processor and memory usage

C. Network traffic

10. CORRECT ANSWERS: A-B-C

Usually, when creating a baseline, you want to make sure that everything that affects the server's performance is tracked so you can determine later if the resource needs to be replaced or upgraded. Any computer can be broken down into four major resources: processor, memory, disk, and network.

FURTHER REVIEW

Table 3.1 shows the different network cables and their distance limitations. Table 3.2 describes the different methods of wireless communication.

TABLE 3.1 **TYPES OF NETWORK CABLES AND THEIR DISTANCE LIMITATIONS**

Cable Description	Limitations
10BASE-T (twisted-pair)	100 meters (328 feet) for Ethernet; 45–200 meters (148–656 feet) for Token-Ring
10BASE-2 (thinnet)	185 meters (607 feet)
10BASE-5 (thicknet)	500 meters (1,650 feet)
10BASE-FL (fiber-optic)	2,000+ meters (66,000+ feet)

TABLE 3.2 **METHODS OF WIRELESS COMMUNICATION**

Transmission Type	Description
Infrared	An infrared light beam is used to carry the signal from one computer to another. These signals need to be very strong because they are highly susceptible to interference from interior lighting and windows. Rates tend to be high because of infrared's high bandwidth, but infrared cannot operate at distances greater than 100 feet.
Laser	Laser is similar to infrared, except that its light is much more intense, which means the signals can travel much farther. Still, like infrared, laser is susceptible to interference from other light sources.
Narrow-band radio	This is similar to a radio station broadcast. Both the transmitter and the receiver must be tuned to a certain frequency. This type of transmission does not require a line-of-site (as do infrared and laser), but because it operates at a high frequency, the transmission cannot pass through steel or load-bearing walls. Narrow-band radio works well over long distances, but is relatively slow at about 4.8Mbps.
Spread-spectrum radio	As the name implies, this signal is transmitted over a range of frequencies.

When you're planning a network, whether it be a new one or an upgrade, it is important that you consider all the resources that can affect the performance of the servers and ultimately the network. The four major resources that all performance relies on (in no particular order) are processor, memory, disk, and network. It can be argued that one is more important than the other, but depending on the role of the server, any one or all of these can negatively affect performance.

For the exam, you need to know the role of the server and consider the resources that will be needed most for it. A file and print server, for example, should have fast disk drives so that large amounts of data can be written to and read from it in the least possible amount of time. A domain controller should have a fast processor for validating logons. An application server should have a fast processor and lots of memory for carrying out remote commands and storing data in memory (as opposed to caching to the disk drive). All servers should have the quickest network adapters possible so that data can pass between the clients and the servers as quickly as possible.

For disaster recovery, be sure to think through the different options for backing up data and what it would take to recover the data. For example, recovering from a disk failure on a Windows NT Server would take a number of steps in most cases:

1. Install new disk drive(s).

2. Install Windows NT Server.

3. Install backup software (if Windows NT's backup software was not used).

4. Restore the entire server, including the Registry.

If a complete backup (including the Registry) was not kept, the administrator has a lot of work to do to rebuild the server.

SUMMARY

The Implementation section of the exam is not made up of hard-and-fast facts like some of the other sections. The Implementation section deals more with logic and familiarity with Microsoft networking. The best advice for preparing for this part of the exam is to work with the products, create networks, and try different configurations and scenarios to understand how the products perform.

CHAPTER 4

Troubleshooting

No matter how much planning you do during implementation, maintenance, and monitoring, some problems will arise that you don't anticipate. Having said that, perhaps the most important attribute a system administrator can possess is the ability to effectively troubleshoot computer and network problems. Some people just naturally have the ability to solve problems, but that does not mean that everyone can *troubleshoot* problems. By following some basic procedures, you can determine the source of just about any problem.

The following is an example of the steps you might follow:

1. Set the problem's priority (more than one problem may exist).

2. Gather as much information about the problem (error messages, applications that don't run, the fact that you can't connect to the network, and so on) as possible.

3. Compile a list of possible problems and their possible solutions.

4. Try one solution at a time, and document the results.

5. Study the results of the tests to identify a solution.

6. Document all solutions tried and the results created. Ensure that the problem and its resolution are recorded in a log for future reference.

7. (Optional, but recommended): Keep a separate maintenance/monitoring/resolution log for each server. Although two servers may have the same hardware and software, each computer is unique.

EXAM TIP

Always check the simple things first. Make sure that cables are securely connected, user accounts are not locked out, and the user has the necessary permissions before starting an in-depth analysis of the problem. Many an hour has been spent in vain because something simple has been overlooked.

These steps are effective in most situations, but you should remember a few additional things. First, documentation is extremely important. Without documentation, you are bound to repeat your mistakes. Second, sometimes you face more than one problem, and the symptoms of one problem might hide the existence of the other problem.

The exam questions on troubleshooting cover all aspects of this book, so it is important to be familiar with networking as a whole.

The Microsoft test objectives for the troubleshooting portion of the exam are as follows:

Identify common errors associated with components required for communications. (Practice questions start on page 169.)

▶ The purpose of this test objective is to make sure you are able to isolate what problems are associated with what components on the network.

Diagnose and resolve common connectivity problems with cards, cables, and related hardware. (Practice questions start on page 180.)

▶ This exam objective reflects the need for you to be able to not only diagnose common connectivity problems with cards, cables and other related hardware, but also to be able to resolve these problems in order to reestablish connectivity on the network.

Resolve broadcast storms. (Practice questions start on page 189.)

▶ This exam objective is designed to ensure that you understand what causes a broadcast storm and methods of resolving these broadcast storms.

Identify and resolve network performance problems. (Practice questions start on page 198.)

▶ This exam objective addresses your ability to use tools and understand issues relating to identifying and resolving poor performance on a network.

IDENTIFYING COMMON ERRORS

1. Scott has heard from a number of users that when they try to dial in from home, they cannot connect to the RAS server. It appears that they have configured their dial-in software correctly, but still they have intermittent problems. Where should Scott start to resolve this problem?

   A. Verify that the users' modems operate at the same speed as the modem in the server.

   B. Use Network Monitor to view the traffic on the network.

   C. Monitor the Event Viewer log to see what happens when people try to connect.

   D. Use Performance Monitor to see how busy the RAS port is.

   E. Verify that the user's accounts have not been locked out for dial-in.

2. You are managing a network that has multiple segments within a single building. When it was decided to move from a single segment to multiple segments, the protocol was switched from NetBEUI to TCP/IP. The only problem seems to be that when the users are in Network Neighborhood, they cannot see a listing of the computers on the other segments. You have tried to PING to the computer names on other segments, and they all respond as expected. How should you try to resolve the problem?

   A. LMHOSTS file

   B. HOSTS file

   C. WINS

   D. DHCP

   E. SNMP

3. ABC Company has just signed a lease for an ISDN line from its local telco company. The speed ABC has ordered is a 64KB line. When the company first installed the router, users were able to connect to the Internet without any problem, but after a day or so, they lost connectivity. The router appears to be configured correctly, but still no traffic is getting in or out. Where should ABC begin to resolve the problem?

   A. Increase the speed of the router.

   B. Decrease the speed of the router.

   C. Increase the memory in the server.

   D. Increase the speed of the line.

   E. Decrease the speed of the line.

4. A company has 200 users on one subnet and 150 users on another. A number of users on both subnets are complaining that they cannot share their files with users on another segment in the network. The current configuration consists of a multi-homed Windows NT 4 server acting as

a router between the two segments. The first NIC is configured with the IP address of 207.29.18.5. The second NIC is configured with both NetBEUI and TCP/IP; its IP address is 207.29.18.254. Both NICs use the default Class C subnet mask. What should be done to resolve the problem?

A. Change the subnet mask for both NICs.

B. Remove NetBEUI from the first NIC.

C. Add NetBEUI to the other NIC.

D. Change the Default Gateway for both NICs.

E. Change the IP address of one NIC.

5. Gail has just finished installing 15 new Windows NT Workstation 4 systems, all of which were configured to be part of the domain CORP. Shortly after they were set up for the users, some users had difficulty getting validated by a domain controller. What should Gail check first? Choose the most correct answer(s).

A. Verify that the user(s) has a valid account.

B. Verify the computer name.

C. Verify that the network adapter card is correct.

D. Verify the computer accounts.

E. None of the above.

6. Evelyn just set up a new printer on a network with a JetDirect card. Mark installed the drivers for the printer on the server,

and now everyone is ready to print. The users are complaining that "the printer is not printing." What areas should Evelyn verify first to make sure that the users can print to the new printer?

A. Verify the computer accounts on the network.

B. Verify that the users have the proper printer driver installed.

C. Verify the configuration of the printer.

D. Verify the configuration of the JetDirect card.

E. Verify that the network card on the server can accommodate duplex printing.

7. Bob has created a share on his Windows 95 computer so that the rest of his office can access the sport pool he has created. He works in an office of 12 sports enthusiasts. Because he will be away when the next pool must be created, Sharon has volunteered to make the document and share it on her computer. This seems to be a great idea because Bob periodically loses data when someone accidentally deletes his files. Sharon, on the other hand, has Windows NT Workstation 4 and can use the NTFS permissions to restrict access. The only problem is that there always seems to be one person who cannot get to the pool on her computer. What could be the problem? Choose the best answer.

A. Sharon has not granted the correct permissions for everyone.

B. All the users are not logging on to the network properly.

C. The application enables only five users to access the file at one time.

D. The person is trying to log on to the network outside of the allotted hours.

E. Sharon is using Windows NT Workstation 4.

8. You have configured one of your Windows NT 4 servers to use both TCP/IP and IPX/SPX so that it can be used as a gateway to a Novell server. When you try to set up the shares for access to the Novell volumes using GSNW (Gateway Services for NetWare), you find that you cannot access the Novell server. What do you suspect is the problem? Choose the most correct answer.

A. The cable lengths you have been using are just over the documented limits and are causing inconsistent results.

B. NDIS 4.0 network cards cannot support both TCP/IP and IPX/SPX when trying to implement GSNW.

C. Routing tables must be created on the GSNW server to enable the users to access the Novell server through the "gateway."

D. The TCP/IP over IPX/SPX option should be selected in the "Gateway Services" dialog box.

E. Check the "frame type" of both the Novell server and the Windows NT server.

9. Dale just installed a new network card in his new Windows 95 system. Upon startup, he was prompted by the system to install new hardware that was detected. After installation, he still could not get his account validated by a domain controller on the network. What is the problem? Choose the most correct answer.

A. The network card came with newer drivers than those supplied on the Windows CD.

B. The driver files came from a demo disk and have a lifespan of only one month.

C. Domain controllers do not validate user accounts. That function is performed by member servers.

D. He does not have an administrative account on the domain and, therefore, cannot install hardware on a computer.

E. None of the above.

10. Nancy runs a network for a company that is in the process of expanding its offices to include a second building. She and the rest of the IT staff have been doing some performance studies to see what should be implemented on the servers. Because of the network's small size and speed, they have concluded that they want to use NetBEUI on all the systems. What concerns would you have using NetBEUI throughout the network?

A. NetBEUI is too fast for most network cards and will cause sporadic results if the speeds are not matched correctly.

B. NetBEUI is too slow and will cause a loss of data.

C. The router has been configured to forward broadcasts.

D. NetBEUI cannot be routed.

E. The routing table has not been configured properly.

ANSWER KEY

1. C-D	5. A-C-D	9. A
2. A-C	6. B-C-D	10. D
3. B	7. E	
4. E	8. E	

IDENTIFYING COMMON ERRORS

1. Scott has heard from a number of users that when they try to dial in from home, they cannot connect to the RAS server. It appears that they have configured their dial-in software correctly, but still they have intermittent problems. Where should Scott start to resolve this problem?

C. Monitor the Event Viewer log to see what happens when people try to connect.

D. Use Performance Monitor to see how busy the RAS port is.

1. CORRECT ANSWERS: C-D

Windows NT Server 4 can accommodate up to 256 RAS connections; Windows NT Workstation 4 can accommodate one inbound RAS connection. In this question, you are not supplied with a great deal of information, but some basic things should always be checked when a problem with RAS arises.

First, the Event Viewer can provide a great deal of information and is often overlooked when people are trying to resolve problems. By looking at the event logs, you can determine who is trying to log on using RAS and when the logon occurred. In addition, if a problem existed, you would have an error code that could explain what the problem was. If multiple problems occurred, they would also be shown in the Event Viewer. However, if you based your diagnosis simply by what the users tell you, you might conclude that they are all having the same problem.

By looking at the event logs, you should be able to tell whether the RAS port has been busy on a constant basis, or whether it just seems to be busy at certain times of the day or week.

As mentioned before, you have not been provided with a great deal of information in this question. Therefore, you also must consider that a multiport card (digiboard, chili-port, and so on) could be attached to the server to provide it with more than one port.

In this case, it would be useful to use Performance Monitor to view the activity on the ports. A log file could be created that would enable you to view the total number of ports available, as well as the total number of ports being used. This may not point to any specific problems occurring when users try to dial in currently, but it could help monitor activity. By analyzing the log file, you could determine when peak usage occurs and develop policy on dial-in use. Additionally, you could predict when more dial-in lines would be needed, as more people work from their home and need to connect to the network.

Performance Monitor could also be used to track how quickly (or slowly) data is transferred across the telephone lines. This could be a determining factor when trying to justify purchasing faster modems.

2. You are managing a network that has multiple segments within a single building. When it was decided to move from a single segment to multiple segments, the protocol was switched from NetBEUI to TCP/IP. The only problem is that when the users are in Network Neighborhood, they cannot see a listing of the computers on the other segments. You have tried to PING to the computer names on other segments, and they all respond as expected. How should you try to resolve the problem?

A. LMHOSTS file

C. WINS

2. CORRECT ANSWERS: A-C

It seems as though browsing the network to see the other computers and resources on the network should be the easiest thing to do, but users always have problems with this task.

Several areas can be checked right up front: the LMHOSTS file and WINS. Both provide a mapping of NetBIOS names to IP addresses. Not all networks utilize these, but most use one or the other.

The LMHOSTS file is a static text file that provides the mapping between an IP address and the NetBIOS name of a computer. When the computer is started, and if any of the lines have #PRE in them, these entries are loaded into the NetBIOS name cache and stay there. If the name is not loaded with the #PRE entry at startup, the LMHOSTS file can be parsed to discover the mapping later. Entries added to the NetBIOS name cache by parsing are flushed from the cache at predetermined intervals (after 2 minutes, if not used again, or after 10 minutes even if used again).

WINS (Windows Internet Naming Service) can also be used to resolve NetBIOS names to IP addresses. Unlike the static text file LMHOSTS, WINS is dynamic. As each computer is started on the network, it announces itself to the WINS server, providing it with its NetBIOS name and IP address. When a computer wants to communicate with a computer whose address is not in its NetBIOS name cache, it sends a request to the WINS server to resolve the name to the IP address for it. Because communication with the WINS server occurs through directed messages, broadcast traffic is reduced and, therefore, overall network traffic decreases.

By using LMHOSTS and/or WINS, communication with the browsers is improved, so you are more likely to be able to view more of the systems and resources on the network.

To test NetBIOS name resolution, try carrying out a NetBIOS command, such as NET VIEW or NET USE. The PING command is a Windows Sockets application and can be used to test host name resolution. The confusing part of these name resolutions is that, on a PC, the host name and the NetBIOS name are often (but not always) the same. When the name is resolved for one, administrators often assume that it is resolved for the other.

3. ABC Company has just signed a lease for an ISDN line from its local telco company. The speed ABC has ordered is a 64KB line. When the company first installed the router, users were able to connect to the Internet without any problem, but after a day or so, they lost connectivity. The router appears to be configured correctly, but still no traffic is getting in or out. Where should ABC begin to resolve the problem?

B. Decrease the speed of the router.

3. CORRECT ANSWER: B

ISDN has become one of the most popular methods for businesses to connect a network to the Internet or to connect a group of WANs. The ISDN router is a proven device that faces very few problems after it has been installed and configured. Along with the stability, a number of options for line speed are available to meet most people's needs. These speeds generally range from around a 56KB line to 512KB and higher, depending on the needs and what is offered.

The lines are generally conditioned to operate at a certain speed, and the routers are configured to operate at that speed.

However, some areas have more reliable power and cables than others. Most providers state that the line speed is a certain rate with a margin of error to accommodate external influences. For example, the provider may supply you with a 64KB line that actually operates at 59KB. If this is the case, and if your router is configured to operate at 64KB, you will probably have problems. However, if you change the configuration on the router to 56KB, the problems will probably disappear.

In this kind of situation, you want to make sure that you get everyone (network administration, telco, and ISDN provider) involved to narrow the problem.

4. A company has 200 users on one subnet and 150 users on another. A number of users on both subnets are complaining that they cannot share their files with users on another segment in the network. The current configuration consists of a multihomed Windows NT 4 server acting as a router between the two segments. The first NIC is configured with the IP address of 207.29.18.5. The second NIC is configured with both NetBEUI and TCP/IP; its IP address is 207.29.18.254. Both NICs use the default Class C subnet mask. What should be done to resolve the problem?

E. Change the IP address of one NIC.

4. CORRECT ANSWER: E

You have not been provided with the configuration of the IP addresses on each of the workstations, but from what you have been given, you know that both NICs in the server have been given IP addresses in the same subnet. This is generally not accepted and will stop packets from being sent to the other subnet.

When a Microsoft client sends packets to another computer, it first resolves whether the receiving address exists on the local subnet or a remote subnet. If the address is determined to be local, the client tries to send the packet directly to it. If the address is determined to be remote, the packet is sent to the Default Gateway. In this case, the packet would never be sent to the Default Gateway.

You know from the number of users on each of the subnets that they could not have subnetted a single class C address. Therefore, you must assume that someone made a mistake when configuring the addresses of the NICs in the server. To resolve the problem, you should check the addresses of the workstations on each subnet and configure the server accordingly.

5. Gail has just finished installing 15 new Windows NT Workstation 4 systems, all of which were configured to be a part of the domain CORP. Shortly after they were set up for the users, some users had difficulty getting validated by a domain controller. What should Gail check first? Choose the most correct answer(s).

A. Verify that the user(s) has a valid account.

C. Verify that the network adapter card is correct.

D. Verify the computer accounts.

5. CORRECT ANSWERS: A-C-D

In a situation in which a person is trying to log on to a Windows NT domain, a number of factors influence what happens.

For Windows NT to operate correctly in a domain, it should have a valid computer account in the domain. When a user in the domain tries to log on, the domain controller verifies not only the user account but the computer account as well.

Without a valid user account, the user cannot gain access to the network and does not have access to the local Windows NT workstation. If the user is at a Windows 95 computer, the user can access the local computer (unless policies have been put in place to restrict this kind of access).

A bad NIC or NIC driver could also prevent a user from logging on to the domain.

6. Evelyn just set up a new printer on a network with a JetDirect card. Mark installed the drivers for the printer on the server, and now everyone is ready to print. The users are complaining that "the printer is not printing." What areas should Evelyn verify first to make sure that the users can print to the new printer?

B. Verify that the users have the proper printer driver installed.

C. Verify the configuration of the printer.

D. Verify the configuration of the JetDirect card.

6. CORRECT ANSWERS: B-C-D

It seems that printing should be the simplest thing to do, yet it seems to be the one action that causes everyone problems.

Anytime a printer has just been set up and users are having difficulty printing, always ask the basic questions first: Are the cables all plugged in, is the printer turned on, and is the printer online? If these all check out okay, go on to the next stage.

Because the printer has just been installed, first make sure that the JetDirect card has been configured correctly and that the IP address is not already in use. This also assumes that you are using TCP/IP as the protocol. If you are not, make sure the DLC protocol is installed on the print server.

If the JetDirect card is correctly configured at the server, you can check to make sure that the proper (and most current drivers) have been installed for the printer.

If the proper driver has been installed correctly, the next obvious place to check is the configuration of the printer. Have the proper permissions been applied to enable people to print to it? Has the printer ever been shared?

These basic questions will solve most problems that arise from printing.

7. Bob has created a share on his Windows 95 computer so that the rest of his office can access the sport pool that he has created. He works in an office of 12 sports enthusiasts. Because he will be away when the next pool must be created, Sharon has volunteered to make the document and share it on her computer. This seems to be a great idea because Bob periodically loses data when someone accidentally deletes his files. Sharon, on the other hand, has Windows NT Workstation 4 and can use the NTFS permissions to restrict access. The only problem is that there always seems to be one person who cannot get to the pool on her computer. What could be the problem? Choose the best answer.

E. Sharon is using Windows NT Workstation 4.

7. CORRECT ANSWER: E

Windows NT Workstation 4 and Server 4 are very similar and differ from each other in only a few subtle areas. One of these areas is that Windows NT Server 4 has no real limits as to how many inbound connections can be made from the network. However, Windows NT Workstation 4 is restricted to 10 inbound connections from the network.

Because 12 people are in the office, the first 10 people will gain access to the share and the 11th person will be denied access. (The 12th person happens to be Sharon, and she doesn't need access because the files are local to her.)

Depending on the networking budget for this office, a definitive solution for this problem might not exist. Windows NT

Server is considerably more expensive (about four or five times as much) than Windows NT Workstation. Therefore, unless the company has a lot of money to spend on upgrading to Windows NT Server, it might be easier (as in, less expensive) to just make sure that users disconnect from the other shares on other computers when they are not actively using them.

8. You have configured one of your Windows NT 4 servers to use both TCP/IP and IPX/SPX so that it can be used as a gateway to a Novell server. When you try to set up the shares for access to the Novell volumes using GSNW (Gateway Services for NetWare), you find that you cannot access the Novell server. What do you suspect is the problem? Choose the most correct answer.

   E. Check the "frame type" of both the Novell server and the Windows NT server.

8. CORRECT ANSWER: E

Novell generally uses the protocol IPX/SPX. Therefore, the Windows NT server that normally will run the Gateway Services for NetWare also must use IPX/SPX.

As with anything else, the IPX/SPX protocol was modified over the years. The IPX/SPX protocol has a configuration for its frames; depending on the version of NetWare that is implemented, the protocol may be using one frame type or another. If the frame type is not set correctly in the IPX/SPX configuration, communication is not guaranteed. Therefore, the most obvious place to look is to see whether the frame types match between the Novell server and the Windows NT server.

9. Dale just installed a new network card in his new Windows 95 system. Upon startup, he was prompted by the system to install new hardware that was detected. After installation, he still could not get his account validated by a domain controller on the network. What is the problem? Choose the most correct answer.

   A. The network card came with newer drivers than those supplied on the Windows CD.

9. CORRECT ANSWER: A

Anytime a new network card (or any new hardware) is installed into a Windows 95 system, it tries to install the hardware and drivers for you. As it installs the drivers, the system prompts you for the location of the original Windows 95 files. If the hardware has newer drivers, they are provided on a disk along with the new hardware. If the Windows 95 CD was used instead of the disk supplied, an older driver may be installed. This older driver may cause problems with the new device and possibly even prevent it from working altogether.

Even if the hardware did not come with a driver disk, it is always a good idea to check with the manufacturer for a newer driver or a patch.

10. Nancy runs a network for a company that is in the process of expanding its offices to include a second building. She and the rest of the IT staff have been doing some performance studies to see what should be implemented on the servers. Because of the network's small size and speed, they have concluded that they want to use NetBEUI on all the systems. What concerns would you have using NetBEUI throughout the network?

D. NetBEUI cannot be routed.

10. CORRECT ANSWER: D

Although NetBEUI is relatively fast and uses small packets, it also has a number of drawbacks.

With NetBEUI, you generally end up with a lot of network traffic because it was designed to use broadcasting a lot. This is fine for a small network, but a great deal of traffic congestion occurs when you grow to 30 or 40 computers.

Also, the small size of NetBEUI becomes a drawback. Without the additional information that TCP/IP and IPX/SPX have, NetBEUI cannot be routed. This means that it is restricted to working in a single subnet.

In the case of Nancy's network, she can't use NetBEUI because everyone would be restricted to communication on individual subnets.

DIAGNOSING AND RESOLVING CONNECTIVITY PROBLEMS

1. Jack has a Windows NT network segment and a Novell NetWare segment that he wants to connect. The Windows NT segment uses Ethernet, and the Novell NetWare segment uses Token-Ring. What device can Jack use to connect the segments so that they can share resources?

   A. Router.

   B. Bridge.

   C. Gateway.

   D. Repeater.

   E. It cannot be done.

2. Sam is having problems adding a new server to the domain MARKET. He just installed Windows NT Server 4 on the computer, but when he tries to join it to the domain, he gets an error indicating that the computer cannot find the domain controller. What areas should Sam check? Choose all appropriate answers.

   A. Windows NT Diagnostics

   B. The Event Viewer

   C. Performance Monitor

   D. Network Card properties

   E. Windows Explorer

3. Carol has been moving workstations in the office due to office expansion. Of the 10 computers she has moved so far, she cannot get one to work on the network. She has tried rebooting the computer a number of times, but she still can't log on to the network. The office uses 100Mbps Ethernet cards with CAT 5 cabling. What should Carol do to troubleshoot her problem? Choose all the correct options.

   A. Replace the network card.

   B. Replace the network cable.

   C. Move the network card to a different slot.

   D. Disable and then reenable the bindings for the network card.

   E. Plug the network cable into a different wall jack.

4. Lyle has just started in the IT department to help with the support of the network. His first task was to label and bundle the cables in the back of the server racks. Lyle was careful to not disconnect any of the cables as he carried out his duties. When he was finished, however, there seemed to be intermittent and inexplicable problems with the servers. When Lyle and the senior administrator checked the cabling, everything seemed fine. What could be causing these intermittent problems?

   A. Electrical interference.

   B. A broken wire.

C. A damaged component from static electricity.

D. A disconnected cable.

E. The servers must be rebooted after the cables have been bundled.

5. To reduce the amount of network traffic, it has been decided that the network should be subnetted. To reduce expenses, two of the existing Windows NT 4 servers will be set up as routers. That way, they can still operate as servers while performing the duties of a router. For simplicity, the three subnets will be referred to as A, B, and C. Computers on subnets A and C can communicate with subnet B. However, subnets A and C cannot communicate with each other. What could be the problem?

   A. Windows NT 4 was not meant to operate as a router.

   B. Windows NT 4 can operate with a maximum of only two subnets.

   C. DHCP must be set up.

   D. Modify the Default Gateway setting in each server.

   E. Add SNMP to each server.

6. Dave is setting up a new server and has installed a number of devices onto it. These include a network card, two SCSI cards, a sound card, and a modem. As he gets to the part of the installation where the networking components are to be initialized, the components fail. He is sure that he has entered the correct domain name and installed the correct drivers. What should Dave check before he tries anything else?

   A. Check the slot where the network card is located to ensure that it has the correct number of pins.

   B. Check the network cable to ensure that it has the correct number of pins.

   C. Check the HCL (Hardware Compatibility List) to ensure that the network cable is on the list.

   D. Remove the Server service because it is interfering with the Workstation service.

   E. Modify the settings in the EISA configuration.

7. Jane is working on a 16Mbps Token-Ring network. Some new computers were delivered last week, and today a number of people are complaining about how poorly the network is functioning. What should Jane look for to resolve the problem?

   A. Verify the routing tables on each of the servers and routers.

   B. Check the configuration of the network cards.

   C. Replace the Token-Ring cards with Ethernet cards.

   D. Replace the CAT 5 network cables with 10BASE-2 cables.

   E. Replace the terminators on the trunk cable.

8. Tom is working with a small network of about 15 computers in a ring topology. This morning the network stopped functioning. What should Tom do to

resolve the problem? Choose all correct answers.

A. Replace all the cables in the network.

B. Replace all the connectors in the network.

C. Remove one computer from the ring and test the network.

D. Remove all the computers from the ring and test the network.

E. Reinstall the network drivers.

9. Alice must move John's computer into the boardroom because he is doing a presentation tomorrow. After setting up the computer in the boardroom, Alice starts to receive a number of calls that people cannot use the network. What could be the problem?

A. They are using a linear bus topology for their network; when Alice removed John's computer from the bus, she did not put a terminator on the connector.

B. Alice forgot to log John's computer off the network, so the server is still trying to verify the computer account.

C. The server is still trying to validate the IP address that John's computer was using.

D. Alice should have removed the network card from John's computer and left it connected to the bus.

E. The MAC address of the network card must be removed from the WINS server.

10. The ACME Co. uses 10BASE-T cabling for its network, and users continually experience problems with a few of their workstations. The office is configured in a star topology with a hub in the middle of the building and the server room in one corner. The distance from the hub to any one of the computers is about 350 feet. The company uses Token-Ring network cards that are configured to operate at 16Mbps. What could be the problem?

A. 10BASE-T cabling cannot be used in a star topology.

B. The network adapter must be configured for the distance from the workstation to the hub.

C. The hub needs additional memory.

D. The distance between the hub and the workstations near the perimeter of the building is too great.

E. A stronger hub must be used.

ANSWER KEY

1. C	5. D	9. A
2. B-D	6. E	10. D
3. B-D-E	7. B	
4. A	8. C	

DIAGNOSING AND RESOLVING CONNECTIVITY PROBLEMS

1. Jack has a Windows NT network segment and a Novell NetWare segment that he wants to connect. The Windows NT segment uses Ethernet, and the Novell NetWare segment uses Token-Ring. What device can Jack use to connect the segments so that they can share resources?

C. Gateway.

1. CORRECT ANSWER: C

Many devices are designed to connect different network segments. Each is used in a slightly different way to accomplish the same basic task—to connect network segments. Table 4.1 shows the differences between the devices.

TABLE 4.1 DEVICES USED TO CONNECT NETWORK SEGMENTS PERFORM SLIGHTLY DIFFERENT TASKS

Device	Description
Repeater	Used to connect segments of different or similar media. The repeater increases the signal and passes all traffic in both directions. It functions at the Physical layer of the OSI model.
Bridge	Has the same features as the repeater, plus many others. The bridge functions at the Data Link layer of the OSI model, so it is capable of acquiring more information about the destination of the packets. Bridges do not work well on WANs slower than 56KB, and they cannot take advantage of multiple paths.
Router	Functions at the Network layer of the OSI model and is capable of acquiring a lot more of the addressing information than a bridge. The biggest differences between a bridge and a router are as follows: ▶ A bridge only recognizes a MAC address on its own segment. ▶ A bridge broadcasts everything it does not recognize and forwards addresses it does know to the appropriate port. ▶ The bridge works with all protocols, whereas the router works only with routable protocols. ▶ Routers filter addresses.
Brouter	Similar to a router, except that it can route selected protocols and can bridge nonroutable protocols.
Gateway	Task-specific device used to connect heterogeneous networks; usually referred to by the particular task it performs. As an example, the Windows NT to SNA gateway takes the data from one environment, strips off the old protocol stack, and repackages it in the protocol stack of the destination network. Depending on the gateway, it may operate in all seven layers of the OSI model or in just a few layers.

2. Sam is having problems adding a new server to the domain MARKET. He just installed Windows NT Server 4 on the computer, but when he tries to join it to the domain, he gets an error indicating that the computer cannot find the domain controller. What areas should Sam check? Choose all appropriate answers.

   B. The Event Viewer

   D. Network Card properties

2. CORRECT ANSWERS: B-D

Whenever a problem occurs on a Windows NT 4 system, first look at the Event Viewer. This log captures most events and assigns an event ID to them. This ID can help determine what is causing the problem—and possibly resolve it as well. If nothing immediately obvious exists in the event logs, the next place to check are the properties of the network card itself. Often, especially when working with TCP/IP, a configuration error arises. If you are assigning static IP addresses and encountering problems, it might be worthwhile to use DHCP.

3. Carol has been moving workstations in the office due to office expansion. Of the 10 computers she has moved so far, she cannot get one to work on the network. She has tried rebooting the computer a number of times, but she still can't log on to the network. The office uses 100Mbps Ethernet cards with CAT 5 cabling. What should Carol do to troubleshoot her problem? Choose all the correct options.

   B. Replace the network cable.

   D. Disable and then reenable the bindings for the network card.

   E. Plug the network cable into a different wall jack.

3. CORRECT ANSWERS: B-D-E

Often, the simplest solution eludes the experienced troubleshooter. When in doubt, replace cables with ones that you know work. Sometimes it is the cable that is faulty, or the cable perhaps did not have good contact and, by taking it out and reconnecting it, you may establish a better connection. This is also true of the wall jacks. Sometimes they are damaged when someone unplugs the cable incorrectly or does work in the area where the cable has been run. Also, if you are not the only administrator, there may be some reason that a network card—or at least a service—may have been disabled. By going through this process, you can ensure that the network card is bound properly to everything.

4. Lyle has just started in the IT department to help with the support of the network. His first task was to label and bundle the cables in the back of the server racks. Lyle was careful to not disconnect any of the cables as he carried out his duties. When he was finished, however, there seemed to be intermittent and inexplicable problems with the servers. When Lyle and the senior administrator checked the cabling, everything seemed fine. What could be causing these intermittent problems?

   A. Electrical interference.

4. CORRECT ANSWER: A

Although Lyle may have been very careful not to disconnect any of the cables, he probably bundled the network cable with the power cables. If the cables are not well-shielded, EMF (electromagnetic frequency) interference may be causing the problems. Lyle should keep the power cables bundled together and keep the network cables separate.

5. To reduce the amount of network traffic, it has been decided that the network should be subnetted. To reduce expenses, two of the existing Windows NT 4 servers will be set up as routers. That way, they can still operate as servers while performing the duties of a router. For simplicity, the three subnets will be referred to as A, B, and C. Computers on subnets A and C can communicate with subnet B. However, subnets A and C cannot communicate with each other. What could be the problem?

D. Modify the Default Gateway setting in each server.

6. Dave is setting up a new server and has installed a number of devices onto it. These include a network card, two SCSI cards, a sound card, and a modem. As he gets to the part of the installation where the networking components are to be initialized, the components fail. He is sure that he has entered the correct domain name and installed the correct drivers. What should Dave check before he tries anything else?

E. Modify the settings in the EISA configuration.

5. CORRECT ANSWER: D

Two types of routers exist: static and dynamic. A dynamic router discovers and adds routes to its configuration automatically. A static router must have routes added to its routing table manually. Windows NT 4 can act as router, but it acts as a static router by default.

To resolve this problem, one of the following must be done:

▶ Configure the Default Gateway of each of the Windows NT 4 servers to point to the address of the other server. That way, if a packet must be sent to a subnet of which the server is not aware, it will go to the other server and on to the far subnet.

▶ Manually add entries to the routing tables of each server.

▶ Install RIP (Routing Information Protocol) on each server, which will enable them to act as dynamic routers.

6. CORRECT ANSWER: E

As soon as you start adding pieces of hardware, you run the chance of hardware conflicts. Often, the sound card and network card will be configured from the manufacturer with a similar IRQ setting. The first thing to do is read the documentation of each card to find out which ones can use more than one IRQ. Usually, most devices have an option to use between two and three or more IRQs.

Determine which devices must use certain IRQs and which are plug-and-play. Set the IRQs for the devices that must use a particular IRQ, and then let the plug-and-play devices choose the IRQ that is not already occupied. Table 4.2 shows the standard IRQ assignments. Of course, these settings may be changed according to additional hardware that is installed.

TABLE 4.2 THE STANDARD IRQ SETTINGS IN A PERSONAL COMPUTER CAN BE CHANGED AS DIFFERENT HARDWARE IS INSTALLED

IRQ	Device Assignment
2 (9)	EGA/VGA (video adapter)
3	Open (unless COM2 or COM4 is used)
4	COM1, COM3
5	Open (sometimes LPT2 or a sound card)
6	Floppy disk controller
7	Parallel port (LPT1)
8	Real-time clock
10	Open
11	Open
12	Mouse (PS/2)
13	Math coprocessor
14	Hard-disk controller
15	Open

7. Jane is working on a 16Mbps Token-Ring network. Some new computers were delivered last week, and today a number of people are complaining about how poorly the network is functioning. What should Jane look for to resolve the problem?

   B. Check the configuration of the network cards.

7. CORRECT ANSWER: B

Experience with Token-Ring can help with this problem. With Ethernet, if some computers are using network adapters that are configured to operate at different rates, only the computer that is configured incorrectly is affected. With Token-Ring, if the network cards on a single subnet are configured to operate at different rates, you may end up with *beaconing*. Beaconing occurs when a system that detects a serious error on the network sends a beacon onto the network. After all computers have received and sent the beacon, a new token is entered onto the network. If the error persists, the network may end up in a hung state.

Most places of business using Token-Ring on their network operate their networks at 16Mbps. However, most manufacturers ship their Token-Ring adapters set at 4Mbps. If the person setting up the computer(s) forgets to change the speed of the adapter before connecting it to the network, the network will start beaconing.

Depending on the type of NOS (Network Operating System) and the applications being used, a variety of symptoms may occur.

8. Tom is working with a small network of about 15 computers that is in a ring topology. This morning the network stopped functioning. What should Tom do to resolve the problem? Choose all correct answers.

    C. Remove one computer from the ring and test the network.

8. CORRECT ANSWER: C

A ring network operates as a single loop in which the signal passes around the loop in a single direction through each computer. As the signal passes through the computer, that computer boosts the signal before passing it to the next computer. If any of the computers fail, the entire network fails. Likewise, if any the connections fail, the entire network fails.

To resolve a network problem in a ring topology, you could try removing a computer and placing a terminator on the T-connector. If the problem still exists, reconnect the computer and try removing the next computer in the line. If this doesn't resolve the problem, try replacing the connectors and the cable segments until the problem is resolved.

9. Alice must move John's computer into the boardroom because he is doing a presentation tomorrow. After setting up the computer in the boardroom, Alice starts to receive a number of calls that people cannot use the network. What could be the problem?

    A. They are using a linear bus topology for their network; when Alice removed John's computer from the bus, she did not put a terminator on the connector.

9. CORRECT ANSWER: A

Although a linear bus network is not affected by the failure of a computer on the network, a cable end that is not plugged into something affects it. If a computer is to be removed from the network, a terminator should be connected to the cable end to which the computer was connected. If a terminator is not added, a signal bounce will occur from the open end of cable, and the network will be functionally down.

10. The ACME Co. uses **10BASE-T** cabling for its network, and users continually experience problems with a few of their workstations. The office is configured in a star topology with a hub in the middle of the building and the server room in one corner. The distance from the hub to any one of the computers is about 350 feet. The company uses Token-Ring network cards that are configured to operate at 16Mbps. What could be the problem?

D. The distance between the hub and the workstations near the perimeter of the building is too great.

10. CORRECT ANSWER: D

10BASE-T cabling is rated for a maximum distance of approximately 328 feet. The layout of this office is not conducive to using a star topology with 10BASE-T cabling. To make this network operate, add more hubs, change the topology, or change the cable type.

RESOLVING BROADCAST STORMS

1. You are working on a Windows NT 4 network and have found that network response has become extremely slow. When you checked the network traffic using Network Monitor, you found that almost the entire bandwidth of the network was being used. You are running an Ethernet network with NetBEUI as the protocol, and the topology is a linear bus. What should be done to resolve the problem?

   A. Add the protocol TCP/IP.

   B. Switch to Token-Ring.

   C. Add TCP/IP and remove NetBEUI.

   D. Change to a star topology.

   E. Add repeaters to the network.

2. Jim has been trying to set up a segmented network but has heard that if he doesn't use the correct device to connect the segments, he might end up with broadcast storms. What is a *broadcast storm*?

   A. A broadcast storm occurs when so many signals are being sent in one direction that the flow of signals in the other direction stops.

   B. A broadcast storm occurs when the connection device (repeater, bridge, router, and gateway) starts to take directed messages and broadcasts them to all addresses.

   C. A broadcast storm is the equivalent to Ethernet networks, as beaconing is to Token-Ring networks.

   D. A broadcast storm occurs when so many broadcast messages are being transmitted that the entire bandwidth of the network is used.

   E. A broadcast storm occurs when messages are sent to specific addresses instead of to all computers on the subnet.

3. Melba has just finished her plan to segment her network. She noticed that network traffic was starting to push the limits of the network, so she thought it would be useful to subnet the network to reduce traffic. Which device(s) could she use to reduce network traffic?

   A. Repeaters

   B. Bridges

   C. Routers

   D. Brouters

   E. Gateways

4. Janet is working with a network that is divided into five segments. An eight-port repeater connects the segments with thin coax cable. She discovered earlier that the bandwidth was at 80-percent capacity. She switched from using IPX/SPX to TCP/IP

but still found that the bandwidth was almost at capacity. Which of the following should Janet think about doing?

A. Replace the repeater with a router.

B. Replace the repeater with a bridge.

C. Replace the repeater with a modem.

D. Replace the repeater with a gateway.

E. Change the cable to thick coax.

5. Adam has been contracted to determine why a client's network seems to be operating so slowly. Just six months ago, the company made the investment to upgrade its LAN cards from 10MB to 100MB, yet it did not see the desired improvement. Adam suspects that a lot of network traffic is being generated by broadcasts on the network. Select the correct option(s) for Adam to verify his hypothesis.

A. Run Performance Monitor on the router to extract details as to what kind of packets are sent, how often they are being sent, and how many are being dropped because of buffer overflow.

B. Run Network Monitor on the router to extract details as to what kind of packets are sent, how often they are being sent, and how many are being dropped because of buffer overflow.

C. Run the SMS version of Network Monitor to see whether SMS is causing a problem on the network.

D. Run the SMS version of Network Monitor from a Windows NT member server to monitor the network traffic.

E. Upgrade the router to reduce broadcast storms.

6. Dan is having difficulty resolving a network traffic problem. So far, he has removed the NetBIOS protocol and has configured his routers to not forward broadcasts. When he monitors the network, he finds that a lot of broadcasts are still taking place. What can Dan do to reduce the amount of broadcasts?

A. Install a WINS server and configure all the client computers to use it.

B. Install a RIP router.

C. Disable browsing on the client computers.

D. Install a DHCP server and configure all the client computers to use it.

E. Add an additional Domain Controller to validate client logons.

7. Jan was told that a router that forwards broadcasts could cause broadcast storms. However, she read that a bridge is more likely to cause broadcast storms than a router. Choose the best explanation(s) for this statement.

A. A router only forwards broadcasts sent to a specific address.

B. Bridges do not cause as much traffic as a router that is configured to forward broadcasts.

C. Bridges filter broadcasts and pass only directed traffic.

D. A bridge forwards broadcasts to every computer on the network through all ports except the port on which it received the broadcast.

E. The router operates at the Network layer of the OSI model, whereas the bridge operates at the Data Link layer of the OSI model.

ANSWER KEY

1. C
2. D
3. C-D-E
4. A
5. D-E
6. A-C
7. D-E

ANSWERS & EXPLANATIONS

RESOLVING BROADCAST STORMS

1. You are working on a Windows NT 4 network and have found that network response has become extremely slow. When you checked the network traffic using Network Monitor, you found that almost the entire bandwidth of the network was being used. You are running an Ethernet network with NetBEUI as the protocol, and the topology is a linear bus. What should be done to resolve the problem?

   C. Add TCP/IP and remove NetBEUI.

1. CORRECT ANSWER: C

NetBEUI is a small, fast protocol that was originally designed for small networks. To keep the size small, a minimum amount of addressing information is included in each package. However, this can create a number of problems as a network grows in size.

For one thing, the NetBEUI protocol cannot be routed. This means that if a company grows past the size of its office, it will reach a physical limitation due to the protocol.

Secondly, NetBEUI relies heavily on broadcasting for a lot of its communication. By not including specific addressing information in the header of a package, the package can maintain a small size. This is fine as long as the network is small, or if it is not subnetted. If the size of the network gets too large, broadcast storms may occur because of the number of computers sending broadcast messages. One way of reducing broadcast storms is to split your network into subnets. However, you must use a different protocol to do this because NetBEUI cannot be routed.

Just adding the TCP/IP network will not help reduce the amount of broadcasts on the network because in most cases, messages are sent for each of the bound protocols. So, if three installed and bound protocols exist, you are probably sending a single message three times. Therefore, by just adding another protocol, you would be increasing traffic, not decreasing it.

Changing to Token-Ring from Ethernet may help reduce traffic, but the difference would probably be insignificant. The largest difference between Token-Ring and Ethernet is that, with Ethernet, collisions may occur when two computers try sending messages at the same time. With Token-Ring, a computer cannot send a message unless it possesses the token. Unless an error arises on the network, only one token should exist.

No matter what type of topology is used, the topology will not prompt a significant change unless the network is broken into subnets, with each subnet being connected through a device such as a router. If a repeater separates the subnets, the traffic will not be reduced or increased. A repeater regenerates all signals it receives to increase the distance they can travel and then passes them to all other segments.

2. Jim has been trying to set up a segmented network but has heard that if he doesn't use the correct device to connect the segments, he might end up with broadcast storms. What is a *broadcast storm*?

    D. A broadcast storm occurs when so many broadcast messages are being transmitted that the entire bandwidth of the network is used.

2. CORRECT ANSWER: D

As the term implies, a broadcast storm occurs when the network bandwidth becomes clogged because so many broadcast messages are being sent. The difference between a broadcast message and a directed message is that a directed message is intended for one or more specific addresses. However, a broadcast message is intended for all computers. Certain protocols use broadcasting more than others, and that is why those protocols are not intended/recommended for networks with a large number of computers. A *multicast* is similar to a broadcast but does not generate as much traffic because, although it is sent to all computers, only those that are of, say, the correct workgroup actually process the message.

Once a message package has been created and transmitted, it cannot change the type of message it is. Therefore, the message starts out as a broadcast message.

As mentioned in the previous question, it doesn't matter whether the network uses Ethernet or Token-Ring; broadcast storms can still occur. Beaconing is a trait of Token-Ring that has nothing to do with broadcast messages. A beacon occurs when an error has occurred on the subnet—such as when network adapters of different speeds are connected to the same subnet—and a computer tries to insert a new token.

3. Melba has just finished her plan to segment her network. She noticed that network traffic was starting to push the limits of the network, so she thought it would be useful to subnet the network to reduce traffic. Which device(s) could she use to reduce network traffic?

   C. Routers

   D. Brouters

   E. Gateways

3. CORRECT ANSWERS: C-D-E

Routers, brouters, and gateways are all good choices for reducing traffic when a network is subnetted, as long as they are configured correctly.

Both routers and brouters will not pass on broadcast messages unless they are configured to do so. However, a repeater regenerates a signal and passes it to all segments that are attached. A bridge passes a signal that it receives to all of its ports, except for the port on which it received the message.

Gateways perform differently than routers and brouters in that they are suited more for specific tasks and are used in situations where networks of different architecture and environments need to be connected. The gateway repackages the packages it receives in the format of the destination computer. As an example, the RAS server on Windows NT can act as gateway between a dial-in client that is configured to use NetBEUI and the network servers that may be configured to use TCP/IP. When the RAS server receives the packages from the remote client, it removes the old protocol stack and repackages it in the protocol stack of the destination computers.

4. Janet is working with a network that is divided into five segments. An eight-port repeater connects the segments with thin coax cable. She discovered earlier that the bandwidth was at 80-percent capacity. She switched from using IPX/SPX to TCP/IP but still found that the bandwidth was almost at capacity. Which of the following should Janet think about doing?

   A. Replace the repeater with a router.

4. CORRECT ANSWER: A

Repeaters pass all packages that they receive to all the subnets to which they are connected, with the exception of the port on which the message was originally received. By doing so, a lot of excess traffic is passed to all subnets. All the extra traffic may be using up network bandwidth.

5. Adam has been contracted to determine why a client's network seems to be operating so slowly. Just six months ago, the company made the investment to upgrade its LAN cards from 10MB to 100MB, yet it did not see the desired improvement. Adam suspects that a lot of network traffic is being generated by broadcasts on the network. Select the correct option(s) for Adam to verify his hypothesis.

D. Run the SMS version of Network Monitor from a Windows NT member server to monitor the network traffic.

E. Upgrade the router to reduce broadcast storms.

5. CORRECT ANSWERS: D-E

By running the System Management Server of Network Monitor on the network, Adam could log and view all the traffic on the network. After the log has been created, the traffic can be viewed and filtered to see which computer(s) are generating the most traffic and to determine whether a problem is causing packets to be retransmitted.

The version of Network Monitor that is shipped with Windows NT Server 4 is capable of monitoring traffic that is sent from or received by the server running the monitor. The version that comes with System Management Server is capable of monitoring all traffic on the network. By using the System Management Server version, Adam would have a better chance of determining what is causing the high amount of network traffic.

Although System Management Server (SMS) is a part of the Microsoft BackOffice suite, SMS need not be installed on the server to run its version of Network Monitor. However, even if System Management Server was installed on the Windows NT Server, it would be unlikely that SMS would be the application causing the problem(s).

6. Dan is having difficulty resolving a network traffic problem. So far, he has removed the NetBIOS protocol and has configured his routers to not forward broadcasts. When he monitors the network, he finds that a lot of broadcasts are still taking place. What can Dan do to reduce the amount of broadcasts?

A. Install a WINS server and configure all the client computers to use it.

C. Disable browsing on the client computers.

6. CORRECT ANSWERS: A-C

A WINS server is used to resolve NetBIOS names to IP addresses. However, WINS is dynamic in how it builds its database because each computer sends a directed message to the WINS server to announce when it is active on the network or when it is being shut down. If WINS is not used, computers broadcast across the network to discover the IP address of the computer with which it is trying to communicate. With WINS implemented, the only time that broadcasting would be used to resolve a NetBIOS name would be when the WINS server does not have an entry for a particular computer name.

Another service that generates a lot of broadcast messages is the Browser Service. Shared network resources are discovered by computers through a series of broadcast messages. These lists of resources are announced on the network through broadcast messages by every computer capable of sharing resources, even if they don't have a share created. By disabling browsing and setting up mapped drives for the clients to the resources that they need, a lot of broadcast traffic can be eliminated.

By disabling the server service on workstation computers, a lot of the broadcast traffic can be removed. For Windows 95 systems, open the Network applet in Control Panel and select File and Printer Sharing. Deselect both options in this dialog box to make sure that the Windows 95 system is not advertising itself as a server. For Windows NT systems, open the Services applet in Control Panel. Select the Server service and then select the Stop button. If the service will not be run automatically, change the startup option to Manual.

Adding a DHCP server or another Backup Domain Controller to the network will not reduce network traffic and may actually increase the amount of broadcast traffic. The DHCP server makes the assignment and administration of IP addresses to each of the computers a lot simpler, but it does increase broadcast traffic.

A Backup Domain Controller may help reduce the validation load during peak logon hours, but it also can increase the amount of broadcast traffic that takes place due to account database synchronization that must take place at regular intervals.

7. Jan was told that a router that forwards broadcasts could cause broadcast storms. However, she read that a bridge is more likely to cause broadcast storms than a router. Choose the best explanation(s) for this statement.

D. A bridge forwards broadcasts to every computer on the network and to all segments except the segment on which it received the broadcast.

E. The router operates at the Network layer of the OSI model, whereas the bridge operates at the Data Link layer of the OSI model.

7. CORRECT ANSWERS: D-E

A bridge is similar to a router in that it operates at a very low level on the OSI model (Data Link layer). Because it operates at such a low level, all messages are sent to the rest of the network. However, one difference between the bridge and the router enables the router to reduce network traffic. The bridge passes messages to all ports except for the port on which the message was received. With a router, the source address is compared to the destination address. If the segment portion of the address is different, the message is passed to the segment. If the segment portion of the address is the same, the message is not sent to that segment.

The biggest difference between a bridge and a router is the layers at which they operate. The router operates at the Network layer and therefore has more information to work with when passing messages to connected segments. A router passes a message (directed or broadcast) only if it knows the destination address or the destination segment address. If it cannot find that information in the message, it does not pass the message. As with the router, if the bridge recognizes the destination address, it either keeps the message local or passes it to the appropriate segment. However, if the bridge does not recognize the Media Access Control address, the message is forwarded to all segments except the segment on which it was received.

IDENTIFYING AND RESOLVING NETWORK PERFORMANCE PROBLEMS

1. Tom has been given the responsibility of determining whether a problem exists on the file and printer server. A total of 55 employees use a mix of Windows 95 and Windows NT Workstation computers. The file and printer server runs Windows NT Server 4 and is configured as a member server. Choose all options that can help determine whether the file and printer server is having a communication problem.

   A. Open Windows NT Diagnostics on the server and view the resource assignments.

   B. Use Performance Monitor to see how often packets are being retransmitted.

   C. View the resource settings in the System applet of Control Panel.

   D. Configure the Server service to start up using the Administrator account instead of the system account.

   E. Monitor the physical memory that is being used on the server.

2. Peter recently went into business for himself as a network consultant/administrator. He just signed his first contract to maintain and optimize a network for a company over the next two years. Because the network is already up and running, what should be the first thing Peter does? Choose the most correct answer(s).

   A. Reboot all the servers and workstations.

   B. Upgrade the network adapters in each server.

   C. Compress the hard drives on the servers to ensure that they do not run out of free disk space.

   D. Create a baseline.

   E. Upgrade the memory in the servers.

3. You are working with a 16MB Token-Ring network that has about 95 computers, including three servers. Three new employees have been hired and will start work next Monday. Your assistant just finished setting up one of the new computers and connected it to the network to test its settings. Shortly after he started his tests, you received a number of calls from users complaining that the network has become very slow. What would you suspect is the cause? Choose the most correct answer.

   A. The new computer was connected to the network using a cable with RJ10 connectors instead of an RJ45 connectors.

B. Token-Ring networks are rated to handle only approximately 90 connections. When this limit is exceeded, performance can degrade.

C. The speed of the new Token-Ring card is configured for 4MB.

D. Although three servers exist on the network, only two are domain controllers. After 90 client computers have been reached, an additional domain controller should be added.

E. WINS should be implemented to reduce the broadcast traffic.

4. User Bill has called the help desk because, although he was logged on to the network this morning, when he tried to log on this afternoon, he received a message that a domain controller cannot be found. What is the first thing you should check?

A. Check to make sure that all his cables are connected correctly and are not damaged.

B. Check to see whether his account is "locked out."

C. Check to see whether his CAPS LOCK is turned on.

D. Ensure that he is logging on to the Primary Domain Controller.

E. Add Bill to the Administrator group to determine whether this is a permission problem.

5. User Sally has had intermittent problems logging on to the network for almost two weeks. How can you determine whether the problem is caused by Sally's computer or the cabling? Choose all that apply.

A. Have Sally power the computer off and on, and then try logging on.

B. Have Sally come in on the weekend or during the evening when everyone else is at home and then have her try logging on.

C. Have Sally log on to the network at another computer.

D. Connect the computer to a different wall jack using a different cable.

E. Connect a different computer to the network using the wall jack and cable that has been connected to the problem computer.

6. One of the computers has been having problems with network connectivity. After doing a number of tests, you have determined that the network card is at fault. What is the best method for resolving the network card problem? Choose the most correct answer.

A. Remove the network drivers, reboot the computer, and then reinstall the network card drivers.

B. Remove the network card, remove the network card drivers, reboot the computer, put the network card back into the computer, and reinstall the drivers.

C. Replace the network card.

D. Move the network card to a different slot in the computer.

E. Download and install new drivers for the network card.

7. Harry has had a number of calls from the users stating that different applications and services have either started to function oddly or have stopped functioning altogether. The users are running Windows NT Workstation in a workgroup. Because only 25 users exist in the network, it was decided that the cost of dedicating a server to act as a domain controller could not be justified. What would you suspect is the problem from the description that has been provided?

   A. Windows NT Workstation functions better in a domain than it does in a workgroup.

   B. The administrator account should be located only on the administrator's computer.

   C. An Emergency Repair Disk was not created when the computer was first set up.

   D. The users have been installing software on their computers.

   E. The PCI bus of each computer is not fast enough for some of the applications that have been installed.

8. You are administering a network that has approximately 150 workstations operating in a domain that has one Primary Domain Controller and one Backup Domain Controller. As new people are hired, new equipment is set up for them. The company is two years old now and is starting to grow as its reputation builds. The only problem is that you seem to be spending a lot of time engineering solutions for the users. What would be the best option to keep the users' downtime to a minimum?

   A. Make each of the users administrators of their own computers so that they can fix problems themselves.

   B. Create install scripts for installing new applications.

   C. Have the users shut down their computers each night to make sure that applications with "leaky" memory are restarted.

   D. Put a business plan together to propose that the company standardize the desktop computers.

   E. Hire additional computer support staff.

9. The ACME Home Business Solutions company has been located in a small office in a strip mall for the past three years. It has noticed a growth in business as the year 2000 approaches and has decided to expand the office to include the vacant space next door. ACME is using a 10BASE-T network that is configured in a star topology. After the expansion, a number of users cannot connect to the network. What is the most likely problem?

   A. The users that have been located in the new space have cables that are too long.

   B. The star topology works only in small areas.

C. The cables need to have new terminators connected to them.

D. CAT 6 cabling must be used.

E. There are too many users for a 10BASE-T network.

ANSWER KEY

1. B	4. C	7. D
2. D	5. A-C-D-E	8. D
3. C	6. C	9. A

ANSWERS & EXPLANATIONS

IDENTIFYING AND RESOLVING NETWORK PERFORMANCE PROBLEMS

1. Tom has been given the responsibility of determining whether a problem exists on the file and printer server. A total of 55 employees use a mix of Windows 95 and Windows NT Workstation computers. The file and printer server runs Windows NT Server 4 and is configured as a member server. Choose all options that can help determine whether the file and printer server is having a communication problem.

   B. Use Performance Monitor to see how often packets are being retransmitted.

1. CORRECT ANSWER: B

Because you don't know what kind of utilities or tools you have been provided, the simplest thing to do is check the Event Viewer to see whether any errors are logged. Then, use Performance Monitor to see whether packets are being retransmitted. Performance Monitor is the only real monitoring tool that is installed by default. Other utilities that come with Windows NT enable the user to view the configuration and resource assignments, but they still do not provide any data as to how the server or network is performing.

2. Peter recently went into business for himself as a network consultant/administrator. He just signed his first contract to maintain and optimize a network for a company over the next two years. Because the network is already up and running, what should be the first thing Peter does? Choose the most correct answer(s).

   D. Create a baseline.

2. CORRECT ANSWER: D

Anytime you will be maintaining a network, always create a baseline for each server, and possibly even the workstations. After a baseline has been established, current activity can always be compared to it to see whether any problems have developed. By comparing activity to a baseline, trends also can be identified and proactive steps can be taken.

Depending on the hardware that has been implemented, it may also be a good idea to set up a schedule for rebooting the servers as part of a regular maintenance schedule. Not very many computers can be left to run indefinitely. If they aren't rebooted, there is the risk that the computers will crash at some point. In other words, it is always nicer to bring a computer down properly than to wait for it to bring itself down.

3. **You are working with a 16MB Token-Ring network that has about 95 computers, including three servers. Three new employees have been hired and will start work next Monday. Your assistant just finished setting up one of the new computers and connected it to the network to test its settings. Shortly after he started his tests, you received a number of calls from users complaining that the network has become very slow. What would you suspect is the cause? Choose the most correct answer.**

C. The speed of the new Token-Ring card is configured for 4MB.

4. **User Bill has called the help desk because, although he was logged on to the network this morning, when he tried to log on this afternoon, he received a message that a domain controller cannot be found. What is the first thing you should check?**

C. Check to see whether his CAPS LOCK is turned on.

3. CORRECT ANSWER: C

Faster is always better when you ask someone about network speeds. So, in most cases, Token-Ring networks are configured to run at 16MB. The only problem with this is that a large number of manufacturers still ship their Token-Ring network cards configured to 4MB as the default. When Token-Ring cards of different speeds are connected to the same segment, beaconing probably occurs and slows the network.

Although Token-Ring networks tend to get slower as the number of workstations increases, they can easily handle well over 100 computers.

4. CORRECT ANSWER: C

Depending on the administrator, a few people might say to check whether the user account is locked out, or see whether something is wrong with the cabling. However, while the user is on the telephone, it is simple to have the user verify that the CAPS LOCK is not turned on. Because passwords in Microsoft networking are case-sensitive, having the CAPS LOCK turned on prevents the user from logging on. If the CAPS LOCK was not turned on, you should probably check to see whether the account is locked out and then verify that the cabling is okay. Even though the user was logged on a short time ago, someone may have tried to log on using his account and locked the account before the user returned.

The possibility also exists that a user's account is not on the domain controller that is trying to validate the user's logon. This can happen occasionally if the user account was just added and the changes had not been synchronized with domain controller validating the logon request. Because the user had been logged on earlier in the day, this is not likely to be the problem.

5. User Sally has had intermittent problems logging on to the network for
almost two weeks. How can you determine whether the problem is caused by
Sally's computer or the cabling?
Choose all that apply.

A. Have Sally power the computer off
and on, and then try logging on.

C. Have Sally log on to the network at
another computer.

D. Connect the computer to a different
wall jack using a different cable.

E. Connect a different computer to the
network using the wall jack and
cable that has been connected to the
problem computer.

5. CORRECT ANSWERS: A-C-D-E

Intermittent problems are always the most difficult to find, let
alone resolve. Try rebooting the computer or connecting the
computer to a different cable. The types of applications the
user has been working with and the process by which the user
has been shutting down the computer can both be factors.
Some applications were not meant to be run on the same computer at the same time. If an application is not written well, it
may have a problem known as *leaky memory*, which means that
over time more memory is used until the system runs out of
free memory. At that time, it may be necessary to either stop
the application and restart it or reboot the computer to free up
the memory.

By connecting the computer to a different cable and logging
on, you can start to determine whether the problem is with
the computer itself or the cabling. Connecting a different
computer (one that is not having problems) to the cable in
question also helps determine whether the cabling is bad. At
times you may come across two problems that give the same
results, such as bad cabling and a problem with the computer.
In this case, it also helps to have the user log on to the network at a computer that works.

6. One of the computers has been having
problems with network connectivity.
After doing a number of tests, you have
determined that the network card is at
fault. What is the best method for
resolving the network card problem?
Choose the most correct answer.

C. Replace the network card.

6. CORRECT ANSWER: C

Ethernet network cards seem to be getting cheaper by the day.
In most cases, when there seems to be a problem with a network that had been functioning properly before, it is most
likely that there is a problem with the network card that you
will not be able to fix. If the problem of a network card cannot
be resolved in a short period of time, it is almost not worth
testing it in different slots or other computers. The only time
that you might want to try to determine the exact problem is
when you suspect that something may be wrong with the
motherboard or some other component in the computer.

7. Harry has had a number of calls from the users stating that different applications and services have either started to function oddly or have stopped functioning altogether. The users are running Windows NT Workstation in a workgroup. Because only 25 users exist in the network, it was decided that the cost of dedicating a server to act as a domain controller could not be justified. What would you suspect is the problem from the description that has been provided?

D. The users have been installing software on their computers.

8. You are administering a network that has approximately 150 workstations operating in a domain that has one Primary Domain Controller and one Backup Domain Controller. As new people are hired, new equipment is set up for them. The company is two years old now and is starting to grow as its reputation builds. The only problem is that you seem to be spending a lot of time engineering solutions for the users. What would be the best option to keep the users' downtime to a minimum?

D. Put a business plan together to propose that the company standardize the desktop computers.

7. CORRECT ANSWER: D

Anytime users are allowed to install software on their computers, you run a greater risk of having problems with drivers, DLLs, and so on. Many different applications use similar DLLs with the same name; if an application with an older DLL or driver is installed, it may cause problems with applications that were already installed. The only way that this can be controlled is by first installing and testing new applications on a "test" machine with different applications already installed. That way, if any problems exist, they do not affect a production machine and steps can be taken to engineer a solution.

8. CORRECT ANSWER: D

Although this may not be the most inexpensive solution, it will probably save the company money in the long run. By standardizing hardware (and possibly software), installations can be automated, troubleshooting becomes much simpler, and software becomes more reliable. Because all the hardware is the same, scripts can be made for installing software with a minimal amount of variables. Troubleshooting becomes simpler because the administrator can become more familiar with the hardware. Finally, the software becomes more reliable because it doesn't need to be configured differently for different machine types.

Additional staff might be an option, except that in the long run it could cost a lot more money. This option would mean that you have more people to solve the same problems, rather than trying to reduce the number of actual problems.

9. The ACME Home Business Solutions company has been located in a small office in a strip mall for the past three years. It has noticed a growth in business as the year 2000 approaches and has decided to expand the office to include the vacant space next door. ACME is using a 10BASE-T network that is configured in a star topology. After the expansion, a number of users cannot connect to the network. What is the most likely problem?

A. The users that have been located in the new space have cables that are too long.

9. CORRECT ANSWER: A

The cables of 10BASE-T networks are limited to 100 meters (about 330 feet). This length was probably exceeded when the company expanded into the new office space. This problem could be resolved in a number of ways, but the least expensive would probably be to add repeaters for the computers that have been installed in the new area. This way, the network cards do not have to be replaced, nor does the existing cabling. Unless the company has expanded at a logarithmic pace, it is unlikely that it has surpassed the limit of 1,024 users.

A few issues are always important to remember
when working with computers:

▶ The OSI model

▶ The IRQs

▶ Cable types and their limitations

▶ Network devices and their uses

TABLE 4.3   THE DIFFERENT LAYERS OF THE OSI MODEL ARE DESCRIBED HERE

Number	Layer	Description
7	Application	This topmost layer serves as an interface to network services for the application processes.
6	Presentation	This layer determines the format to be used to exchange data between computers. It is responsible for converting protocols, translating data, encrypting data, compressing data, converting the character set, and expanding graphics commands.
5	Session	This layer enables two computers to start, use, and end a connection (session). Name recognition and security functions are carried out so that two applications can communicate over the network.
4	Transport	The Transport layer provides an additional connection level below the Session layer. This layer ensures that the data arrives error-free, in sequence, and with no duplicates or losses. Messages are repackaged to accommodate efficient transmission of the data.
3	Network	Addressing messages and translating logical addresses and names into physical addresses is carried out at the Network layer. This layer also manages traffic problems on the network, such as routing traffic to control data flow.
2	Data Link	Sends data frames to the Physical layer. When a frame is received, the Data Link layer packages the raw bits from the Physical layer into data frames. A data frame is an organized, logical structure for the data that usually consists of the destination ID, Sender ID, Control, Data, and CRC.
1	Physical	The bottom layer is responsible for transmitting the raw data bit stream over the medium (network cable) to the destination computer.

TABLE 4.4   THESE BASIC TYPES OF NETWORK CABLE ARE USED FOR BOTH ETHERNET AND TOKEN-RING NETWORKS

Cable Type	Description
UTP (unshielded twisted-pair)	This twisted-pair wire does not have any shielding. The more twists per inch in the cable, the less cross-talk occurs. Telephone wire is an example of UTP cable.
STP (shielded twisted-pair)	This is the same as UTP, except that the wire is shielded to reduce interference from other cables.

continues

TABLE 4.4 CONTINUED

Cable Type	Description
Thinnet (thin coaxial)	This cable has a conductor core surrounded by an insulating layer, which is surrounded by a shielding layer, which is surrounded by an outer shell. This cable is very well shielded, can conduct farther than UTP (STP), and is relatively inexpensive.
Thicknet (thick coaxial)	Thicknet cable, as the name implies, has a larger diameter than thinnet, which improves on its distances and tolerances.
Fiber-optic cable	Fiber-optic cable is made from a strand of glass or plastic. Instead of an electric current being transmitted, light pulses are used to transmit. Because of the reduced interference and quality of the medium, fiber-optic segments have the potential to be miles in length.

The most important point to remember when troubleshooting a problem is to think of the simple things first. It is far too easy to get caught up looking at complex problems and solutions when the answer to the problem is very simple. This also applies to any exam. A lot of the questions will have extra information in them that may confuse the issue. This is done to test your ability to look at all the information and determine what is pertinent—while ignoring the rest.

By being able to determine what is relevant to the situation at hand, you will become much more efficient in your job and when taking the exam.

SUMMARY

The process of troubleshooting network problems is the same as troubleshooting any kind of problem. Some basics steps should always be followed:

1. Assign priority to your problems to determine which ones should get the most attention.

2. Gather as much information about the symptoms of the problem as possible.

3. Speculate as to what could be causing the problem(s).

4. Test each possibility.

5. Observe and record the results of each test to determine a solution and document what you did.

These five steps—plus using common sense and not jumping to conclusions—will help you through just about any crisis.

> **EXAM TIP**
>
> Always remember to document everything that you do as you do it. Many an administrator has ended up repeating steps because he or she could not remember what had been tried or in what order things were tried.
>
> Good documentation helps to resolve problems that reoccur eight months later, when you have forgotten what you did to resolve the problem in the first place.

This exam covers four major topics: standards and terminology, planning, implementation, and troubleshooting. You have 75 minutes to complete this test. Remember that time is a factor. Answer each of the questions that you can answer in a relatively short period of time. If you are unsure of a question, do not spend a lot of time trying to work through it. Mark the question and go on to the next question. When you have gone through the entire exam, go back and work through the questions that you marked.

Before the actual exam begins, the exam program will give you the option of taking a sample orientation exam to familiarize yourself with the way the exam operates. If you have never taken a Microsoft exam before, you should take this orientation exam. If you are unsure about how to use the testing equipment or software, or if you have any questions about the rules for the exam, ask the exam administrator before the exam begins.

PRACTICE QUESTIONS

1. **Carol wants to set up an infrared network in her office. One of her coworkers disagrees with this idea because she has read that Token-Ring would be faster. At what speed can infrared transmit data?**

   A. 10Mbps

   B. 100Mbps

   C. 1Mbps

   D. 1.544Mbps

   E. 2Mbps

2. **Thicknet is used as a backbone in some installations to connect a number of thinnet-based networks. Why would it be an advantage to use thicknet cabling as a backbone for a thinnet network?**

   A. Thicknet has a faster transfer rate than thinnet cable.

   B. Thicknet can use longer segment lengths than thinnet cable.

   C. You cannot mix thicknet and thinnet cable.

   D. Thicknet is less expensive and easier to install than thinnet.

   E. Thicknet is the most common type of cable used in most networks.

3. **Max is thinking of implementing infrared in a small office that has 12 computers in an area of about 50 feet by 50 feet. There are a few ways to implement infrared, and Max must determine which implementation is the best for this particular office. Select all possible types of infrared networks.**

   A. Reflective

   B. Line-of-sight

   C. Scatter transmissions

   D. Spread-spectrum

   E. Broadband optical

4. Cheryl is in the process of converting her network from using NetBEUI to using TCP/IP. The reason for changing was so that the users could split the network into different segments. The only problem is that she has not had a lot of experience with TCP/IP and is not sure of all the configurations. Cheryl needs to know what is used in the TCP/IP protocol to isolate the host ID from the network ID. Select the correct answer.

   A. Network address

   B. Node address

   C. Default gateway

   D. Subnet mask

   E. Host name

5. You have been supporting a Windows 95 peer-to-peer network for the past three years, and now a Windows NT domain has been set up. Which utility in the Windows NT operating system is used to create accounts on the domain?

   A. User Profile Editor

   B. User Manager for Domains

   C. Server Manager for Domains

   D. Policy Editor

   E. Registry Editor

6. You are using thinnet cable in your network and have a couple of segments that are going to be quite long. You are afraid that the signal will not be able to transmit along the entire length of the segment. How far can the correct data

frames be transmitted before the data signal degrades?

   A. 500 meters

   B. 250 meters

   C. 100 meters

   D. 75 meters

   E. 185 meters

7. Primary-rate ISDN systems have three ports on them. Two B channels can be used separately or combined to double your throughput. The third channel is referred to as the D channel. What is the D channel used for?

   A. 16Kbps transmission

   B. 64Kbps transmission

   C. Signaling and link-management data

   D. Voice, data, and images

   E. Handshaking only

8. Jack is in charge of the office expansion currently taking place. The office is increasing from 2,000 square feet to 3,500 square feet, and one of the concerns from the IT department is *attenuation*. Jack checked with the cabling specifications and was sure that there would not be a problem. What is attenuation?

   A. The signal crossover from one wire to another.

   B. The signal overflow from an adjacent wire.

   C. The decrease in signal strength as the data signal travels through the wire.

D. The electrical current that travels through the wire.

E. The signal increase in a data packet in a long-distance cable run.

9. **Adam is relatively new to working with Windows NT and has been trying to read up on how the operating system functions, both locally and on the network. One service that he has heard of is the *redirector*. What is the redirector, and what is it used for? Select the best answer.**

A. It is a service that operates in Disk Administrator to divide the hard disk into multiple sectors.

B. It is a service to determine whether the resource is on the local computer, or whether the request should be sent to the remote computer on the network.

C. It is used to redirect SMB blocks into NetWare NCP blocks.

D. It is a utility that can capture hardware requests and redirect them to the Windows NT kernel.

E. It determines the degree of resource sharing on the network.

10. **You are part of a new test group within your company that is having ISDN lines put into your home so that you can work at home. Your service provider was in the process of installing a 64Kbps service on B channel in your home. What other channel would be connected if you wanted to double your speed?**

A. Y channel

B. D channel

C. C channel

D. A channel

E. B channel

11. **A training company with more than 15 offices across the continent is looking to set up a WAN connection between each of its sites. It had previously tried using the Internet as a virtual private network, but ran into a number of problems. To improve speed and quality of signal, it also wanted to use dedicated digital lines. What is the most common type of digital line being used?**

A. T1

B. 56Kbps

C. CAT 5

D. E1

E. T3

12. **Many different types of connectors exist for cabling networks. Each type of cable generally has only one type of connector that can be used for it. The RJ-45 connector is used with UTP and STP cabling, and it looks very similar to a telephone jack. How many wires are used in an RJ-45 connector?**

A. Two

B. Three

C. Four

D. Six

E. Eight

13. Mark has just been hired to take over an Ethernet network of approximately 250 computers. There are four servers, with one a file server, one a print server, one an application server, and the other server a network services server (DHCP, WINS, and so on). One of the tools that the previous administrator had in the hardware cabinet was a Time Domain-Reflectometer. What is the Time Domain-Reflectometer (TDR) used for?

   A. TDR is an advanced cable tester used for WANs.

   B. TDR sends SONAR to locate breaks or shorts in a cable run.

   C. TDR sends light to locate breaks or shorts in a cable run.

   D. TDR sends a laser signal to locate breaks or shorts in a cable run.

   E. TDR is used to measure the amount of signal that reflects back off the terminator at the end of a backbone cable.

14. A number of different RAID configurations are available for all servers. Of all the configurations, one provides fault tolerance as well as a slight performance enhancement. Which level of RAID writes data equally across drives in 64KB blocks and also provides fault tolerance?

   A. RAID 0

   B. RAID 1

   C. RAID 2

   D. RAID 5

   E. RAID 6

15. Because Tony's network will have a substantial number of users as well as a large amount of data, it is important that the backup strategy enables him to reduce the amount of network traffic. A number of Windows NT and UNIX servers must be backed up by a single backup server. What is the best strategy to keep network traffic to a minimum on the network?

   A. Do a full backup once a month.

   B. Schedule backups after business hours.

   C. Only back up the operating system.

   D. Only back up files and directories.

   E. Place the backup server on an isolated network.

16. You are working with an application that must interact with a remote computer on your network. As the application makes the request for additional data on the other computer, at which layer of the OSI model does the assembly of the requesting packet begin?

   A. Network

   B. Application

   C. Session

   D. Physical

   E. Presentation

17. As the purchaser for your company, you have placed orders for everything from a toilet and sink to the servers used in the network. Now that the network is expanding to include 20 more computers, you have been requested to order more 10BASE-T cable. What type of cable is used in a 10BASE-T network?

A. Thicknet

B. Thinnet

C. RJ-11

D. Fiber

E. Unshielded twisted-pair (UTP)

18. **In reference to the previous question, before you were able to order the additional cable, you were shipped cable from one of your eastern offices that had purchased too much cable. However, the cable sent is 100BASE-TX cable. Which category of UTP cable is required?**

   A. CAT 5

   B. CAT 4

   C. CAT 3

   D. CAT 2

   E. CAT 1

The next four questions deal with the same situation.

19. **Jerry is setting up a temporary office and must ensure that he has the correct wiring installed for the computers and network adapters that he already has. His network adapters support 10BASE-T. Select all the cable types that support 10BASE-T.**

   A. CAT 1

   B. CAT 2

   C. CAT 3

   D. CAT 4

   E. CAT 5

20. **Jerry already has computers with network adapters that are 10BASE-T–**

compliant. He felt that by buying the cable needed for the network cards, he would save the most money. However, before he purchased the cable, he spoke to another vendor to determine the price of cable in case there was a dramatic savings if a different cable were used. Which of the cables listed would be the least expensive to purchase?

   A. Fiber

   B. Thicknet

   C. Thinnet

   D. UTP

   E. STP

21. **Now that Jerry has analyzed his network adapters (the type of cable available onsite) and determined which cable would be least expensive, what should Jerry do to set up the network in the temporary office? Select the best answer.**

   A. Use the existing cable and replace the network adapters with a card that is compatible with the cable.

   B. Leave everything as is.

   C. Replace the cable with a type that is compatible with the existing network adapters.

   D. Leave the existing cable and network adapters, and purchase crossover cables that can be used to convert from one cable type to another.

   E. Leave the cable and network adapters as they are, and replace the connectors on the existing cable so that they will connect with the network adapters.

22. Jerry needs to set up a temporary office so that expansion and remodeling can take place at his existing office. Because of the new space being added (a warehouse), some of the cable segments will increase substantially. One segment will be close to 400 meters in length. What kind of cabling is needed in the office?

    A. 10BASE-2

    B. 10BASE-5

    C. 10BASE-FL

    D. 10BASE-T

    E. Infrared

23. As a recommendation from your network consultant, you have had DHCP implemented on your Windows NT domain. You were told that it would reduce overhead and save you money. That was all your operations manager needed to know to agree with the installation. What exactly does a DHCP server do?

    A. It is an Internet Server service.

    B. It acts as a gateway service to a UNIX server.

    C. It resolves network adapter hardware addresses as a service.

    D. It is a TCP/IP service that provides TCP/IP configurations.

    E. It is a service to resolve NetBIOS names to IP addresses.

24. To help ensure that a packet of data is transferred to the proper location and without errors, a number of components are added to the data packet. Which of the following is contained inside a packet header frame?

    A. DA (destination address)

    B. TTL

    C. SA (source address)

    D. CRC

    E. Alert signal

25. Many times, the need arises to have network connections in places where it is not feasible to run cable. In those cases, wireless transmission may be used. Different wireless techniques provide different speeds. Which wireless transmission technique is the slowest method of transmitting a data packet from location A to location B?

    A. Infrared

    B. Laser

    C. Narrow-band radio

    D. Spread-spectrum radio

    E. 10BASE-T

26. As a systems integration consultant, you often recommend different types of hardware and software for your clients. For example, to save your client money, you may propose to use 10BASE-T cable (because it is cheaper), but find that the length of the segments is too great. What is the maximum cable length for 10BASE-T?

    A. 100 meters (328 feet)

    B. 185 meters (607 feet)

C. 50 meters (164 feet)

D. 500 meters (1,640 feet)

E. 25 meters (82 feet)

27. **You are switching to using Windows 95 clients in your network. A NetWare 4.11 Server is being used as an application server. What must be installed and configured to enable the Windows 95 clients to access the applications on the Novell NetWare server?**

    A. NDS

    B. NWLink with FPNW

    C. NWLink with GSNW

    D. NWLink with CSNW

    E. IPX/SPX with Microsoft Client for NetWare

28. **Ethernet is the most commonly used network architecture in the world. It is reliable, flexible, fast, and it is easy to configure. It also follows specific methods and standards for the way it communicates. One of the standards is CSMA/CD. What is the function of CSMA/CD?**

    A. It's part of Token-Ring algorithm.

    B. It breaks data into smaller formats.

    C. It's an Ethernet tool for finding wiring faults.

    D. It regulates traffic on the segment.

    E. It is a cable repeater system.

29. *Impedance* **is a consideration in just about every type of cable. If impedance is**
not taken into account, a number of problems could arise on the network. Select the best definition of impedance.

    A. The flow of electrons along the cable; it can also be referred to as current.

    B. Signal overflow errors.

    C. The resistance to the flow of direct current.

    D. The resistance to the flow of alternating current.

    E. The unit of measure used for terminators.

30. **Many methods exist for preserving the data on your servers. Some methods provide good security for your data but make data retrieval difficult. Others provide speed of retrieval, but with a relatively high cost. Then, there are others that provide good access speed with a relatively low cost. Which of these systems provides fast access with a relatively low cost per disk?**

    A. UPS system

    B. RAID 5

    C. RAID 0

    D. Tape backup

    E. RAID 1

31. **For each type of cable, different types of connectors are used. When you were ordering connectors for the 10BASE-2 cable already on hand, you needed to consult your hardware catalogs to see which should be used. What type of connector assembly is used by 10BASE-2 for**

connection to a standard Network
Adapter Card?

   A. A BNC barrel connector assembly

   B. A BNC T connector assembly

   C. An RJ-11 connector assembly

   D. An RJ-45 connector assembly

   E. An AUI connector assembly

32. The IEEE standards were agreed upon in
the early 1980s so that products would
be consistent from one manufacturer to
another. Which media access method is
defined by the IEEE 802.3 standard?

   A. CDMS/CA

   B. Ethernet-passing

   C. Token-passing

   D. Demand priority

   E. CSMA/CD

33. A number of protocols were developed
over the years by different manufacturers
to meet their own needs. After a while,
two or three protocols remain, while
most others are falling off in popularity.
Often, a protocol's limitations cause a
protocol to become less popular. Which
of the following transport protocols cannot be routed?

   A. NetBEUI

   B. DLC

   C. IPX

   D. IP

   E. AppleTalk

34. Each layer of the OSI model has specific
functions in the task to transmit data to
and from other computers. One layer is
responsible for converting raw data bits
into data frames that are then passed to
the next level in the OSI model. Select
the OSI layer that is responsible for converting the raw data to data packets.

   A. Transport

   B. Session

   C. Physical

   D. Presentation

   E. Data Link

35. Ethernet networks can be configured in
many topologies, depending on the cable
used and the layout of the environment
where the network is to be located.
Which statement is true of a star topology design?

   A. A star has a central point of failure.

   B. A star is more difficult to configure
than a ring design.

   C. A star provides centralized monitoring
and management control.

   D. A star requires less cable than a bus
design.

   E. A star does not require any additional
hardware other than cable and network adapters.

36. Along with converting data from raw
form to data packets, another layer of the
OSI performs the translation of the data
format. Select the layer that is responsible

for translating the data format and performing compression.

    A. Application

    B. Physical

    C. Data Link

    D. Communication

    E. Presentation

37. Novell developed its own protocols for use on its networks. For other network operating systems to interact with a NetWare server, they must use a compatible protocol. This involved either using the same protocol as NetWare or using an equivalent that emulated the NetWare protocol. Select the protocol that is an NDIS-compliant version of the Internetwork Packet Exchange protocol.

    A. IP

    B. SMB

    C. NCP

    D. NWLink

    E. NetBEUI

38. The Data Link layer is somewhat different than most of the other layers of the OSI. A number of years after the OSI model had been developed, it was modified due to changes in technology. The Data Link layer was given two distinct sublayers. Which sublayer directly communicates with the Network Adapter Card assembly?

    A. Logical Link Control

    B. Logical Address Control

    C. Media Access Control

    D. Direct Address Control

    E. Media Address Control

39. In Windows NT, many services are used for controlling the flow of data and ensuring that requests are answered correctly. When a request is made to access a file, a service determines whether the request is intended for the local computer or for a remote computer. Select the service that determines where the request should be directed.

    A. The frame type

    B. The networking protocol

    C. The redirector

    D. The transceiver

    E. The TDI

40. Until recent years, the NetBEUI protocol had been the default choice for Microsoft networking. Because of this and the many other network operating systems, NetBEUI has a very large install base to this day. Although it has been very popular, it has some drawbacks. Select the statement that is true of NetBEUI.

    A. NetBEUI is routable.

    B. NetBEUI is slow in a LAN environment.

    C. NetBEUI is a NetWare protocol only.

    D. NetBEUI is a small, fast protocol.

    E. NetBEUI is slow in a WAN environment.

41. Most hardware devices that are used in networks are associated with a particular layer of the OSI model. However, one device uses all seven layers of the OSI model. Select the device that can use all seven layers.

    A. Bridges

    B. Routers

    C. Repeaters

    D. Gateways

    E. Modems

42. Topology refers to the way in which the cables of a network are run. Different cable types are used with different topologies as well. Select the type of network that typically uses a star bus topology.

    A. 10BASE-T

    B. 10BASE-5

    C. 100BASE-5

    D. 100BASE-X

    E. 100BASE-VG-AnyLAN

43. Dial-Up Networking is an inexpensive means to enable remote users to access the central network. It is meant to allow occasional connectivity; otherwise, the users would need a dedicated line brought to their location or some other more expensive solution. Select the protocols used for dial-up communications.

    A. SLIP

    B. PPP

    C. FTP

    D. ATM

    E. TCP

44. Sometimes there is a need to not only pass a signal to the next segment, but also to convert the signal from one type to another. When two companies merge, one may have been using a Windows NT network and the other a mainframe network. To enable the two networks to communicate without having to make major changes to one set of computers, a device can be used to translate the data from one protocol to the other. Select the device that is capable of protocol conversions.

    A. Gateways

    B. Routers

    C. Bridges

    D. Brouters

    E. Repeaters

45. Jill is planning to switch her network from 10Mbps to 100Mbps. She has already purchased the new network adapters, but is not sure whether she needs to upgrade the cable currently being used. She has 75 computers connected using CAT 3 cable and 45 newer computers connected using CAT 5 cable. Select the cable types that can support 100Mbps networks.

    A. CAT 2

    B. CAT 1

    C. CAT 3

D. CAT 5

E. CAT 4

46. **Mary is working with an Ethernet network that has one very long segment. One segment will be close to 1,000 meters without a repeater. Select the cable type that can work with a segment that is 1,000 meters in length.**

    A. CAT 3

    B. CAT 5

    C. 10BASE-XL

    D. 10BASE-5

    E. Fiber-optic

47. **Jonathon is studying for his Networking Essentials exam and has purchased a set of practice exams to help him study. One of the questions asks him to select the true statements about the capabilities of a bridge. Select the tasks that a bridge can perform.**

    A. Connect a 10BASE-T segment with a 10BASE-5 segment.

    B. Translate network protocols.

    C. Segment a network to isolate traffic.

    D. Connect a 10BASE-T segment with a 10BASE-2 segment.

    E. Join a network using IPX/SPX with a network using NetBEUI.

48. **Gail is using a 10BASE-2 network and must increase the strength of the baseband signal over a long cable. Select the** device that would be used to increase the signal strength in a 10BASE-2 network.

    A. Repeater

    B. Router

    C. Amplifier

    D. Multiplexer

    E. Switch

49. **Originally, to meet the need of connecting remote sites to mainframe servers, a method of packet switching was developed. Now, a number of different media exist in which to connect remote sites, depending on a number of factors. Select all those that implement packet-switching technology.**

    A. ISDN

    B. Modem

    C. ATM

    D. X.25

    E. T1

50. **You have just finished a design that combines a UNIX server and its terminals with a Windows NT network and its workstations. Which protocol should be used in your design to enable communication between the two systems?**

    A. NetBEUI

    B. DLC

    C. NWLink

    D. TCP/IP

    E. FDDI

51. You want to convert the parallel data stream used on the computer's PCI bus into a serial data stream that can be sent along a cable. Select the device in your computer that is responsible for this conversion.

    A. Hub

    B. Terminator

    C. Bridge

    D. Multiplexer

    E. Transceiver

52. Routers by themselves can use static routing tables to direct traffic that passes through them. However, protocols can be used at the router to enable them to dynamically determine the routes that signals should follow to reach their destination. Select the protocol that uses a distance-vector algorithm to determine routes.

    A. RIP

    B. NFS

    C. SNA

    D. DLC

    E. XNS

53. TCP/IP is a suite of protocols that can perform many different functions. Some of these functions include transferring files, monitoring the network, and resolving addresses. The protocol for monitoring a network is rudimentary but very useful. Select the protocol that is used for monitoring networks.

    A. SMP

    B. NCP

    C. SMTP

    D. SNMP

    E. FTAM

54. You are setting up a network in your new office. The office space has existed for about five years, but the previous tenants did not have a network. Therefore, no cabling exists in the building. You now must consider what type of cabling should be installed for your network. Which type of cabling should you consider first?

    A. Thicknet

    B. Thinnet

    C. CAT 5

    D. UTP

    E. Fiber-optic

55. You have 65 users in your network that are using Windows 95 at the desktop. Your administration manager wants the users to be able to allow other users to access each other's resources (disk drives) freely, but you also want to protect them with special passwords. Which of the following security models should you implement?

    A. Domain-level security

    B. Share-level security

    C. User-level security

    D. Server-level security

    E. Group-level security

ANSWERS AND EXPLANATIONS

1. **A**   An infrared network normally operates at 10Mbps.

2. **B**   Thicknet can support the same data over longer distances than thinnet, which is 10BASE-2 cabling.

3. **A-B-E**   Reflective, line-of-sight, and broadband optical are used in the transmission of infrared data.

4. **D**   The subnet mask is used to "mask" or hide the network ID so that the host is visible. In many cases, a company may receive a class B or C license and then create its own custom subnet mask to split its network into more subnets. These custom subnet masks basically extend the network address.

5. **B**   User Manager for Domains is the utility used to create accounts and groups.

6. **E**   The specification is 185 meters for 10BASE-2 (thinnet cable).

7. **C**   The D channel is used only for signaling (handshaking) and link-management data at 16Kbps speed.

8. **C**   Due to the impedance of the wire (the resistance to electricity flowing), the strength of the signal decreases as the distance increases. After a certain distance (which is different for each type of cable), the signal gets so weak that degradation takes place.

9. **B**   The redirector is also sometimes known as the *workstation service*. This service determines whether the request to access a resource is a local request or a remote request. If it is not a local device that is accessed, it then passes the request to the appropriate computer.

10. **E**   B channel is described as 64Kbps. When two channels are used, the total combination is 128Kbps, which consists of two B channels.

11. **A**   T1 is the most common type of digital line and can operate at 1.544Mbps.

12. **E**   RJ-45 cable has eight connections and four pairs of wire assembly.

13. **B**   TDR sends a SONAR signal to locate breaks or shorts in a cable run. It can be an excellent troubleshooting tool for suspected bad cabling.

14. **D**   RAID 5 divides the data into 64KB blocks of equal increments across disks. These disks must be three physical drives or greater for RAID 5 to function.

15. **E**   By placing the server on an isolated network, you can reduce the amount of traffic on the network. This is also called segmentation of network traffic.

16. **B**   The Application layer is layer number seven in the OSI model, which is where the packet assembly begins and transcends to the lowest layer (the Physical layer—number one).

17. **E**   UTP is a four-pair cable that 10BASE-T topology uses.

18. **A**   CAT 5 cabling uses 10BASE-T, 100BASE-TX, and 100BASE-T.

19. **C-D-E**   CAT 3, CAT 4, and CAT 5 cable all support 10BASE-T networks. All are standards for twisted-pair cabling and use the RJ-45 connector.

20. **D**   Unshielded twisted-pair (UTP) cable is cheaper than shielded twisted-pair, coaxial (thicknet and thinnet), and fiber-optic cable.

21. **B**   10BASE-T refers to an Ethernet network that uses UTP (STP) cabling. Because twisted-pair cable is the least expensive cable, UTP cable is already in the temporary space, and the existing network adapters already use UTP cable. Nothing has to be done except connect the computers.

22. **B**   10BASE-5 or thicknet cable is thick coaxial cable that can have a network segment up to 500 meters in length.

23. **D**   DHCP is a service that provides IP addresses for client computers. In addition to IP addresses, the DHCP server can also provide subnet masks, default gateways, WINS server addresses, DNS addresses, and so on.

24. **A-C-E**   The destination address, source address, and alert signal are all required fields in the header frame of a packet.

25. **D**   Spread-spectrum radio has a maximum output between 2Mbps and 10Mbps, whereas infrared can scale over 10Mbps, and laser can scale at the speed of light.

26. **A**   100 meters, or 328 feet, is the exact IEEE specification for CAT 5 cable with 10BASE-T cable.

27. **E**   You must load IPX/SPX protocol with a Windows 95 client. You must also load Microsoft Client for NetWare, which is a service under Windows 95. GSNW is Gateway Services for NetWare and is part of the Windows NT server service. CSNW (Client Services for NetWare) is used in the Windows NT workstation product. FPNW (File and Printer Services for NetWare) is installed on a Windows NT server to make it appear as NetWare server to NetWare clients.

28. **D**   CSMA/CD (which stands for Carrier-Sense Multiple Access with Collision Detection) regulates traffic on the segment. When a computer senses that no signals exist on the wire, it assumes that it can transmit. If more than one computer transmits at the same time, a collision occurs and transmissions must be re-sent.

29. **D**   Impedance is the opposite of conduction. In signals flowing in a network cable, impedance is the resistance factor to AC (alternating current). AC is the type of voltage sent in network cabling topologies.

30. **B**   RAID 5 provides complete access to your data online, even when a disk failure occurs.

31. **B**   For 10BASE-2 (termed thinnet), a BNC T connector is used to basically join the network interface card in the local computer to the cable assembly in the form of a coaxial cable.

32. **E**   The term CSMA/CD is a standard called Carrier-Sense Multiple Access with Collision Detection and is a media-access method used in Ethernet networks. With

CSMA/CD, a computer listens to the physical medium to determine whether another computer is transmitting the data frame.

33. **A-B**   NetBEUI was a popular transport protocol used in small, nonroutable networks. It is very fast but cannot be routed because it does not have the header information that other protocols have. DLC is another protocol that cannot be routed; it is used mainly for controlling network printers.

34. **E**   At the Data Link layer, the conversion of data frames from raw bits takes place. This layer is also responsible for transferring frames from one computer to another. After the Data Link layer sends a frame, it waits for ACK, which is an acknowledgment from the receiving computer.

35. **A**   In a star design, cable segments to a centralized component device called a hub that connects the computers. Signals transmitted by a computer on the star pass through the hub to all computers on the network. If the hub goes down, all communication on the network stops.

36. **E**   The Presentation layer is responsible for translating data from the Application layer into an intermediary format. The Presentation layer is also responsible for security issues and the compression of data.

37. **D**   NWLINK is an NDIS-compliant version of the IPX protocol used with Microsoft products.

38. **C**   The MAC (Media Access Control) layer communicates directly with the network adapter card and is responsible for

delivering error-free data between two computers on the network.

39. **C**   The redirector is a small section of the code in the NOS (network operating system) that intercepts requests in the computer and determines whether the requests should be local or redirected out to the network computer.

40. **D**   NetBEUI is a small, efficient, and fast Transport layer protocol. It is very dynamic in the way it can be optimized for very high performance when used in mostly departmental LANs that are not routable.

41. **D**   Gateways are used to connect networks using different protocols so that information can be passed from one system to another. For example, Microsoft SNA Server for Windows NT is a gateway product that connects one form of protocol to another for connectivity to a mainframe system.

42. **A-D**   100BASE-X Ethernet uses the CSMA/CD in a star-wired bus design, similar to 10BASE-T in that all cables are attached to a hub. Also, 10BASE-T and 100BASE-X are configured in a star pattern, but internally they use a bus signaling system as other Ethernet configurations do.

43. **A-B**   SLIP and PPP are two protocols adopted by the Internet community to transmit Internet Protocol (IP) datagram over serial lines. Other protocols, such as CSLIP and PPTP, are also used, but SLIP and PPP are the most common.

44. **A**   A gateway can perform protocol conversions and act as a translator between two systems that do not use the same

communication protocols, data-formatting structures, languages, or architecture.

45. **D** CAT 5 supports speeds up to and including 100Mbps in an unshielded twisted-pair design. CAT 3 supports signal speeds up to 10Mbps in unshielded twisted-pair designs. CAT 4 supports speeds up to 16Mbps.

46. **E** Fiber optics can transmit speeds in excess of 100Mbps in a distance of 1,000 meters to 2,000 meters without any special fiber repeaters.

47. **A-C-D** Bridges can perform the same functions as repeaters, but they can also reduce traffic by segmenting the network. Bridges can join dissimilar physical media, such as twisted-pair and coaxial networks.

48. **A** A repeater is an amplifier that increases the power factor of the electrical signal so that it can travel beyond the specification of the cable length, depending on the type of cable. A repeater strengthens baseband signals in LANs.

49. **C-D** ATM (Asynchronous Transfer Mode) is a packet-switch technology that provides high-speed data transmission rates for sending fixed-size cells over broadband LANs or WANs. X.25 is a set of protocols used in a packet-switching network. This is a slower method of packet switching because it incorporates a large amount of error checking to handle poor or noisy cabling (telephone lines).

50. **D** TCP/IP is a standard routable protocol and is the most complete and accepted

protocol available to connect dissimilar systems such as UNIX and Windows NT.

51. **E** A transceiver is a device that connects a computer to the network. The term *transceiver* is derived from the words *transmitter* and *receiver*, so a transceiver is basically a device that receives data and transmits the signal.

52. **A** Routing Information Protocol (RIP) uses a distance-vector algorithm to determine routes. With RIP, routers transfer information among other routers to update their internal routing tables, and they use that information to determine the best routes.

53. **D** SNMP (Simple Network Management Protocol) is a TCP/IP protocol for monitoring networks. In SNMP, agents monitor the network traffic and gather statistical data, which they put into a management information base called (MIB).

54. **C** CAT 5 cable design would be appropriate because it can support transmission speeds of 100Mbps, and because all new installations have CAT 5 cable as a de facto standard in cable designs. CAT 5 can support video, multimedia, and imaging at higher data-transfer speeds than other categories of cable.

55. **B** Implementation of share-level security involves assigning a password to each shared resource. Access to a shared resource is granted when a user enters the appropriate password.

This exam covers four major topics: standards and terminology, planning, implementation, and troubleshooting. You have 75 minutes to complete this test. Remember that time is a factor. Answer each of the questions you can answer in a relatively short period of time. If you are unsure of a question, do not spend a lot of time trying to work through it. Mark the question and go on to the next question. When you have gone through the entire exam, go back and work through the questions that you marked.

Before the actual exam begins, the exam program will give you the option of taking a sample orientation exam to familiarize yourself with the way the exam operates. You should take this orientation exam before you take your first exam. If you are unsure about how to use the testing equipment or software, or if you have any questions about the rules for the exam, ask the exam administrator before the exam begins.

PRACTICE QUESTIONS

The first three questions use the following scenario.

You must design a simple network given the following parameters:

- ▶ Five users are located in offices on one floor and are less than 100 meters apart.
- ▶ These users do not have dedicated network cabling.
- ▶ Additional telephone wiring (CAT 3) is available at each of their desks.
- ▶ The users want to share each other's files and printers.
- ▶ The users do not want to have their applications file-served.

Practice Exam 2

- ▶ All users use Windows 95 in a standalone environment.
- ▶ No official budget exists for this project.

1. **Which network cabling scheme should you implement?**
    A. Thicknet
    B. Twisted-pair
    C. Wireless
    D. Infrared
    E. Thinnet

2. **Which operating system should you use?**
    A. Windows NT domain
    B. NetWare 4.11
    C. Windows 95 Workgroup
    D. Lantastic Peer-to-Peer
    E. Windows NT Workgroup

3. **Based on your answer to question number 1, which type of networking equipment would support your cable solution?**
    A. A repeater
    B. A hub
    C. A transmitter

D. A router

E. A switch

4. **From the types of cable listed, which can be used for a LAN with a maximum distance of 370 feet between network devices?**

   A. Thicknet

   B. Thinnet

   C. Twisted-pair

   D. Fiber-optic

   E. Coaxial

5. **As with transmitting over cable, transmissions using wireless networking also differ in speed. Ted has a wireless network that he is connecting, and he wants to use a method with the lowest transmission speed. Select the LAN transmission method that typically has the lowest speed.**

   A. Laser

   B. Narrow-band radio

   C. Spread-spectrum radio

   D. Infrared

   E. Reflective

The next two questions use the following scenario.

You have a small office with three users who are located six feet apart and are separated by half-wall cubicles. You do not have an existing network, and there are no spare pairs in the phone cable. You want to share files and printers, and all applications reside on the desktops. All users are using

Windows 95. The budget is very limited.

6. **Based on the scenario, which network cabling scheme makes the most sense?**

   A. Thinnet

   B. Twisted-pair

   C. Fiber

   D. Microwave

   E. Thicknet

7. **Which network operating system would work best?**

   A. Windows 95 Workgroup

   B. Windows NT domain

   C. NetWare

   D. Appleshare

   E. Windows NT Workgroup

8. **Many differences and similarities exist between peer-to-peer networks and server-based networks. When installing a new network, it is important to consider what is important for your situation. Select three attributes of a server-based network.**

   A. Individual users are responsible for the security of their resources.

   B. A dedicated server exists.

   C. Files are stored on a central file server.

   D. Applications are centrally managed on a central file server.

   E. System managers are responsible for the security and protection of resources.

9. **The redirector service (or a form of it) operates on every computer that makes requests to use resources. Select two functions of a network operating system's redirector.**

   A. To determine the level of sharing between network resources

   B. To segment the hard disk into different areas

   C. To intercept requests and forward them to the computer

   D. To assign a letter to a shared resource

   E. To determine whether a task should be left on a local computer or sent to another server on the network

10. **The ISO developed the OSI model to define a standard for the functions that must take place for communication between two computers. As the communication takes place, a packet is created and information is added to the packet as it travels through the different layers. Which layer of the OSI model initiates the packet creation?**

    A. Physical

    B. Network

    C. Transport

    D. Session

    E. Application

11. **As mentioned in question 10, a packet is created and information is added to the header as the packet passes through the layers of the OSI model. Select the three things added to the header.**

    A. Source address

    B. Destination address

    C. Alert signal

    D. Actual address

    E. Cyclical Redundancy Check

12. **In local area networks, a limited number of ways exist by which to control the number of computing devices that can communicate on the wire at one time. In a bus topology, how many computing devices can communicate at one time?**

    A. Ten

    B. Two

    C. All computing devices

    D. One

    E. Only the computing device with the token

The next two questions use the following scenario.

Imagine an office with 20 people who have an open CAT 5 cable next to their phone connections. All the CAT 5 cable is run into a central wiring closet. The users currently use Windows 95. Applications are to be hosted on a central server. The TCP/IP configurations for the desktop computers are to be managed centrally. The power to the building is questionable at times. A reasonable budget has been allocated to implement this solution.

13. **Which type of network cabling scheme would work best?**

    A. Fiber-optic

    B. Thinnet

C. Twisted-pair

D. Microwave

E. Thicknet

14. **Your supervisor has requested that you centrally manage the IP addresses in your network. Which service could you use to perform this task?**

    A. ARP

    B. HTTP

    C. SLIP

    D. WINS

    E. DHCP

15. **You're planning to expand your current network by connecting two networks on different floors of a multifloor building. Your main objective with this design is to reduce the risk of someone tapping into your network. Select the medium that would work best in this scenario.**

    A. Coaxial cable

    B. UTP cable

    C. Wireless

    D. STP cable

    E. Fiber-optic cable

The next four questions use the following scenario.

You are assigned the task of designing a network for a lab at a local school. Listed here are your operating conditions:

▶ You will network 10 workstations together (all IBM-compatibles).

▶ The workstations are currently operating as standalones.

▶ The workstations are all in a row on four tables.

▶ There will not be a dedicated file server.

▶ You want to run applications locally but share printers and files.

▶ You will be connected to an Internet provider and given the IP addresses 134.93.4.10–134.93.4.25.

▶ This design should be built to expand in the future to include other network cabling schemes, where appropriate.

▶ You are contracted to install this network, but the librarian (who is Windows 95 literate) will manage it after installation.

16. **When preparing to install this network, select the three questions that would be of the greatest concern to you.**

    A. What type of experience does the librarian have?

    B. How old is the school?

    C. How does the school want to implement security?

    D. What are the minimum hardware levels for each of the computers to be networked?

    E. How old are the students who will be using the network?

17. **What type of network cabling would be the simplest to install and the most cost-effective?**

A. Fiber-optic

B. Thinnet

C. Twisted-pair

D. Wireless

E. Thicknet

18. **Based on the requirement for future expansion, what type of network card would be appropriate?**

    A. Token-Ring

    B. Combo card with fiber-optic and twisted-pair

    C. Twisted-pair only

    D. Combo card with coaxial and twisted-pair

    E. Coaxial only

19. **Which network operating system would be the best choice?**

    A. LANtastic

    B. Windows NT

    C. Windows 95

    D. Novell Lite

    E. OS/2

20. **Thinnet cable has been a very popular type of network cable for Ethernet networks. It is inexpensive and relatively easy to work with. In addition, it has good shielding to prevent interference from other cables. Thinnet also can carry a signal over a reasonable distance before**

the signal is degraded. How far can a signal be reliable when transmitted over a thinnet cable?

    A. 100 meters

    B. 50 meters

    C. 250 meters

    D. 185 meters

    E. 200 meters

21. **Every type of cable has both accepted limits and theoretical limits. The accepted limit of STP cable is 100Mbps in Ethernet networks. What is the theoretical capacity of STP cable?**

    A. 200Mbps

    B. 400Mbps

    C. 500Mbps

    D. 100Mbps

    E. 300Mbps

22. **CAT 3 cable is commonly used for both networking and telephone communication. Although commonly used for both Ethernet and Token-Ring networks, it does have some limitations. Select all statements that are true of CAT 3 cable.**

    A. CAT 3 cable is suitable for 100Mbps data rates.

    B. CAT 3 cable is suitable for 4Mbps data rates.

    C. CAT 3 cable is considered to be the lowest data-grade cable.

D. CAT 3 cable uses four twisted pairs with three twists per foot.

E. CAT 3 can refer to both twisted-pair and coaxial cable, but is most commonly associated with twisted-pair.

23. **Each type of cable generally needs its own type of connector. The only exception is twisted-pair cable, which generally uses the same type of connector for networking situations. Select the most common type of connector used with twisted-pair cabling.**

A. RJ-11

B. RJ-24

C. RJ-45

D. RJ-8

E. RJ-58

24. **Different environments call for different networking solutions. As most of us have found, there are different reasons for choosing the different types of cable for networks. Select three reasons for implementing wireless networking.**

A. People move around a lot within their work environments.

B. You want temporary installations within your network.

C. Cabling would be impossible or inconvenient to implement.

D. Some people want to use their cell phones to contact their resources at work.

E. You want to increase network security.

25. **Whenever a network is being planned, physical limitations are always a consideration. One major consideration is the maximum distance within which the different media can operate. Select the typical maximum transmission distance for infrared.**

A. 10 feet

B. 50 feet

C. 100 feet

D. 150 feet

E. 200 feet

26. **As with infrared, spread-spectrum radio transmission also has its limits. Because of its frequency, it has a greater range than that of infrared. What is the outdoor operating range of a frequency-hopping scheme under a spread-spectrum radio transmission?**

A. 100 feet

B. 500 feet

C. 1 mile

D. 2 miles

E. 5 miles

27. **Suppose you are implementing a network with the following requirements:**

Servers: Six that run Microsoft Windows NT; three that run Novell NetWare 3.12

Client computers: 800 that run Windows 95

Hubs: 40

Routers: Six

Desktops: All have access to the Internet

Which protocols should you configure on each router for traffic to pass freely across your network?

A. NetBEUI, TCP/IP

B. AppleTalk, TCP/IP

C. IPX, TCP/IP

D. TCP/IP, AppleTalk

E. NetBEUI, IPX

28. Your existing 10BASE-2 Ethernet cable is 185 meters. You are planning to extend your network by adding another 100 meters of cable. Therefore, the total length of the cable will be 285 meters. If the network uses NetBEUI, which of the following devices should you use?

A. Gateway

B. Hub

C. Repeater

D. Router

E. Switch

29. It has been recommended that you use 10BASE-5 cabling for the network you are having installed. The costs quoted seem reasonable for the entire project, but you still want to find out more about this type of network. Select three statements that are true of 10BASE-5.

A. It can operate at a 10Mbps data rate.

B. The signal range is up to 500 meters per cable segment.

C. It uses thin coaxial cable.

D. It is often referred to as thicknet.

E. 10BASE-5 uses RJ-45 connectors.

30. When Windows NT Server and Windows NT Workstation are installed, four groups are automatically created and always exist. The Administrator cannot create, delete, or modify these groups. Select the four Windows NT special groups created during the installation of Windows NT.

A. Active user

B. Everyone

C. Network

D. Interactive

E. Creator-owner

31. Each of the network devices operates at different layers of the OSI model. Select the layer at which a repeater operates.

A. Physical

B. Network

C. Session

D. Transport

E. Presentation

32. To ensure against the loss of data, it is important that data is backed up and that a good backup schedule is devised and maintained. There is never one correct schedule for performing backups—it depends on the network, the data, the users, and many other factors. Because of this, a combination of different backups is usually implemented. Select three types of backups identified by Microsoft.

A. Full backup

B. Semi-contingent backup

C. Incremental backup

D. Differential backup

E. Biweekly backup

33. **From the list, select three network standards that employ token-passing access control.**

   A. FDDI

   B. IEEE Standard 802.3

   C. IEEE Standard 802.4

   D. Token-Ring

   E. IEEE Standard 802.5

34. **Many reasons can exist for using either a peer-to-peer network or a server-based network. Select four statements that describe benefits to using a dedicated file server.**

   A. Files are stored in a central location, where they can be reliably archived.

   B. Central file servers can be managed more efficiently, with user and security data located in a single database.

   C. Dedicated file servers have a single point of failure.

   D. Dedicated file servers allow data backups to be implemented more easily.

   E. The cost of specialized file server technology is shared by a large number of users.

35. **You can ensure that the data on a computer disk is safe from disaster in several ways. Some of the solutions are** implemented through hardware, others are through software, and others through either hardware or software. One option is to use disk mirroring. Select the statement that best describes disk mirroring.

   A. The function of simultaneously writing data to two disks using one channel on one disk controller

   B. The function of simultaneously writing data to two disks on different servers

   C. The function of simultaneously writing data to two disks using separate channels

   D. The function of writing data across two disks to balance the load

   E. The function of writing data to one disk while preserving the directory structure on another

36. **RAID 5 is also referred to as stripe set with parity. This means that while data is being written in the stripe, parity information is also being written. If one disk fails, the computer could continue to operate (slowly) while the missing information is derived from the parity information. What is the minimum number of disks needed to configure a stripe set with parity on a Windows NT server?**

   A. Seven

   B. Two

   C. Three

   D. Four

   E. Five

37. Most people realize that they need a network adapter to communicate on the network. However, very few users know what exactly the network adapter does to enable them to communicate on the network. Select three duties of a network adapter.

   A. Format and prepare data.

   B. Control the flow of data in and out of the computer.

   C. Send the data on to the cable.

   D. Identify network cabling issues within the network.

   E. Filter the actual data from the header information.

38. A characteristic of Ethernet networks is that data flows from the network adapter card to the transmission medium in a particular form. Select the form in which the data is sent to the medium.

   A. Serial

   B. Parallel

   C. Both serial and parallel

   D. Neither parallel nor serial

   E. Pulse

39. Whenever new hardware is added to a computer, the installer must be aware of certain settings. With the advent of plug-and-play, this is not quite as crucial in most cases. However, in certain situations it is an essential part of troubleshooting to know the settings for resources. Select three typical resource settings that may need to be configured when installing new hardware.

   A. Interrupt request

   B. SQA

   C. Base I/O port addresses

   D. Base memory address

   E. Sequence number

40. Suppose you're designing a network and need to install network adapters in 10 ISA computers. Which rule must you follow when installing the NICs?

   A. All network adapters in all computers on the same network must be set to different IRQs.

   B. All adapters in a computer, including the network adapter, must be set to the same IRQ.

   C. All network adapters in all computers on the same network must be set to the same IRQ.

   D. All adapters in a computer, including the network adapter, must be set to different IRQs.

   E. The network adapter can be set to use the same IRQ as the printer.

41. Many tools can be used to monitor a Windows NT network and its computers. Microsoft provides some of these tools; third-party companies develop others. What tool helps a network administrator view operations in real-time for processors, hard disks, memory, network utilization, and the network as a whole on a Windows NT server?

A. Network-management tools for software vendors

B. Problem device

C. Performance Monitor

D. Network Monitor

E. Systems Management Server

42. **Sometimes no problems affect the operating system but target the physical medium used to connect the network. Which tool would you use to check the physical condition of the cable including excess collisions and congestion errors?**

A. DV

B. Protocol analyzer

C. Advanced cable tester

D. Digital Multimeter

E. TDR

43. **The CCITT (Comitée Consultatif Internationale de Télégraphie et Téléphonie) is an organization based in Geneva, Switzerland, that recommends use of communication standards for networks, modems, and facsimile transmissions. Select the set of message-handling standards developed by the CCITT.**

A. X.400

B. MHS

C. SMTP

D. SNMP

E. X.500

44. **Sera has a network of Macintosh computers that she wants to bring into a Windows NT network so that files can be shared and backed up centrally. What service would you need to install on the Windows NT server to enable the Macintosh users to access the disk drive on the Windows NT server?**

A. Gateway.

B. GSNW.

C. Services for Macintosh.

D. Nothing needs to be loaded on the Windows NT server, as the files from Microsoft Office are now in the same format.

E. Redirector.

45. **What Microsoft tool provides a broader scope on network systems management with centralized administration of all computers in a WAN?**

A. Performance Monitor

B. TraceRoute

C. Ping

D. SMS

E. SQL Server

46. **What happens in the Network layer if the network adapter on the router cannot transmit a data chunk as large as the source computer sends?**

A. It causes network activity failure.

B. It retransmits the data chunk.

C. It breaks the data into smaller units.

D. A broadcast storm occurs.

E. It organizes the data frame.

47. **A terminal sends a request for information to a mainframe. The mainframe retrieves the information and displays it on the terminal. What type of computing has taken place?**

    A. Client-server

    B. Peer-to-peer

    C. Centralized

    D. Workgroup

    E. Decentralized

The next three questions use the following scenario.

You are in charge of installing cables for an Ethernet network in your office. Your building has limited workspace, and the cable will have to share an existing conduit with the phone system cable. The maximum length of a cable segment is 320 feet.

48. **Which type of cable should you install in this situation?**

    A. Fiber-optic

    B. Thicknet coaxial

    C. CAT 3 UTP

    D. Thinnet coaxial

    E. CAT 1 UTP

49. **How many pairs are needed to connect to a 10BASE-T network?**

    A. 1 pair

    B. 2 pairs

C. 3 pairs

D 4 pairs

E. 8 pairs

50. **If you choose Ethernet and use 10BASE-T, what type of cable connector would you need to use?**

    A. RJ-11

    B. RJ-45

    C. RJ-6

    D. RJ-12

    E. RJ-58

51. **Your company has a corporate-wide Windows NT network using the TCP/IP protocol. There have been numerous complaints that clients are having IP address conflicts. It seems that after their computers are installed, users make changes to their configurations for one reason or another and end up entering an address that is already in use. Select the Microsoft solution to this problem.**

    A. Increase the TCP window size.

    B. Implement a DHCP server.

    C. Change the MAC address for each network.

    D. Enable WINS on each client computer so they automatically receive their IP configuration.

    E. Manually configure IP addresses on each computer.

52. **Which two layers of the OSI model define how multiple computers can**

simultaneously use the network without interfering with one another?

A. Media Access Control and Logical Link Control

B. Session and Transport

C. Physical and Data Link

D. Media Access Control and Logical Link Control

E. Transport and Network

53. The IP address assigned to each computer that uses the TCP/IP protocol suite is actually made of two components. One component is the network address, and the other component is the host (network device) address. Select what is used to block out the network portion of the IP address so that TCP/IP can determine whether a host exists on the local or remote segment.

A. Node number

B. Subnet mask

C. Default gateway

D. Scope ID

E. Network address

54. Sometimes, problems determine whether a host is available across a WAN. Both NetBIOS and sockets tools can be used to access remote nodes. Select two tools that assist in validating hosts that are active on the Internet.

A. Ping

B. FTP

C. TraceRoute

D. Net Use

E. Multihoming

55. Most people are familiar with using email in their own office environment. However, when they send email messages to people outside their network using the Internet, a different standard must be followed. Select the email standard that is used on the Internet and is part of the TCP/IP protocol.

A. MHS

B. SNMP

C. X.400

D. SMTP

E. X.25

ANSWERS AND EXPLANATIONS

1. **B** Because there are open Category 3 pairs from the phone system, the fastest and most cost-effective approach is to implement a twisted-pair network solution. Another important piece of information here is that the users are fewer than 100 meters apart, which means a twisted-pair solution would work fine.

2. **C** Because each of the users currently uses Windows 95 and the only requirement is to share one another's files and printers, Windows 95 Workgroup is the clear choice. Choosing Windows 95 is the most cost-effective solution. Another advantage here is that the learning curve for the end user is smaller because all currently use the Windows 95 interface.

3. **B** In a twisted-pair network, hubs are a requirement for connectivity.

4. **A-B-D** All these cables have been tested and approved to operate at or above the 370 foot requirement. Twisted-pair cabling is guaranteed to work reliably at 362 feet. With newer technology in twisted-pair cabling (CAT 5), vendors claim longer distances for twisted-pair; however, the IEEE recommendation for twisted-pair is still 362 feet.

5. **C** Spread-spectrum radio transmission speeds are typically 250Kbps or slower.

6. **A** Because the users are close together and their cubicles are half-walled, it makes sense to choose a thinnet solution. Other major factors in this decision are that no available twisted-pair cables exist in the phone cable, and this network must be installed at minimum cost.

7. **A** Because each of the users currently uses Windows 95 and the only requirement for networking is to share one another's files and printers, the logical solution here is to implement Windows 95 Workgroup networking.

8. **B-C-E** Server-based networks consist of dedicated servers, centrally located files on one or many servers, and centrally managed applications. Server-based networks also put more responsibility on systems managers for the security and protection of system resources and files.

9. **C-E** A network operating system's redirector intercepts requests and forwards them to the computer. The redirector also determines whether a task should be left on a local computer or sent to another server on the network.

10. **E** The Application layer is the first layer where the raw data is housed. In layers under the Application layer, the major focus is shaking hands both electronically and physically.

11. **A-B-C** A packet header consists of a source address, a destination address, and an alert signal.

12. **D** In a bus topology, only the computing device with the assigned token can communicate at one time.

13. **C** Because an available twisted-pair cable exists in each office and all run to a central wiring closet, the most logical choice here is twisted-pair cabling.

14. **E** Windows NT's DHCP enables you to distribute and manage your IP addresses centrally and automatically.

15. **E** Fiber-optic cable would be the best choice here because tapping into it is virtually impossible. Fiber connectivity requires a high level of expertise; the other media types are easier to connect.

16. **A-C-D** When planning a network such as the one described here, you must first diagnose your existing hardware to make sure you understand the current operating environment. This information establishes a base from which to plan. You also should be concerned with the level of knowledge the librarian has to ensure that he or she will be able to manage your solution without having to rely on you. The issue of security should always be discussed.

17. **B** In this situation, thinnet seems to be appropriate because the workstations are all lined up in a row in the same room. This would be the simplest and most cost-effective approach. Thinnet is also less expensive than thicknet cable.

18. **D** Because the CPUs are together in a line, coaxial would be the current cable of choice. To plan for future expansion, a combo card with coaxial and twisted-pair would be the best choice because a combo of fiber-optic and twisted-pair card is not available.

19. **C** Because the librarian is familiar with Windows 95—and because peer-to-peer networking will solve all the networking issues—the best choice for this situation is Windows 95.

20. **D** A signal transmitted over thinnet can reliably run 185 meters.

21. **C** The theoretical capacity of STP cable is 500Mbps.

22. **A-B-C-D** Category 3 cabling is the lowest data-grade cable. This type of cable is generally suited for data rates up to 10Mbps, although some innovative schemes enable the cable to support data rates up to 100Mbps. Category 3 cabling uses four twisted pairs with three twists per foot and is now considered to be the standard cable for most telephone systems.

23. **C** RJ-45 connectors are the most common type of connector used with UTP cables.

24. **A-B-C** Wireless networks offer great solutions for people who move around a lot within their environments and for temporary installations within networks. Wireless networks are also great solutions where cabling would be impossible or inconvenient to implement.

25. **C** The maximum transmission distance for infrared signals is 100 feet.

26. **D** The outdoor operating range of a frequency-hopping scheme under a spread-spectrum radio transmission is two miles.

27. **C** To access NetWare servers, IPX must be routed across routers. Windows NT can be accessed by TCP/IP, IPX, and NetBEUI. Therefore, the only answer that works in this situation is C because of the IPX for NetWare resources.

28. **C**   Because the maximum signal distance of a 10BASE-2 segment is 185 meters, you would want to add a repeater in this scenario to regenerate the signal.

29. **A-B-D**   10BASE-5 has a data rate of 10Mbs, with a signal range of 500 meters per cable segment. This type of cable is also referred to as thicknet.

30. **B-C-D-E**   Windows NT creates four special groups, each of which has special uses and access privileges. These groups are Everyone, Network, Interactive, and Creator-owner.

31. **A**   Repeaters operate at the Physical layer of the OSI model.

32. **A-C-D**   Microsoft identifies the following backup types: full, incremental, and differential.

33. **A-C-D-E**   Four network standards that employ token-passing access control (where only the computer that possesses the token can transmit on the network) are FDDI (Fiber Distributed Data Interface), which operates at 100Mbps transmission rates on networks using the Token-Ring standard; IEEE Standard 802.4, which is defined for token-bus networks; Token-Ring, of course; and 802.5, which is the IEEE standard definition for Token-Ring.

34. **A-B-D-E**   Benefits of using dedicated file servers include:

   ▶ Files are stored in a specific place, where they can be reliably archived.

   ▶ Central file servers can be managed more efficiently with user and security data located in a single database.

   ▶ Dedicated file servers enable data backup to be implemented more easily.

   ▶ The cost of specialized file server technology can be shared by a larger number of users.

35. **A**   Disk mirroring is the function of simultaneously writing data to separate disks using one channel on one disk controller.

36. **C**   Three disks is the minimum number needed to configure a stripe set with parity on a Windows NT server.

37. **A-B-C**   Network adapters format and prepare data, control the flow of data in and out of the computer, and send data to other resources.

38. **A**   Data travels on the network in serial form, one bit at a time.

39. **A-C-D**   Typical resource settings are IRQs, base I/O port addresses, and base memory addresses.

40. **D**   The rule for IRQs is that no two components can use an IRQ at the same time. Therefore, option D is the only viable answer here.

41. **C**   Windows NT uses Performance Monitor to track these resources.

42. **C**   An advanced cable tester will provide more information, including stats on collisions and congestion errors, than a TDR.

43. **A**   The CCITT standards committee is responsible for developing and maintaining the X.400 set of message-handling standards.

44. **C** After loading Services for Macintosh on a Windows NT server, you must define special shares on the server so that Macintosh computers can access the directories and files.

45. **D** Microsoft uses its Systems Management Server product to monitor Windows NT networks, as well as to push software to the client computers.

46. **C** When a router is sent a data stream that is larger than it can handle in one session, it breaks the data into smaller units and transmits them in smaller units.

47. **C** In a centralized network model, terminals send requests for data to a mainframe. The mainframe then retrieves the data and displays it on the requesting terminal.

48. **C** The length of the maximum cable run meets the requirement of CAT 3, and 95% of all existing phone systems use CAT 3 cabling. Therefore, CAT 3 UTP is the best choice for this situation.

49. **B** Because the logical choice for cabling here is twisted-pair, you need two pairs (four wires) to comply with 10BASE-T connectivity.

50. **B** RJ-45s are required connectors for 10BASE-T specifications.

51. **B** By implementing a DHCP server, you guarantee that no duplicate addresses will ever be served.

52. **C** In the OSI model, the Physical and Data Link layers are responsible for enabling multiple computers to simultaneously access the network without interfering with one another.

53. **B** A subnet mask is used to block out a portion of the IP address so that TCP/IP can distinguish the network ID from the host ID.

54. **A-C** These two tools enable a user or network administrator to validate host machines that are active.

55. **D** SMTP is the email standard used on the Internet. SMTP is also part of the TCP/IP protocol.

Exam Strategies

You must pass rigorous certification exams to become a Microsoft Certified Professional. These closed-book exams provide a valid and reliable measure of your technical proficiency and expertise. Developed in consultation with computer industry professionals who have on-the-job experience with Microsoft products in the workplace, the exams are conducted by two independent organizations. Sylvan Prometric offers the exams at more than 1,400 Authorized Prometric Testing Centers around the world. Virtual University Enterprises (VUE) testing centers offer exams as well.

To schedule an exam, call Sylvan Prometric Testing Centers at 800-755-EXAM (3926) or VUE at 888-837-8616.

This appendix is divided into two main sections. First, it describes the different certification options provided by Microsoft, and how you can achieve those certifications. The second portion highlights the different kinds of examinations and the best ways to prepare for those different exam and question styles.

TYPES OF CERTIFICATION

Currently Microsoft offers seven types of certification, based on specific areas of expertise:

- **Microsoft Certified Professional (MCP).** Qualified to provide installation, configuration, and support for users of at least one Microsoft desktop operating system, such as Windows NT Workstation. Candidates can take elective exams to develop areas of specialization. MCP is the base level of expertise.

- **Microsoft Certified Professional+Internet (MCP+Internet).** Qualified to plan security, install and configure server products, manage server resources, extend service to run CGI scripts or ISAPI scripts, monitor and analyze performance, and troubleshoot problems. Expertise is similar to that of an MCP, but with a focus on the Internet.

- **Microsoft Certified Professional+Site Building (MCP+Site Building).** Qualified to plan, build, maintain, and manage Web sites by using Microsoft technologies and products. The credential is appropriate for people who manage sophisticated, interactive Web sites that include database connectivity, multimedia, and searchable content.

- **Microsoft Certified Systems Engineer (MCSE).** Qualified to effectively plan, implement, maintain, and support information systems with Microsoft Windows NT and other Microsoft advanced systems and workgroup products, such as Microsoft Office and Microsoft BackOffice. MCSE is a second level of expertise.

- **Microsoft Certified Systems Engineer+ Internet (MCSE+Internet).** Qualified in the core MCSE areas, and also qualified to enhance, deploy, and manage sophisticated intranet and Internet solutions that include a browser, proxy server, host servers, database, and messaging and commerce components. An MCSE+Internet–certified professional is able to manage and analyze Web sites.

- **Microsoft Certified Solution Developer (MCSD).** Qualified to design and develop custom business solutions by using Microsoft development tools, technologies, and platforms, including Microsoft Office and Microsoft BackOffice. MCSD is a second level of expertise, with a focus on software development.

- **Microsoft Certified Trainer (MCT).** Instructionally and technically qualified by Microsoft to deliver Microsoft Education Courses at Microsoft-authorized sites. An MCT must be employed by a Microsoft Solution Provider Authorized Technical Education Center or a Microsoft Authorized Academic Training site.

▼ **NOTE**

For the most up-to-date information about each type of certification, visit the Microsoft Training and Certification Web site at http://www.microsoft.com/train_cert. You also can call or email the following sources:

- Microsoft Certified Professional Program: 800-636-7544

- mcp@msprograms.com

- Microsoft Online Institute (MOLI): 800-449-9333

CERTIFICATION REQUIREMENTS

The requirements for certification in each of the seven areas are detailed below. An asterisk after an exam indicates that the exam is slated for retirement.

How to Become a Microsoft Certified Professional

Passing any Microsoft exam (with the exception of Networking Essentials) is all you need to do to become certified as an MCP.

How to Become a Microsoft Certified Professional+Internet

You must pass the following exams to become an MCP specializing in Internet technology:

- Internetworking Microsoft TCP/IP on Microsoft Windows NT 4.0, #70-059

- Implementing and Supporting Microsoft Windows NT Server 4.0, #70-067

- Implementing and Supporting Microsoft Internet Information Server 3.0 and Microsoft Index Server 1.1, #70-077

  OR Implementing and Supporting Microsoft Internet Information Server 4.0, #70-087

How to Become a Microsoft Certified Professional+Site Building

You need to pass two of the following exams in order to be certified as an MCP+Site Building:

- Designing and Implementing Web Sites with Microsoft FrontPage 98, #70-055

- Designing and Implementing Commerce Solutions with Microsoft Site Server 3.0, Commerce Edition, #70-057

- Designing and Implementing Web Solutions with Microsoft Visual InterDev 6.0, #70-152

How to Become a Microsoft Certified Systems Engineer

You must pass four operating system exams and two elective exams to become an MCSE. The MCSE certification path is divided into two tracks: the Windows NT 3.51 track and the Windows NT 4.0 track.

The following lists show the core requirements (four operating system exams) for both the Windows NT 3.51 and 4.0 tracks, and the elective courses (two exams) you can take for either track.

The four Windows NT 3.51 Track Core Requirements for MCSE certification are as follows:

- Implementing and Supporting Microsoft Windows NT Server 3.51, #70-043*

- Implementing and Supporting Microsoft Windows NT Workstation 3.51, #70-042*

- Microsoft Windows 3.1, #70-030*

  OR Microsoft Windows for Workgroups 3.11, #70-048*

  OR Implementing and Supporting Microsoft Windows 95, #70-064

  OR Implementing and Supporting Microsoft Windows 98, #70-098

- Networking Essentials, #70-058

The four Windows NT 4.0 Track Core Requirements for MCSE certification are as follows:

- Implementing and Supporting Microsoft Windows NT Server 4.0, #70-067

- Implementing and Supporting Microsoft Windows NT Server 4.0 in the Enterprise, #70-068

- Microsoft Windows 3.1, #70-030*

  OR Microsoft Windows for Workgroups 3.11, #70-048*

  OR Implementing and Supporting Microsoft Windows 95, #70-064

  OR Implementing and Supporting Microsoft Windows NT Workstation 4.0, #70-073

  OR Implementing and Supporting Microsoft Windows 98, #70-098

- Networking Essentials, #70-058

For both the Windows NT 3.51 and the 4.0 tracks, you must pass two of the following elective exams for MCSE certification:

- Implementing and Supporting Microsoft SNA Server 3.0, #70-013

  OR Implementing and Supporting Microsoft SNA Server 4.0, #70-085

- Implementing and Supporting Microsoft Systems Management Server 1.0, #70-014*

  OR Implementing and Supporting Microsoft Systems Management Server 1.2, #70-018

  OR Implementing and Supporting Microsoft Systems Management Server 2.0, #70-086

- Microsoft SQL Server 4.2 Database Implementation, #70-021

  OR Implementing a Database Design on Microsoft SQL Server 6.5, #70-027

  OR Implementing a Database Design on Microsoft SQL Server 7.0, #70-029

- Microsoft SQL Server 4.2 Database Administration for Microsoft Windows NT, #70-022

  OR System Administration for Microsoft SQL Server 6.5 (or 6.0), #70-026

  OR System Administration for Microsoft SQL Server 7.0, #70-028

- Microsoft Mail for PC Networks 3.2-Enterprise, #70-037

- Internetworking with Microsoft TCP/IP on Microsoft Windows NT (3.5-3.51), #70-053

  OR Internetworking with Microsoft TCP/IP on Microsoft Windows NT 4.0, #70-059

- Implementing and Supporting Microsoft Exchange Server 4.0, #70-075*

  OR Implementing and Supporting Microsoft Exchange Server 5.0, #70-076

  OR Implementing and Supporting Microsoft Exchange Server 5.5, #70-081

- Implementing and Supporting Microsoft Internet Information Server 3.0 and Microsoft Index Server 1.1, #70-077

  OR Implementing and Supporting Microsoft Internet Information Server 4.0, #70-087

- Implementing and Supporting Microsoft Proxy Server 1.0, #70-078

  OR Implementing and Supporting Microsoft Proxy Server 2.0, #70-088

- Implementing and Supporting Microsoft Internet Explorer 4.0 by Using the Internet Explorer Resource Kit, #70-079

How to Become a Microsoft Certified Systems Engineer+ Internet

You must pass seven operating system exams and two elective exams to become an MCSE specializing in Internet technology.

The seven MCSE+Internet core exams required for certification are as follows:

- Networking Essentials, #70-058

- Internetworking with Microsoft TCP/IP on Microsoft Windows NT 4.0, #70-059

- Implementing and Supporting Microsoft Windows 95, #70-064

  OR Implementing and Supporting Microsoft Windows NT Workstation 4.0, #70-073

  OR Implementing and Supporting Microsoft Windows 98, #70-098

- Implementing and Supporting Microsoft Windows NT Server 4.0, #70-067

- Implementing and Supporting Microsoft Windows NT Server 4.0 in the Enterprise, #70-068

- Implementing and Supporting Microsoft Internet Information Server 3.0 and Microsoft Index Server 1.1, #70-077

  OR Implementing and Supporting Microsoft Internet Information Server 4.0, #70-087

- Implementing and Supporting Microsoft Internet Explorer 4.0 by Using the Internet Explorer Resource Kit, #70-079

You must also pass two of the following elective exams for MCSE+Internet certification:

- System Administration for Microsoft SQL Server 6.5, #70-026

- Implementing a Database Design on Microsoft SQL Server 6.5, #70-027

- Implementing and Supporting Web Sites Using Microsoft Site Server 3.0, # 70-056

- Implementing and Supporting Microsoft Exchange Server 5.0, #70-076

  OR Implementing and Supporting Microsoft Exchange Server 5.5, #70-081

- Implementing and Supporting Microsoft Proxy Server 1.0, #70-078

  OR Implementing and Supporting Microsoft Proxy Server 2.0, #70-088

- Implementing and Supporting Microsoft SNA Server 4.0, #70-085

How to Become a Microsoft Certified Solution Developer

The MCSD certification is undergoing substantial revision. Listed next are the requirements for the new track (available fourth quarter 1998), as well as the old.

For the new track, you must pass three core exams and one elective exam.

The core exams include the following:

Desktop Applications Development (1 required)

- Designing and Implementing Desktop Applications with Microsoft Visual C++ 6.0, #70-016

  OR Designing and Implementing Desktop Applications with Microsoft Visual Basic 6.0, #70-176

Distributed Applications Development (1 required)

- Designing and Implementing Distributed Applications with Microsoft Visual C++ 6.0, #70-015

  OR Designing and Implementing Distributed Applications with Microsoft Visual Basic 6.0, #70-175

Solution Architecture (required)

- Analyzing Requirements and Defining Solution Architectures, #70-100

Elective Exams

You must also pass one of the following elective exams:

- Designing and Implementing Distributed Applications with Microsoft Visual C++ 6.0, #70-015

  OR Designing and Implementing Desktop Applications with Microsoft Visual C++ 6.0, #70-016

  OR Microsoft SQL Server 4.2 Database Implementation, #70-021*

- Implementing a Database Design on Microsoft SQL Server 6.5, #70-027

  OR Implementing a Database Design on Microsoft SQL Server 7.0, #70-029

- Developing Applications with C++ Using the Microsoft Foundation Class Library, #70-024

- Implementing OLE in Microsoft Foundation Class Applications, #70-025

- Designing and Implementing Web Sites with Microsoft FrontPage 98, #70-055

- Designing and Implementing Commerce Solutions with Microsoft Site Server 3.0, Commerce Edition, #70-057

- Programming with Microsoft Visual Basic 4.0, #70-065

  OR Developing Applications with Microsoft Visual Basic 5.0, #70-165

  OR Designing and Implementing Distributed Applications with Microsoft Visual Basic 6.0, #70-175

  OR Designing and Implementing Desktop Applications with Microsoft Visual Basic 6.0, #70-176

- Microsoft Access for Windows 95 and the Microsoft Access Development Toolkit, #70-069

- Designing and Implementing Solutions with Microsoft Office (Code-named Office 9) and Microsoft Visual Basic for Applications, #70-091

- Designing and Implementing Web Solutions with Microsoft Visual InterDev 6.0, #70-152

Former MCSD Track

For the old track, you must pass two core technology exams and two elective exams for MCSD certification. The following lists show the required technology exams and elective exams needed to become an MCSD.

You must pass the following two core technology exams to qualify for MCSD certification:

- Microsoft Windows Architecture I, #70-160*

- Microsoft Windows Architecture II, #70-161*

You must also pass two of the following elective exams to become an MSCD:

- Designing and Implementing Distributed Applications with Microsoft Visual C++ 6.0, #70-015

- Designing and Implementing Desktop Applications with Microsoft Visual C++ 6.0, #70-016

- Microsoft SQL Server 4.2 Database Implementation, #70-021*

  OR Implementing a Database Design on Microsoft SQL Server 6.5, #70-027

  OR Implementing a Database Design on Microsoft SQL Server 7.0, #70-029

- Developing Applications with C++ Using the Microsoft Foundation Class Library, #70-024

- Implementing OLE in Microsoft Foundation Class Applications, #70-025

- Programming with Microsoft Visual Basic 4.0, #70-065

OR Developing Applications with Microsoft Visual Basic 5.0, #70-165

OR Designing and Implementing Distributed Applications with Microsoft Visual Basic 6.0, #70-175

OR Designing and Implementing Desktop Applications with Microsoft Visual Basic 6.0, #70-176

- Microsoft Access 2.0 for Windows-Application Development, #70-051

OR Microsoft Access for Windows 95 and the Microsoft Access Development Toolkit, #70-069

- Developing Applications with Microsoft Excel 5.0 Using Visual Basic for Applications, #70-052

- Programming in Microsoft Visual FoxPro 3.0 for Windows, #70-054

- Designing and Implementing Web Sites with Microsoft FrontPage 98, #70-055

- Designing and Implementing Commerce Solutions with Microsoft Site Server 3.0, Commerce Edition, #70-057

- Designing and Implementing Solutions with Microsoft Office (Code-named Office 9) and Microsoft Visual Basic for Applications, #70-091

- Designing and Implementing Web Solutions with Microsoft Visual InterDev 6.0, #70-152

Becoming a Microsoft Certified Trainer

To understand the requirements and process for becoming an MCT, you need to obtain the Microsoft Certified Trainer Guide document from the following site:

```
http://www.microsoft.com/train_cert/mct/
```

At this site, you can read the document as Web pages or display and download it as a Word file. The MCT Guide explains the four-step process of becoming an MCT. The general steps for the MCT certification are as follows:

1. Complete and mail a Microsoft Certified Trainer application to Microsoft. You must include proof of your skills for presenting instructional material. The options for doing so are described in the MCT Guide.

2. Obtain and study the Microsoft Trainer Kit for the Microsoft Official Curricula (MOC) courses for which you want to be certified. Microsoft Trainer Kits can be ordered by calling 800-688-0496 in North America. Interested parties in other regions should review the MCT Guide for information on how to order a Trainer Kit.

3. Take the Microsoft certification exam for the product about which you want to be certified to teach.

4. Attend the MOC course for the course for which you want to be certified. This is done so you can understand how the course is structured, how labs are completed, and how the course flows.

◆ **WARNING**

You should consider the preceding steps a general overview of the MCT certification process. The precise steps that you need to take are described in detail on the Web site mentioned earlier. Do not misinterpret the preceding steps as the exact process you need to undergo.

If you are interested in becoming an MCT, you can receive more information by visiting the Microsoft Certified Training Web site at `http://www.microsoft.com/train_cert/mct/` or by calling 800-688-0496.

STUDY AND EXAM PREPARATION TIPS

This part of the appendix provides you with some general guidelines for preparing for the exam. It is organized into three sections. The first section, "Study Tips," addresses your pre-exam preparation activities, covering general study tips. This is followed by "Exam Prep Tips," an extended look at the Microsoft Certification exams, including a number of specific tips that apply to the Microsoft exam formats. Finally, "Putting It All Together" discusses changes in Microsoft's testing policies and how they might affect you.

To better understand the nature of preparation for the test, it is important to understand learning as a process. You probably are aware of how you best learn new material. You may find that outlining works best for you, or you may need to see things as a visual learner. Whatever your learning style, test preparation takes place over time. Although it is obvious that you can't start studying for these exams the night before you take them, it is very important to understand that learning is a devel-opmental process. Understanding it as a process helps you focus on what you know and what you have yet to learn.

Thinking about how you learn should help you to recognize that learning takes place when you are able to match new information to old. You have some previous experience with computers and networking, and now you are preparing for this certification exam. Using this book, software, and supplementary materials will not just add incrementally to what you know. As you study, you actually change the organization of your knowledge as you integrate this new information into your existing knowledge base. This will lead you to a more comprehensive understanding of the tasks and concepts outlined in the objectives, and of computing in general. Again, this happens as an iterative process rather than a singular event. Keep this model of learning in mind as you prepare for the exam, and you will make better decisions about what to study and how much more studying you need to do.

Study Tips

There are many ways to approach studying, just as there are many different types of material to study. However, the tips that follow should prepare you well for the type of material covered on the certification exams.

Study Strategies

Individuals vary in the ways they learn information. Some basic principles of learning apply to everyone, however; you should adopt some study strategies that take advantage of these principles. One of these principles is that learning can be broken into various depths. Recognition (of terms, for example) exemplifies a more surface level of learning—you rely on a prompt of some sort to elicit recall. Comprehension or understanding (of the concepts behind the terms, for instance) represents a deeper level of learning. The ability to analyze a concept and apply your understanding of it in a new way or novel setting represents an even further depth of learning.

Your learning strategy should enable you to understand the material at a level or two deeper than mere recognition. This will help you to do well on the exam(s). You will know the material so thoroughly that you can easily handle the recognition-level types of questions used in multiple-choice testing. You will also be able to apply your knowledge to solve novel problems.

Macro and Micro Study Strategies

One strategy that can lead to this deeper learning includes preparing an outline that covers all the objectives and subobjectives for the particular exam you are working on. You should delve a bit further into the material and include a level or two of detail beyond the stated objectives and subobjectives for the exam. Then flesh out the outline by coming up with a statement of definition or a summary for each point in the outline.

This outline provides two approaches to studying. First, you can study the outline by focusing on the organization of the material. Work your way through the points and subpoints of your outline with the goal of learning how they relate to one another. For example, be sure you understand how each of the main objective areas is similar to and different from another. Then do the same thing with the subobjectives; be sure you know which subobjectives pertain to each objective area and how they relate to one another.

Next, you can work through the outline, focusing on learning the details. Memorize and understand terms and their definitions, facts, rules and strategies, advantages and disadvantages, and so on. In this pass through the outline, attempt to learn detail rather than the big picture (the organizational information that you worked on in the first pass through the outline).

Research has shown that attempting to assimilate both types of information at the same time seems to interfere with the overall learning process. Separate your studying into these two approaches, and you will perform better on the exam than if you attempt to study the material in a more conventional manner.

Active Study Strategies

In addition, the process of writing down and defining the objectives, subobjectives, terms, facts, and definitions promotes a more active learning strategy than merely reading the material. In human information-processing terms, writing forces you to engage in more active encoding of the information. Simply reading over it constitutes more passive processing.

Next, determine whether you can apply the information you have learned by attempting to create examples and scenarios of your own. Think about how or where you could apply the concepts you are learning. Again, write down this information to process the facts and concepts in a more active fashion.

The hands-on nature of the step-by-step tutorials and exercises at the ends of the chapters provide further active learning opportunities that will reinforce concepts as well.

Common-sense Strategies

Finally, you should follow common-sense practices in studying. Study when you are alert, reduce or eliminate distractions, take breaks when you become fatigued, and so on.

Pre-testing Yourself

Pre-testing allows you to assess how well you are learning. One of the most important aspects of learning is what has been called meta-learning. *Meta-learning* has to do with realizing when you know something well or when you need to study more. In other words, you recognize how well or how poorly you have learned the material you are studying. For most people, this can be difficult to assess objectively on their own. Practice tests are useful in that they reveal more objectively what you have learned and what you have not learned. You should use this information to guide review and further studying. Developmental learning takes place as you cycle through studying, assessing how well you have learned, reviewing, assessing again, until you feel you are ready to take the exam.

You may have noticed the practice exams included in this book. Use them as part of this process.

Exam Prep Tips

Having mastered the subject matter, your final preparatory step is to understand how the exam will be presented. Make no mistake about it—a Microsoft Certified Professional (MCP) exam will challenge both your knowledge and test-taking skills! This section starts with the basics of exam design, reviews a new type of exam format, and concludes with hints that are targeted to each of the exam formats.

The MCP Exams

Every MCP exam is released in one of two basic formats. What's being called exam format here is really little more than a combination of the overall exam structure and the presentation method for exam questions.

Each exam format utilizes the same types of questions. These types or styles of questions include multiple-rating (or scenario-based) questions, traditional multiple-choice questions, and simulation-based questions. It's important to understand the types of questions you will be presented with and the actions required to properly answer them.

Understanding the exam formats is key to good preparation because the format determines the number of questions presented, the difficulty of those questions, and the amount of time allowed to complete the exam.

Exam Formats

There are two basic formats for the MCP exams: the traditional fixed-form exam and the adaptive form. As its name implies, the fixed-form exam presents a fixed set of questions during the exam session. The adaptive format, however, uses only a subset of questions drawn from a larger pool during any given exam session.

Fixed-form

A fixed-form, computerized exam is based on a fixed set of exam questions. The individual questions are presented in random order during a test session. If you take the same exam more than once, you won't necessarily see the exact same questions. This is because two to three final forms are typically assembled for every fixed-form exam Microsoft releases. These are usually labeled Forms A, B, and C.

The final forms of a fixed-form exam are identical in terms of content coverage, number of questions, and allotted time, but the questions themselves are different. You may have noticed, however, that some of the same questions appear on, or rather are shared across, different final forms. When questions are shared across multiple final forms of an exam, the percentage of sharing is generally small. Many final forms share no questions, but some older exams may have a ten to fifteen percent duplication of exam questions on the final exam forms.

Fixed-form exams also have a fixed time limit in which you must complete the exam.

Finally, the score you achieve on a fixed-form exam, which is always reported for MCP exams on a scale of 0 to 1000, is based on the number of questions you answer correctly. The exam passing score is the same for all final forms of a given fixed-form exam.

The typical format for the fixed-form exam is as follows:

- 50–60 questions
- 75–90 minute testing time
- Question review allowed, including the opportunity to change your answers

Adaptive Form

An adaptive form exam has the same appearance as a fixed-form exam, but differs in both how questions are selected for presentation and how many questions actually are presented. Although the statistics of adaptive testing are fairly complex, the process is concerned with determining your level of skill or ability with the exam subject matter. This ability assessment begins by presenting questions of varying levels of difficulty and ascertaining at what difficulty level you can reliably answer them. Finally, the ability assessment determines if that ability level is above or below the level required to pass that exam.

Examinees at different levels of ability will then see quite different sets of questions. Those who demonstrate little expertise with the subject matter will continue to be presented with relatively easy questions. Examinees who demonstrate a higher level of expertise will be presented progressively more difficult questions. Both individuals may answer the same number of questions correctly, but because the exam-taker with the higher level of expertise can correctly answer more difficult questions, he or she will receive a higher score, and is more likely to pass the exam.

The typical design for the adaptive form exam is as follows:

- 20–25 questions
- 90-minute testing time, although this is likely to be reduced to 45–60 minutes in the near future
- Question review not allowed, providing no opportunity to change your answers

Your first adaptive exam will be unlike any other testing experience you have had. In fact, many examinees have difficulty accepting the adaptive testing process because they feel that they are not provided the opportunity to adequately demonstrate their full expertise.

You can take consolation in the fact that adaptive exams are painstakingly put together after months of data gathering and analysis and are just as valid as a fixed-form exam. The rigor introduced through the adaptive testing methodology means that there is nothing arbitrary about what you'll see! It is also a more efficient means of testing, requiring less time to conduct and complete.

As you can see from Figure A.1, there are a number of statistical measures that drive the adaptive examination process. The most immediately relevant to you is the ability estimate. Accompanying this test statistic are the standard error of measurement, the item characteristic curve, and the test information curve.

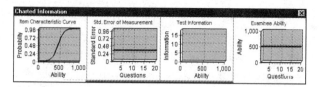

FIGURE A.1
Microsoft's Adaptive Testing Demonstration Program.

The standard error, which is the key factor in determining when an adaptive exam will terminate, reflects the degree of error in the exam ability estimate. The item characteristic curve reflects the probability of a correct response relative to examinee ability. Finally, the test information statistic provides a measure of the information contained in the set of questions the examinee has answered, again relative to the ability level of the individual examinee.

When you begin an adaptive exam, the standard error has already been assigned a target value below which it must drop for the exam to conclude. This target value reflects a particular level of statistical confidence in the process. The examinee ability is initially set to the mean possible exam score: 500 for MCP exams.

As the adaptive exam progresses, questions of varying difficulty are presented. Based on your

pattern of responses to these questions, the ability estimate is recalculated. Simultaneously, the standard error estimate is refined from its first estimated value of one toward the target value. When the standard error reaches its target value, the exam terminates. Thus, the more consistently you answer questions of the same degree of difficulty, the more quickly the standard error estimate drops, and the fewer questions you will end up seeing during the exam session. This situation is depicted in Figure A.2.

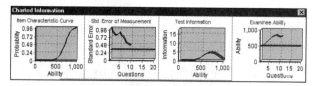

FIGURE A.2
The changing statistics in an adaptive exam.

As you might suspect, one good piece of advice for taking an adaptive exam is to treat every exam question as if it were the most important. The adaptive scoring algorithm is attempting to discover a pattern of responses that reflects some level of proficiency with the subject matter. Incorrect responses almost guarantee that additional questions must be answered (unless, of course, you get every question wrong). This is because the scoring algorithm must adjust to information that is not consistent with the emerging pattern.

New Question Types

A variety of question types can appear on MCP exams. Examples of multiple-choice questions and scenario-based questions appear throughout this book. They appear in the Top Score software as well. Simulation-based questions are new to the MCP exam series.

Simulation Questions

Simulation-based questions reproduce the look and feel of key Microsoft product features for the purpose of testing. The simulation software used in MCP exams has been designed to look and act, as much as possible, just like the actual product. Consequently, answering simulation questions in an MCP exam entails completing one or more tasks just as if you were using the product itself.

The format of a typical Microsoft simulation question is straightforward. It presents a brief scenario or problem statement along with one or more tasks that must be completed to solve the problem. An example of a simulation question for MCP exams is shown in the following section.

A Typical Simulation Question

It sounds obvious, but the first step when you encounter a simulation is to carefully read the question (see Figure A.3). Do not go straight to the simulation application! Assess the problem being presented and identify the conditions that make up the problem scenario. Note the tasks that must be performed or outcomes that must be achieved to answer the question, and review any instructions about how to proceed.

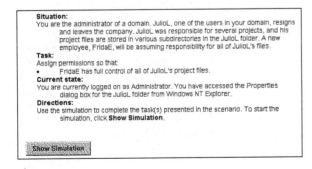

Situation:
You are the administrator of a domain. JulioL, one of the users in your domain, resigns and leaves the company. JulioL was responsible for several projects, and his project files are stored in various subdirectories in the JulioL folder. A new employee, FridaE, will be assuming responsibility for all of JulioL's files.
Task:
Assign permissions so that:
• FridaE has full control of all of JulioL's project files.
Current state:
You are currently logged on as Administrator. You have accessed the Properties dialog box for the JulioL folder from Windows NT Explorer.
Directions:
Use the simulation to complete the task(s) presented in the scenario. To start the simulation, click **Show Simulation**.

Show Simulation

FIGURE A.3
Typical MCP exam simulation question with directions.

The next step is to launch the simulator. Click the Show Simulation button to see a feature of the product, such as the dialog box shown in Figure A.4. The simulation application partially covers the question text on many test center machines. Feel free to reposition the simulation or to move between the question text screen and the simulation using hot keys, point-and-click navigation, or even by clicking the simulation launch button again.

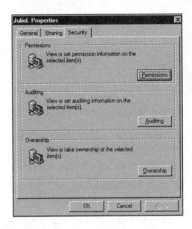

FIGURE A.4
Launching the simulation application.

It is important to understand that your answer to the simulation question is not recorded until you move on to the next exam question. This gives you the added capability to close and reopen the simulation application (using the launch button) on the same question without losing any partial answer you may have made.

The third step is to use the simulator as you would the actual product to solve the problem or perform the defined tasks. Again, the simulation software is designed to function, within reason, just as the product does. But don't expect the simulation to reproduce product behavior perfectly.

Most importantly, do not allow yourself to become flustered if the simulation does not look or act exactly like the product. Figure A.5 shows the solution to the example simulation problem.

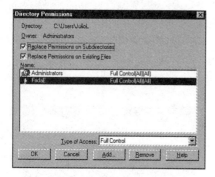

FIGURE A.5
The solution to the simulation example.

There are two final points that will help you tackle simulation questions. First, respond only to what is being asked in the question. Do not solve problems that you are not asked to solve. Second, accept what is being asked of you. You may not entirely agree with conditions in the problem statement, the quality of the desired solution, or the sufficiency of defined tasks to adequately solve the problem. Always remember that you are being tested on your ability to solve the problem as it has been presented.

The solution to the simulation problem shown in Figure A.5 perfectly illustrates both of these points. As you'll recall from the question scenario (refer to Figure A.3), you were asked to assign appropriate permissions to a new user, FridaE. You were not instructed to make any other changes in permissions. Thus, if you had modified or removed Administrators permissions, this item would have been scored as incorrect on an MCP exam.

Putting It All Together

Given all these different pieces of information, the task is now to assemble a set of tips that will help you successfully tackle the different types of MCP exams.

More Pre-exam Preparation Tips

Generic exam preparation advice is always useful. Tips include the following:

- Become familiar with the product. Hands-on experience is one of the keys to success on any MCP exam. Review the exercises and the step-by-step activities in the book.

- Review the current exam preparation guide on the Microsoft MCP Web site. The documentation Microsoft makes publicly available over the Web identifies the skills every exam is intended to test.

- Memorize foundational technical detail as appropriate. Remember that MCP exams are generally heavy on problem solving and application of knowledge rather than just questions that only require rote memorization.

- Take any of the available practice tests. We recommend the ones included in this book and the ones you can create using New Riders' exclusive Top Score Test Simulation software suite, available through your local bookstore or software distributor. Although these are fixed-format exams, they provide practice that is valuable for preparing for an adaptive exam. Because of the interactive nature of adaptive testing, it is not possible to provide examples of the adaptive format in the included practice exams. However, fixed-format exams do provide the same types of questions as found on adaptive exams and are the most effective way to prepare for either type of exam. As a supplement to the material bound with this book, also try the free practice tests available on the Microsoft MCP Web site.

- Look on the Microsoft MCP Web site for samples and demonstration items. These tend to be particularly valuable for one significant reason: They allow you to become familiar with any new testing technologies before you encounter them on an MCP exam.

During the Exam Session

Similarly, the generic exam-taking advice you've heard for years applies when taking an MCP exam:

- Take a deep breath and try to relax when you first sit down for your exam session. It is very important to control the pressure you may (naturally) feel when taking exams.

- You will be provided scratch paper. Take a moment to write down any factual information and technical detail that you've committed to short-term memory.

- Carefully read all information and instruction screens. These displays have been put together to give you information relevant to the exam you are taking.

- Accept the Non-Disclosure Agreement and preliminary survey as part of the examination process. Complete them accurately and quickly move on.

- Read the exam questions carefully. Reread each question to identify all relevant detail.

- Tackle the questions in the order they are presented. Skipping around won't build your confidence; the clock is always counting down.

- Don't rush, but similarly, don't linger on difficult questions. The questions vary in degree of difficulty. Don't let yourself be flustered by a particularly difficult or verbose question.

Fixed-form Exams

Building from this basic preparation and test-taking advice, you also need to consider the challenges presented by the different exam designs. Because a fixed-form exam is composed of a fixed, finite set of questions, add these tips to your strategy for taking a fixed-form exam:

- Note the time allotted and the number of questions appearing on the exam you are taking. Make a rough calculation of how many minutes you can spend on each question and use this to pace yourself through the exam.

- Take advantage of the fact that you can return to and review skipped or previously answered questions. Mark the questions you can't answer confidently, noting the relative difficulty of each question on the scratch paper provided. When you reach the end of the exam, return to the more difficult questions.

- If there is session time remaining after you have completed all questions (and you aren't too fatigued!), review your answers. Pay particular attention to questions that seem to have a lot of detail or that required graphics.

- As for changing your answers, the rule of thumb here is *don't*! If you read the question carefully and completely, and you felt like you knew the right answer, you probably did. Don't second-guess yourself. If, as you check your answers, one stands out as clearly marked incorrectly, however, you should change it in that instance. If you are at all unsure, go with your first impression.

Adaptive Exams

If you are planning to take an adaptive exam, keep these additional tips in mind:

- Read and answer every question with great care. When reading a question, identify every relevant detail, requirement, or task that must be performed and double-check your answer to be sure you have addressed every one of them.

- If you cannot answer a question, use the process of elimination to reduce the set of potential answers, then take your best guess. Stupid mistakes invariably mean additional questions will be presented.

- Forget about reviewing questions and changing your answers. After you leave a question, whether you've answered it or not, you cannot return to it. Do not skip a question, either; if you do, it's counted as incorrect!

Simulation Questions

You may encounter simulation questions on either the fixed-form or adaptive form exam. If you do, keep these tips in mind:

- Avoid changing any simulation settings that don't pertain directly to the problem solution. Solve the problem you are being asked to solve, and nothing more.

- Assume default settings when related information has not been provided. If something has not been mentioned or defined, it is a non-critical detail that does not factor in to the correct solution.

- Be sure your entries are syntactically correct, paying particular attention to your spelling. Enter relevant information just as the product would require it.

- Close all simulation application windows after completing the simulation tasks. The testing system software is designed to trap errors that could result when using the simulation application, but trust yourself over the testing software.

- If simulations are part of a fixed-form exam, you can return to skipped or previously answered questions and review your answers. However, if you choose to change your answer to a simulation question, or even attempt to review the settings you've made in the simulation application, your previous response to that simulation question will be deleted. If simulations are part of an adaptive exam, you cannot return to previous questions.

FINAL CONSIDERATIONS

There are a number of changes in the MCP program that will impact how frequently you can repeat an exam and what you will see when you do.

- Microsoft has instituted a new exam retake policy. This new rule is "two and two, then one and two." That is, you can attempt any exam two times with no restrictions on the time between attempts. But after the second attempt, you must wait two weeks before you can attempt that exam again. After that, you will be required to wait two weeks between any subsequent attempts. Plan to pass the exam in two attempts, or plan to increase your time horizon for receiving an MCP credential.

- New questions are being seeded into the MCP exams. After performance data has been gathered on new questions, they will replace older questions on all exam forms. This means that the questions appearing on exams are regularly changing.

- Many of the current MCP exams will be republished in adaptive format in the coming months. Prepare yourself for this significant change in testing format; it is entirely likely that this will become the new preferred MCP exam format.

These changes mean that the brute-force strategies for passing MCP exams may soon completely lose their viability. So if you don't pass an exam on the first or second attempt, it is entirely possible that the exam will change significantly in form. It could be updated to adaptive form from fixed-form or have a different set of questions or question types.

The intention of Microsoft is clearly not to make the exams more difficult by introducing unwanted change. Their intent is to create and maintain valid measures of the technical skills and knowledge associated with the different MCP credentials. Preparing for an MCP exam has always involved not only studying the subject matter, but also planning for the testing experience itself. With these changes, this is now more true than ever.

Glossary

10BASE-2 An Ethernet topology that supports 10Mbps, uses baseband signals and can span 200 meters. Also called Thinnet.

10BASE-5 An Ethernet topology that supports 10Mbps, uses baseband signals and can span 500 meters. Also called Thicknet.

10BASE-FL An Ethernet topology that supports 10Mbps, uses baseband signals and fiber-optic cable.

10BASE-T An Ethernet topology that supports 10Mbps, uses baseband signals and twisted-pair wiring. Also known as UTP.

100BASE-X 100BASE-X provides a data transmission speed of 100Mbps using baseband. 100BASE-X supports many different cable standards.

100VG-AnyLAN Defined in the IEEE 802.12 standard for the transmitting of Ethernet and Token-Ring packets at 100Mbps. Uses four twisted-pair cables.

802.2 frame The default frame type used on Ethernet networks by all NetWare versions 3.12 and later.

802.3 frame This was the default frame type used in all Novell NetWare products versions 3.11 and earlier.

A

active hub A hub that has the ability to act as a repeater at the same time.

Address Resolution Protocol (ARP) ARP determines the physical address used by the device containing the IP address. ARP maintains tables of address resolution data and can broadcast packets to discover addresses on the network segment or use previously cached entries.

analog signal Analog signals constantly vary in one or more values, and these changes in values can be used to represent data. Analog waveforms frequently take the form of sine waves.

AppleTalk   AppleTalk is the computing architecture developed by Apple Computer for the Macintosh family of personal computers. Although AppleTalk originally supported only Apple's proprietary LocalTalk cabling system, the suite has been expanded to incorporate both Ethernet and Token-Ring Physical layers. Within Microsoft operating systems, AppleTalk is only supported by Windows NT Server.

Application layer   The seventh and top layer of the OSI model. This layer is concerned with the services provided on a network.

application server   A server that provides some high end application used by many different computers.

ARCNet   An older architecture that physically followed a physical bus or star topology and used a form of token passing to transmit data.

Asymmetric Digital Subscriber Line (ADSL) One new type of broadband WAN connectivity that is being tested by the telephone companies. Available only since 1997, ADSL is a Physical layer standard of sending data across existing telephone wires. By using a special ADSL modem, users can receive data at rates over 8Mbps and send data at rates of up to 640Kbps.

asynchronous modems   Do not use a clocking mechanism to keep the sending and receiving devices synchronized. Instead, this type of transmission uses bit synchronization to synchronize the devices for each frame that is transmitted.

Asynchronous Transfer Mode (ATM)   A high-bandwidth switching technology developed by the ITU Telecommunications Standards Sector (ITU-TSS). An organization called the ATM Forum is responsible for defining ATM implementation characteristics. ATM can be layered on other Physical layer technologies, such as Fiber Distributed Data Interface (FDDI) and SONET.

attenuation   The degradation of a signal, caused by travelling too far of a distance.

auditing   The process of creating a database that records particular events that occur on your network.

B

Backup Domain Controller (BDC)   The Backup Domain Controller's user account database is a replicated copy of that from the PDC.

bandwidth   The amount of data that a transmission medium can transfer.

base I/O port address   Defines a memory address through which data will flow to and from the adapter.

base memory address   A place in the computer's memory that marks the beginning of a buffer area reserved for the network adapter.

baseband   The entire bandwidth is used by a signal. Found in digital communications.

baseline   A sampling of how the network functions in its equilibrium state.

Basic Rate ISDN (BRI)   Basic Rate ISDN uses three channels. Two channels (called B channels) carry the digital data at 64Kbps. A third channel (called the D channel) provides link and signaling information at 16Kbps. Basic Rate ISDN thus is referred to as 2B+D. A single PC transmitting through ISDN can use both B channels simultaneously, providing a maximum data rate of 128Kbps (or higher with compression).

bindery An administrative model that is used by Novell NetWare versions up to NetWare 3.2 (all Novell servers that are version 4 or higher use directory services).

block interleaving A process that involves distributing the data block-by-block across the disk array in the same location across each disk. This is used by RAID 0.

Boot PROM Boot PROM allows the network card to boot up and connect over the network, as the Boot PROM has the necessary connection software to use.

bounded media A physical form of media, such as a cable.

boundless media A wireless form of media, such as radio waves.

bridges Bridges know the side of the bridge on which a node is located. A bridge passes only packets addressed to computers across the bridge, so a bridge can thus filter traffic, reducing the load on the transmission medium.

broadband The bandwidth contains many signals at once.

Broadband ISDN (B-ISDN) A refinement of ISDN that is defined to support higher-bandwidth applications, such as video, imaging, and

multimedia. Physical layer support for B-ISDN is provided by Asynchronous Transfer Mode (ATM) and the Synchronous Optical Network (SONET).

broadcast storm A sudden flood of broadcast messages that clogs the transmission medium, approaching use of 100 percent of the bandwidth. Broadcast storms cause performance to decline and, in the worst case, computers cannot even access the network.

brouter A device that is a combination of a bridge and router.

bus topology A topology in which all devices connect to a common shared cable.

C

cable modem This device allows networks to interconnect through existing cable TV lines. Some areas that offer this service have a full duplex version that allows transmission rates of 4- to 10Mbps. Other areas have cable standards in place that only allow the coaxial TV cable to receive data, relying upon an analog dial-up connection to be used to send data.

campus area network (CAN) A network that spans a campus.

centralized computing A form of computing where all the processing is done by one central computer.

circuit switching A mechanism for moving data requiring a constant physical circuit.

client/server   A networking model where a specific role of providing services or acting as a client (but not both) is performed by a computer.

clocking   The mechanism used to count and pace the number of signals being sent and received.

coaxial cable   A type of cabling using a solid metal core surrounded by a plastic sheath.

collaborative or cooperative computing   A form of computing where certain tasks are processed by one computer, and other specific tasks are performed by other computers.

concentrator   This is a term for a hub or MSAU. A connectivity device used to connect multiple twisted-pair cables together.

connection oriented   In connection-oriented mode, the chain of links between the source and destination nodes forms a kind of logical pathway connection. The nodes forwarding the data packet can track which packet is part of which connection. This enables the internal nodes to provide flow control as the data moves along the path.

connectionless   Connectionless mode does not provide elaborate internal control mechanisms; instead, connectionless mode relegates all error-correcting and retransmitting processes to the source and destination nodes. The end nodes acknowledge the receipt of packets and retransmit if necessary, but internal nodes do not participate in flow control and error correction (other than simply forwarding messages between the end nodes).

connector type   The connection between the network adapter card and the transmission media.

contention   Computers contend for use of the transmission medium. Any computer in the network can transmit at any time (first come, first serve).

Copy   This is a Microsoft NT NTBACKUP utility–specific command. This command backs up all selected files, but does not modify the archive bit of those files being backed up. This is a useful option if you wish to do a backup outside the regular backup schedule and do not wish to alter the normal backup routine.

current state   A mechanism that uses the clock count to analyze the current state of the signal during that count. Thus the signal is either "on" or "off" during the clock count.

D

Daily Copy   This is a Microsoft NT NTBACKUP utility–specific command. This command backs up only those files that were changed the day that this option is selected, when doing a Daily Copy backup, and does not modify the archive bit of the files being backed up. This is a useful option if you wish to do a backup outside the regular back up schedule and do not wish to alter the normal backup routine.

data bus   A pathway inside your computer that carries data between the hardware components.

Data Link Control (DLC)   DLC is not a protocol that can be used to connect Windows NT or 95 computers together.

Data Link layer   The second from the bottom layer of the OSI model. This layer is concerned with relating the access methods to the transmission media.

data migration   The moving of data from one location to another.

data striping   The capability of arranging data in different sequences across drives. Microsoft calls this disk striping.

database service   A service that provides access to a database by many different computers.

datagram packet switching   Datagram services treat each packet as an independent message. Each packet is routed through the internetwork independently, and each switch node determines which network segment should be used for the next step in the packet's route. This capability enables switches to bypass busy segments and take other steps to speed packets through the internetwork.

differential backup   Backs up the specified files if the files have changed since the last backup. This type doesn't mark the files as having been backed up, however. (A differential backup is somewhat like a copy command. Because the file is not marked as having been backed up, a later differential or incremental backup will back up the file again.)

Digital Data Service (DDS)   A very basic form of digital service. DDS transmits point-to-point at 2.4-, 4.8-, 9.6-, or 56Kbps. In its most basic form, DDS provides a dedicated line.

digital signal   Signals that have two discrete states. These states are either "off" or "on."

digital volt meters   Hand-held electronic measuring tools that enable you to check the voltage of network cables. They also can be used to check the resistance of terminators.

directory services   A hierarchical distributed database model. This model allows for the management of all resources through one utility as well as providing a high level of fault tolerance within the system.

directory services   A service that provides location information of devices and services on the network. Also known as x.500.

disk duplexing   Disk mirroring when adding a separate drive controller for each drive. Duplexing is a form of mirroring that enables you to configure a more robust hardware environment. Known also as RAID 1.

disk mirroring   Two hard drives—one primary, one secondary—that use the same disk channel or controller cards and cable. Disk mirroring is most commonly configured by using disk drives contained in the server. Known also as RAID 1.

disk striping   See data striping.

disk striping with parity   Also known as RAID 5, this form of fault-tolerance requires three or more drives. It involves striping data and a parity across all drives being used. If any one drive fails, the data on that drive can be reconstructed by using the parity bits and data found on the other drives.

distance vector routing   A routing algorithm that utilizes constant broadcasts to send out routing tables to other routers.

distributed computing   A form of computing where all the processing is shared by many different computers.

DMA channel   The DMA or Direct Memory Access channel is an address used for quicker access to the CPU by the adapter card.

domain   A security model that uses a flat user account database similar to the bindery model. The main difference is that this database is stored on one or more computers known as Domain Controllers.

Domain Name System (DNS)   The Domain Name System (DNS) protocol provides host name and IP address resolution as a service to client applications. DNS servers enable humans to use logical node names, utilizing a fully qualified domain name structure, to access network resources. Host names can be up to 260 characters long.

Dynamic Host Configuration Protocol (DHCP)   DHCP allows for the automatic assignment of IP addresses. This is usually performed by one or more computers (DHCP servers) that will assign IP addresses and subnet masks, along with other configuration information, to a computer as a computer initializes on the network.

dynamic router   A router that can utilize a routing protocol to exchange information with other routers to build a routing table.

E

ElectroMagnetic Interference (EMI)
Interference caused by electromagnetic waves.

electromagnetic spectrum   The range of electromagnetic waves.

email   Electronic mail.

encryption   Encryption codes the information sent on the network using a special algorithm and then decodes it on the other end. This technique offers varying degrees of safety, largely based on the length and complexity of the code used to encrypt the data.

Ethernet   A network architecture that follows the IEEE 802.3 set of standards.

Ethernet II frame type   Ethernet II frame types are similar to 802.3 frame types, except they contain a type field instead of a length field. This frame type can also be used with TCP/IP and AppleTalk.

Ethernet_SNAP frame   Ethernet_SNAP can be used for TCP/IP and AppleTalk Phase II transport protocols, as well as for IPX/SPX on Ethernet networks.

Event Viewer   A Windows NT utility that creates logs containing a record of previous errors, warnings, and other messages from the system. Studying the event log can help you find recurring errors and discover when a problem first appeared.

F

fax service   Services providing a shared fax to many computers.

FDDI   A token passing architecture that uses fiber-optic cable.

fiber-optic cable A type of cable that uses light to transmit data.

file archiving The movement of files to a near or off-line storage.

file service Services allowing for the storage and access of files.

file transfer The moving of a file from one location to another.

File Transfer Protocol (FTP) FTP is a protocol for sharing files between networked hosts. FTP enables users to log on to remote hosts. Logged-on users can inspect directories, manipulate files, execute commands, and perform other commands on the host. FTP also has the capability of transferring files between dissimilar hosts by supporting a file request structure that is independent of specific operating systems.

file-level security Security applied to files and directories on NTFS partitions.

file-update synchronization The updating of many copies of a file at once.

Frame Relay Designed to support the Broadband Integrated Services Digital Network (B-ISDN), which was discussed in the previous section. The specifications for Frame Relay address some of the limitations of X.25. As with X.25, Frame Relay is a packet-switching network service, but Frame Relay was designed around newer, faster fiber-optic networks.

frequency-division multiplexing Multiplexing that sends different data using different signals.

full backup Backs up all specified files.

G

gateway A device that can translate the different protocols used by different networks. Gateways can be implemented starting at the Network layer or at higher layers in the OSI model, depending on where the protocol translation is required. A gateway replaces the necessary protocol layers of a packet so that the packet can circulate in the destination environment.

global groups Created only on the Primary Domain Controller of a Microsoft domain. Backup Domain Controllers receive a copy of this database, thus they also contain global groups. These groups function primarily as containers for user accounts. Global Groups are designed to contain general groupings of people, such as Sales, Accounting, or the IS department. Global groups cannot contain other groups; only users from the domain the global group is created in, are permitted to be part of a global group.

groups Administrative units that are comprised of one or more users with similar needs for network resources. Often users are placed into groups, and resource access is managed on a group basis, as opposed to an individual user basis.

groupware An application that allows access to many users at once for the distribution of information.

H

hop count This method describes the number of routers that a message might cross before it reaches its destination. If all hops are assumed to take the same amount of time, the optimum path is the path with the smallest hop count.

I, J, K

IBM cabling   Another name for STP cabling.

IEEE   The Institute of Electronic and Electrical Engineers. This is an international body that sets standards for electronic devices.

IEEE 802 family   A set of networking standards developed by the IEEE.

incremental backup   Backs up only those files that have changed since the last full or incremental backup.

infrared transmissions   Infrared transmissions typically are limited to 100 feet. Within this range, however, infrared is relatively fast. Infrared's high bandwidth supports transmission speeds of up to 10Mbps.

Integrated Services Digital Network (ISDN) A group of ITU (CCITT) standards designed to provide voice, video, and data transmission services on digital telephone networks. ISDN uses multiplexing to support multiple channels on high-bandwidth circuits.

intelligent hub   A hub that can allow management and/or the ability to perform switching.

International Standards Organization (ISO) International body responsible for setting standards for many things, including certain network standards.

Internet   The term used to describe the far-flung, worldwide set of services provided by the interconnection of LANs and WANs through the TCP/IP networking protocol.

Internet Control Message Protocol (ICMP) ICMP enhances the error control provided by IP. Connectionless protocols, such as IP, cannot detect internetwork errors, such as congestion or path failures. ICMP can detect such errors and notify IP and upper-layer protocols.

Internet Protocol (IP)   A connectionless protocol that provides datagram service, and IP packets are most commonly referred to as IP datagrams. IP is a packet-switching protocol that performs the addressing and route selection. IP operates at the Network layer of the OSI model.

internetwork   Multiple independent networks that are connected and can share remote resources.

Internetwork Packet Exchange (IPX)   A Network layer protocol that provides connectionless (datagram) service. IPX is responsible for internetwork routing and maintaining network logical addresses.

intranet   A term used to describe your network.

IPX/SPX   A protocol suite developed by Xerox and used by Novell operating systems.

IRQ   The IRQ (Interrupt Request Line) setting reserves an interrupt request line for the adapter to use when contacting the CPU.

L

laser transmissions   High-powered laser transmitters can transmit data for several thousand yards when line-of-sight communication is possible. Lasers can be used in many of the same situations as microwave links without requiring an FCC license.

learning bridge   Also known as a transparent bridge. This type of bridge is transparent to the device sending the packet. At the same time, this bridge will learn over time what devices exist on each side of it.

leased lines   Telephone lines that are leased for dedicated use by a company or individual.

link state routing   A routing algorithm that only sends out route table changes.

local area network (LAN)   A network characterized by high throughput, short distances to be traveled, and all systems controlled by the company owning the network.

local groups   Local groups can be created on Windows NT Server or Workstation and can include both user accounts and global groups. Moreover, these groups are assigned permissions.

logical topology   Describes the logical pathway a signal follows as it passes among the network nodes.

M

MAC address   These addresses are hexadecimal in nature and are unique for each card. Each MAC address is assigned by the manufacturer. It is sometimes referred to as the network adapter card's hardware address.

Management Information Base (MIB)   A MIB is a database of information that can be read by management software designed to work with SNMP. Some examples of this management software is IBM's OpenView.

mesh topology   A topology in which every device is connected to every other device on the network. When a new device is added, a connection to all existing devices must be made.

message switching   A store-and-forward mechanism of moving data.

message/communication services   A service that transfers messages and or communications to many different computers.

modem   A device that converts a computer's digital signal to an analog signal for transmission of information over a telephone line.

multiplexing   The ability to send many different signals over a single transmission media.

municipal area network (MAN)   A network that spans a municipality.

N

narrow-band radio   In narrow-band radio communications (also called single-frequency radio), transmissions occur at a single radio frequency.

NDIS (Network Data Link Interface Standard)   A Microsoft standard for network card drivers.

NetBEUI   A transport protocol that serves as an extension to Microsoft's Network Basic Input/Output System (NetBIOS). Because NetBEUI was developed for an earlier generation of DOS-based PCs, it is small, easy to implement, and fast. NetBEUI is non-routable, making it somewhat anachronistic in today's diverse and interconnected networking environment.

NetBEUI is also a broadcast-based protocol, which can cause congestion in larger networks.

NetWare Core Protocol (NCP)   The NetWare Core Protocol provides numerous function calls that support network services, such as file service, printing, name management, file locking, and synchronization. NetWare client software interfaces with NCP to access NetWare services.

NetWare Link Services Protocol (NLSP)   A link state routing protocol used by routers (NetWare servers with two or more adapter cards can act as routers) to advertise networks when their address tables change.

network   A set of interconnected systems with something to share.

Network File System (NFS)   Developed by Sun Microsystems, NFS is a family of file-access protocols that are a considerable advancement over FTP and Telnet. Since Sun made the NFS specifications available for public use, NFS has achieved a high level of popularity.

Network layer   The third layer of the OSI model. This layer is is concerned with the addressing locations on the network.

Network Monitor   A Microsoft program that analyzes frames coming and going, in real time, from the computer on which they run. Network Monitor records a number of statistics, including the percent of network utilization and the broadcasts per second. In addition, Network Monitor tabulates frame statistics (such as frames sent and received) for each network address.

NWLink   Microsoft's implementation of the IPX/SPX protocol suite.

O

ODI   Open Data Link Interface. A Novell standard for network card drivers.

Open Shortest Path First (OSPF)   The OSPF protocol is a link-state route-discovery protocol that is designed to overcome the limitations of RIP. On large internetworks, OSPF can identify the internetwork topology and improve performance by implementing load balancing and class-of-service routing.

oscilloscope   An oscilloscope measures fluctuations in signal voltage and can help find faulty or damaged cabling. Oscilloscopes are often more expensive electronic devices that show the signal fluctuations on a monitor.

OSI   The Open Systems Interconnection model. A reference model developed by the ISO to provide a framework for explaining networking concepts.

P, Q

packet   A unit of data that is transmitted across the transmission media.

packet switching   A mechanism for moving data by breaking the data down into many small packets. These packets are transported over many different routes and are reassembled at their destination.

peer-to-peer   A networking model where both the services and the client are performed by the same computer.

Performance Monitor   A Windows NT program that lets you monitor important system parameters for the computers on your network in real time. Performance Monitor can keep an eye on a large number of system parameters, providing a graphical or tabular profile of system and network trends.

Permanent Virtual Circuit (PVC)   A permanent route through the network that is always available to the customer. With a PVC, charges are still billed on a per-use basis.

Physical layer   Bottom layer of the OSI model. This layer of the OSI model deals with the transmission media.

physical topology   Describes the actual layout of the network transmission media.

Point-to-Point Protocol (PPP)   A standard similar to SLIP, but more robust. This standard will support NetBEUI and NWLink as well as TCP/IP.

polling   One device is responsible for polling the other devices to see if they are ready for the transmission or reception of data.

Presentation layer   The sixth layer from the bottom of the OSI model. This layer is concerned with hiding the bottom layers from the Application layer of the OSI model.

Primary Domain Controller (PDC)   Primary and Backup Domain Controllers perform essentially the same function. It is their role to store the user account database. The difference is that a PDC stores the master copy of this database. It is on this master copy that changes can occur. When a new user is added, the PDC's database is affected.

Primary Rate   Primary Rate supports 23 64Kbps B channels and one 64Kbps D channel. The D channel is used for signaling and management, and the B channels provide the data throughput.

printing services   Services that allow the sharing of a printer.

protocol   A set of rules used for communications.

protocol analyzers   Hardware or software products that are used to monitor network traffic, track network performance, and analyze packets. Protocol analyzers can identify bottlenecks, protocol problems, and malfunctioning network components.

PSTN (Public Switched Telephone Network)   Your typical phone system.

R

redirector service   A service that provides connectivity to a server service.

relative expense   This method calculates any defined measure of the cost (including the monetary cost) to use a given link.

Remote Terminal Emulation (Telnet)   Telnet enables PCs and workstations to function as dumb terminals in sessions with hosts on internetworks. Telnet implementations are available for most end-user platforms, including UNIX (of course), DOS, Windows, and Macintosh OS.

repeaters   Repeaters regenerate a signal and are used to expand LANs beyond cabling limits.

resource   Any component that you would like to use on the network. This could be anything from a file on another machine, to a printer located at the end of the hall, to even a certain task available by a specific program.

ring speed   The data transfer speed of a Token-Ring network. Possible values are 8Mbps and 16Mbps.

ring topology   Ring topologies are wired in a circle. Each node is connected to its neighbors on either side, and data passes around the ring in one direction only.

routers   Routers forward packets based on a logical (as opposed to a physical) address. Some routers can determine the best path for a packet based on routing algorithms.

Routing Information Protocol (RIP)   A protocol used in both the TCP/IP and IPX/SPX protocol suites for the automatic building and distribution of routing tables.

S

satellite microwave   Satellite microwave systems relay transmissions through communication satellites that operate in geosynchronous orbits 22,300 miles above the earth.

security   The process of giving "rights" or "permissions" to groups or users, so that they can access resources on the network. Different network operating systems use different terms to describe these types of security issues.

security service   A service that provides security on the network.

Sequenced Packet Exchange (SPX)   A Transport layer protocol that extends IPX to provide connection-oriented service with reliable delivery. Reliable delivery is ensured by retransmitting packets in the event of an error.

Serial Line Internet Protocol (SLIP)   This is a standard for moving data across a telephone line using the TCP/IP transport protocol.

Server Messaging Blocks (SMB)   Microsoft's equivalent to NCP packets. Like NCP packets, SMBs operate at the Application layer of the OSI model. SMBs allow machines on a Microsoft network to communicate with one another. Through the use of SMBs, file and print services can be shared. SMBs can use TCP/IP, NWLink (IPX/SPX), or NetBEUI.

server mirroring   The capability to have one server completely mirrored in all forms to another server. This would mean that if Server A went down for any reason whatsoever, such as a failed hard drive, a failed network card, or even a blown motherboard, the mirrored Server B would take over the duties of Server A.

server service   A service on Microsoft NT computers that provides file and print services.

Service Advertising Protocol (SAP)   The Service Advertising Protocol (SAP) provides location information by a device indicating what services it is offering. Devices can see each other on the network by listing the SAPs each server issues.

Session layer   This is the fifth layer from the bottom of the OSI model. This layer addresses session establishment between computers.

share-level security   Security applied to resources such as directories and printers that have been shared on the network.

sharing   Only by specifying that you want to grant others access to a resource—be it a directory, a CD-ROM drive, or a printer—do you make the resource available for use from remote computers and devices. A shared resource is simply a resource whose owner has leveraged networking to make it available for use by others.

shielded twisted-pair cable (STP)   A form of twisted-pair cabling that has EMI shielding.

Simple Mail Transport Protocol (SMTP)   A protocol for routing mail through internetworks. SMTP uses the TCP and IP protocols.

Simple Network Management Protocol (SNMP)   A general purpose method of managing remote devices on the network.

spanning tree algorithm   Enables complex Ethernet networks to use bridges while redundant routes exist. The algorithm enables the bridges to communicate and construct a logical network without redundant paths. The logical network is reconfigured if one of the paths fails.

spread-spectrum radio   Spread-spectrum radio transmission is a technique originally developed by the military to solve several communication problems. Spread-spectrum improves reliability, reduces sensitivity to interference and jamming, and is less vulnerable to eavesdropping than single-frequency radio.

star topology   Star topologies require that all devices connect to a central hub. The hub receives signals from other network devices and routes the signals to the proper destinations.

state transmission   State transmission relies on the change of the state of a network signal to represent a new transmission of data.

static router   A router that must have a manually programmed routing table.

Super Server   A hardware solution offered by several different hardware manufacturers. The idea behind a Super Server is that almost any piece of equipment can be changed on the Super Server without needing to shut down the server.

Switched 56   A dial-up version of the 56Kbps DDS. With Switched 56, users can dial other Switched 56 sites and pay only for the connect time.

Switched Multimegabit Digital Service (SMDS) Developed by Bell Communications Research in 1991, SMDS technology is related to ATM in that it transports data in 53-byte cells. SMDS is a connectionless Data Link layer service that supports cell switching at data rates of 1.544- to 45Mbps.

Switched Virtual Circuit (SVC)   SVC is created for a specific communication session and then disappears after the session. The next time the computers communicate, a different virtual circuit might be used.

synchronous modems   A simple, inexpensive technology ideally suited for transmitting small frames at irregular intervals by using start, stop, and parity bits added to each character being transmitted. Overhead for asynchronous transmission is high, often in the neighborhood of nearly 20 to 30 percent.

Synchronous Optical Network (SONET)   Bell Communications Research developed SONET, which has been accepted as an ANSI standard. As the "optical" in the name implies, SONET is a standard for communication over fiber-optic networks. Data rates for SONET are organized in a hierarchy based on the Optical Carrier (OC) speed and the corresponding Synchronous Transport Signals (STS) employed. The basic OC and STS data rate is 51.84Mbps, but higher data rates are provided in multiples of the basic rate.

System Monitor   A program that collects information on a Windows 95 machine in real time. System Manager collects information on different categories of items on the system.

T

T-connector   A T-shaped device used to connect network cards to thinnet cable.

T1   This leased line provides point-to-point connections and transmits a total of 24 channels across two wire pairs—one pair for sending and one for receiving—for a transmission rate of 1.544Mbps. A T1 is known as an E1 line in Europe.

T3   (E3 in Europe) is similar to T1, but T3 has an even higher capacity. In fact, a T3 line can transmit at up to 45Mbps. This is because a T3 line is made up of 672 64Kbps channels.

TCP/IP   Transmission Control Protocol / Internet Protocol. A set of protocols (protocol suite) and services used by many different operating systems and the Internet.

terrestrial microwave   Terrestrial microwave communication employs Earth-based transmitters and receivers. The frequencies used are in the low-gigahertz range, which limits all communications to line-of-sight.

thicknet   A form of coaxial cable that's thicker than thinnet.

thinnet   A form of coaxial cable that's thinner than thicknet.

tic count   This method provides an actual time estimate used in routers. A tic is a time unit as defined by the routing implementation.

time-division multiplexing   Multiplexing using different time intervals to send data.

Time-Domain Reflectometer (TDM)   TDMs send sound waves along a cable and look for imperfections that might be caused by a break or a short in the line. A good TDR will often be able to detect faults on a cable to within a few feet.

token passing   The computers take turns using the transmission medium. This is facilitated by the passing of a token. The machine in possession of the token is allowed to transmit.

Token-Ring   A network architecture that follows the IEEE 802.5 set of standards.

Token-Ring frame   There are two types of Token-Ring frames. One is used to carry management information, and the other is used to transfer data. Token-Ring frames are used on Token-Ring networks, and not Ethernet networks.

Token-Ring_SNAP frame The Token-Ring_SNAP provides a similar function as the Ethernet_SNAP frame type, but for Token-Ring networks.

Transmission Control Protocol (TCP) An internetwork connection-oriented protocol that corresponds to the OSI Transport layer. TCP provides full-duplex end-to-end connections.

transmission medium A pathway used to connect different resources on a network.

transparent bridge See learning bridge.

Transport layer The fourth layer of the OSI model. This layer covers the movement of data on the network.

twisted-pair cable A type of cable that has two or more wires twisted around each other. Telephone wire is a twisted-pair cable.

U, V

Uninterruptible Power Supply (UPS) A special battery (or sometimes a generator) that supplies power to an electronic device in the event of a power failure.

unshielded twisted-pair cable (UTP) A form of twisted-pair that has no shielding from EMI.

user Anyone who requests network resources. In most cases, you assign a unique username and password to every individual on your network.

User Datagram Protocol (UDP) The User Datagram Protocol (UDP) is a connectionless Transport (host-to-host) layer protocol. UDP does not provide message acknowledgments; rather, it simply transports datagrams. UDP operates at the Transport layer of the OSI model.

vampire clamp A device used to connect drop cables to Thicknet cables.

virtual circuit packet switching Virtual circuits operate by establishing a formal connection between two devices in communication. When devices begin a session, they negotiate communication parameters, such as maximum message size, communication windows, and network paths. This negotiation establishes a virtual circuit, which is a well-defined path through the internetwork by which the devices communicate. This virtual circuit generally remains in effect until the devices stop communicating.

viruses Viruses are created intentionally with the aim of injuring or altering your machines. Viruses can be spread through computer systems in many ways, but the most common is through an executable file.

voice mail The storage and movement of voice messages.

W, X, Y, Z

wide area network (WAN) A network characterized by low throughput, long distances to be traveled, and not all systems controlled by the company owning the network.

Windows Internet Naming Service (WINS)
WINS provides a function similar to that of DNS, with the exception that it provides NetBIOS names to IP address resolution.

wireless media   Transmission media that does not use a cable to transmit data.

workgroup   An administrative model used by peer-to-peer networking systems such as Windows 95 and Windows for Workgroups.

X.25   A packet-switching network standard developed by the International Telegraph and Telephone Consultative Committee (CCITT), which has been renamed the International Telecommunications Union (ITU). The standard, referred to as Recommendation X.25, was introduced in 1974 and is now implemented most commonly in WANs.

zone   An AppleTalk version of a workgroup. Multiple network segments can be joined to form a single zone, and a single segment can have multiple zones.

The contents of this book have examined the objectives and components of the Microsoft Networking Essentials exam. Now, what is it that you really need to know before gambling your $100 and pride?

The following material covers the salient points of the four previous chapters and the points that make excellent test fodder. Although there is no substitute for real-world, hands-on experience, knowing what to expect on the exam can be equally meaningful. The information that follows is the networking equivalent of Cliffs Notes, providing the information you must know in each of the four sections to pass the exam. Don't just memorize the concepts given; attempt to understand the reason why they are so and you will have no difficulties passing the exam.

STANDARDS AND TERMINOLOGY

The Standards and Terminology section is designed to test your understanding and knowledge of terms used in networking, as well as some of the more common standards that have been implemented in the industry.

Define Common Networking Terms for LANs and WANs

The Networking Essentials exam does not really test definitions of terms. Rather, the questions you are asked will be the basis for the next set of questions, and you will need to understand the definitions of the terms used in order to successfully answer them.

The best mechanism to study this area would be to review the key terms found in every chapter and provide the correct definition for each term. Below is a list of some of the more general networking terms of which you should be aware:

- **peer-to-peer networking**—a networking model where both the services and the client are performed by the same computer.

- **client/server networking**—a networking model where a specific role of providing services or acting as a client (not both) is performed by a computer.

- **centralized computing**—a form of computing where all the processing is done by one central computer.

- **distributed computing**—a form of computing where all the processing is shared by many different computers.

- **file services**—services allowing for the storage and access of files.

- **printer services**—services that allow the sharing of a printer.

- **file and printer server**—a server that provides file and printer services.

- **application server**—a server that provides some high-end application used by many different computers.

- **Token-Ring network**—a network that follows a logical topology of a ring, but a physical topology of a star. The computers are connected to a concentrator known as an MSAU or MAU. Computers rely on the possession of a token before the transmission of data on the network. This type of network is known as a deterministic network.

- **Ethernet network**—a type of a network that is run as a logical bus, but can take on the physical topology of a bus or a star. The concentrator used by these computers, when in a star topology, is called a hub. This type of network is known as a contention-based network because each device contends with every other device for network access.

- **LAN**—also known as a local area network. Often characterized by fast transmission speeds and short distances between devices, and by the fact that the company running the network has control over all devices and transmission media.

- **WAN**—also known as a wide area network. When compared to a LAN, a WAN is often characterized by lower data transmission rates and the coverage of long distances, and by the fact that a third party is involved with the supply and maintenance of the transmission media.

Compare a File and Printer Server with an Application Server

A file server is a service that is involved with giving access to files and directories on the network. The purpose of the file server is to give large numbers of users access to a centrally stored set of files and directories.

A printer server is a computer or device that gives large number of users access to a centrally maintained printing device. A computer that is a file server often acts as printer server, too. These types of computers are known as file and printer servers.

An application server is responsible for running applications such as Exchange Server or SQL Server on the network. Application servers perform services that often require a more advanced level of processing than a user's personal computer is able to provide.

Compare User-Level Security with Access Permission Assigned to a Shared Directory on a Server

User-level security is a security model in which access to resources is given on a user-by-user basis, a group-by-group basis, or both. This type of access restriction allows an administrator to grant access to resources and affords users seamless access to those resources. User-level security is offered by Windows NT in both the workgroup and domain models.

The permissions to a shared directory are:

- Read. The user is allowed to read files within a share. He can also see all files and subdirectories.

- Change. The user can modify existing files and directories and create new files and directories within the share.

- Full Control. The user can see, modify, delete, and take ownership of all files and directories within the share.

- No Access. The user cannot access any files or directories within the share.

Share-level permissions apply to anyone accessing the share over the network and do not apply to users who are interactive on the computer where the share resides. Share-level permissions can be set on both FAT and NTFS partitions.

Compare a Client/Server Network with a Peer-to-Peer Network

A client/server network is one in which a computer has a specific role. A server is a computer, often with more RAM, more hard drive space, and a faster CPU than the other machines. A server services requests from clients. These requests could be for the use of files and printers, application services, communication services, and database services.

Clients are the computers on which users work. These computers typically are not as powerful as servers. Client computers are designed to submit requests to the server.

Peer-to-peer networks are made up of several computers that play the roles of both a client and a server; thus there is no dedicated computer running file and printer services, application services, communication services, or database services.

Compare the Implications of Using Connection-Oriented Communications with Connectionless Communications

In general, connection-oriented communication differs from connectionless communication as follows:

- Connection-oriented mode. Error correction and flow control are provided at internal nodes along the message path.

- Connectionless mode. Internal nodes along the message path do not participate in error correction and flow control.

In connection-oriented mode, the chain of links between the source and destination nodes forms a kind of logical pathway connection. The nodes forwarding the data packet can track which packet is part of which connection. This enables the internal nodes to provide flow control as the data moves along the path. For example, if an internal node determines that a link is malfunctioning, the node can send a notification message backward through the path to the source computer. Furthermore, because the internal node distinguishes among individual, concurrent connections in which it participates, this node can transmit (or forward) a "stop sending" message for one of its connections without stopping all communications through the node. Another feature of connection-oriented communication is that internal nodes provide error correction at each link in the chain. Therefore, if a node detects an error, it asks the preceding node to retransmit.

SPX and TCP are two major examples of connection-oriented protocols.

Connectionless mode does not provide these elaborate internal control mechanisms; instead, connectionless mode relegates all error-correcting and retransmitting processes to the source and destination nodes. The end nodes acknowledge the receipt of packets and retransmit if necessary, but internal nodes do not participate in flow control and error correction (other than simply forwarding messages between the end nodes).

IPX and UDP are two major examples of connection-oriented protocols.

The advantage of connectionless mode is that connectionless communications can be processed more quickly and more simply because the internal nodes only forward data and thus don't have to track connections or provide retransmission or flow control.

Distinguish Whether SLIP or PPP Is Used as the Communications Protocol for Various Situations

Two other standards vital to network communication are Serial Line Internet Protocol (SLIP) and Point-to-Point Protocol (PPP). SLIP and PPP were designed to support dial-up access to networks based on the Internet transport protocols. SLIP is a simple protocol that functions at the Physical layer, whereas PPP is a considerably enhanced protocol that provides Physical layer and Data Link layer functionality.

Windows NT supports both SLIP and PPP from the client end using the Dial-Up Networking application. On the server end, Windows NT RAS (Remote Access Service) supports PPP but doesn't support SLIP. In other words, Windows NT can act as a PPP server but not as a SLIP server.

PPP

PPP was defined by the Internet Engineering Task Force (IETF) to improve on SLIP by providing the following features:

- Security using password logon
- Simultaneous support for multiple protocols on the same link
- Dynamic IP addressing
- Improved error control

Different PPP implementations might offer different levels of service and negotiate service levels when connections are made. Because of its versatility, interoperability, and additional features, PPP has surpassed SLIP as the most popular serial-line protocol.

SLIP

Developed to provide dial-up TCP/IP connections, SLIP is an extremely rudimentary protocol that suffers from a lack of rigid standardization in the industry, which sometimes hinders different vendor implementations of SLIP from operating with each other.

SLIP is most commonly used on older systems or for dial-up connections to the Internet via SLIP-server Internet hosts.

Certain dial-up configurations cannot use SLIP for the following reasons:

- SLIP supports the TCP/IP transport protocol only. PPP, however, supports TCP/IP, as well as a number of other transport protocols, such as NetBEUI, IPX, AppleTalk, and DECnet. In addition, PPP can support multiple protocols over the same link.

- SLIP requires static IP addresses. Because SLIP requires static, or preconfigured, IP addresses, SLIP servers do not support the Dynamic Host Configuration Protocol (DHCP), which assigns IP addresses dynamically or when requested. (DHCP enables clients to share IP addresses so that a relatively small number of IP addresses can serve a larger user base.) If the dial-up server uses DHCP to assign an IP address to the client, the dial-up connection won't use SLIP.

- SLIP does not support dynamic addressing through DHCP so SLIP connections cannot dynamically assign a WINS or DNS server.

Define the Communication Devices that Communicate at Each Level of the OSI Model

- Repeater. Operates at the Physical layer of the OSI model. The purpose of a repeater is to regenerate a signal, allowing a signal to travel beyond the maximum distance specified by the transmission media.

- Hub. Operates at the Physical layer. A hub is a concentrator that connects 10BASE-T cabling together on an Ethernet network. Some hubs also have the capability to act as a repeater.

- MSAU. Operates at the Physical layer. An MSAU performs the same purpose of a hub, but is used on token-ring networks.

- Network Interface Card (NIC). Operates at the Data Link layer. A NIC is responsible

for converting information in a computer to a signal that will be sent on the transmission media.

- Bridge. Operates at the Data Link layer of the OSI mode. A bridge is responsible for isolating network traffic on a cable segment. It performs this task by building address tables that contain the MAC address or hardware addresses of devices on ether side of it.

- Router. Operates at the Network layer of the OSI model. It is responsible for connecting different segments that have dissimilar logical network addresses.

- Gateway. Can appear at any level of the OSI model but is primarily seen at the Network layer and higher. The purpose of a gateway is to convert one network protocol to another.

Describe the Characteristics and Purpose of the Media Used in IEEE 802.3 and IEEE 802.5 Standards

The various media types used by the IEEE 802.3 and 802.5 are discussed below.

IEEE 802.3

This standard defines characteristics related to the MAC sublayer of the Data Link layer and the OSI Physical layer. Except for one minor distinction—frame type—IEEE 802.3 Ethernet functions identically to DIX Ethernet v.2.

The MAC sublayer uses a type of contention access called Carrier Sense Multiple Access with Collision Detection (CSMA/CD). This technique reduces the incidence of collision by having each device listen to the network to determine whether it is quiet ("carrier sensing"); a device attempts to transmit only when the network is quiescent. This reduces but does not eliminate collisions because signals take some time to propagate through the network. As devices transmit, they continue to listen so they can detect a collision should it occur. When a collision occurs, all devices cease transmitting and send a "jamming" signal that notifies all stations of the collision. Each device then waits a random amount of time before attempting to transmit again. This combination of safeguards significantly reduces collisions on all but the busiest networks.

The IEEE 802.3 Physical layer definition describes signaling methods (both baseband and broadband), data rates, media, and topologies. Several Physical layer variants also have been defined. Each variant is named following a convention that states the signaling rate (1 or 10) in Mbps, baseband (BASE) or broadband (BROAD) mode, and a designation of the media characteristics.

The following list details the IEEE 802.3 variants of transmission media:

- lBASE-5. This 1Mbps network utilizes UTP cable with a signal range up to 500 meters (250 meters per segment). A star physical topology is used.

- 10BASE-5. Typically called Thick Ethernet, or Thicknet, this variant uses a large diameter (10mm) "thick" coaxial cable with a 50ohm impedance. A data rate of 10Mbps is supported with a signaling range of 500 meters per cable segment on a physical bus topology.

- 10BASE-2. Similar to Thicknet, this variant uses a thinner coaxial cable that can support cable runs of 185 meters. (In this case, the "2" only indicates an approximate cable range.) The transmission rate remains at 10Mbps, and the physical topology is a bus. This variant typically is called Thin Ethernet, or Thinnet.

- 10BASE-F. This variant uses fiber-optic cables to support 10Mbps signaling with a range of four kilometers. Three subcategories include 10BASE-FL (fiber link), 10BASE-FB (fiber backbone), and 10BASE-FP (fiber passive).

- 10BROAD36. This broadband standard supports channel signal rates of 10Mbps. A 75ohm coaxial cable supports cable runs of 1,800 meters (up to 3,600 meters in a dual-cable configuration) using a physical bus topology.

- 10BASE-T. This variant uses UTP cable in a star physical topology. The signaling rate remains at 10Mbps, and devices can be up to 100 meters from a wiring hub.

- 100BASE-X. This proposed standard is similar to 10BASE-T but supports 100Mbps data rates.

IEEE 802.5

The IEEE 802.5 standard was derived from IBM's Token-Ring network, which employs a ring logical topology and token-based media-access control. Data rates of 1-, 4-, and 16Mbps have been defined for this standard.

Explain the Purpose of NDIS and Novell ODI Network Standards

The Network Driver Interface Specification (NDIS), a standard developed by Microsoft and the 3Com Corporation, describes the interface between the network transport protocol and the Data Link layer network adapter driver. The following list details the goals of NDIS:

- To provide a vendor-neutral boundary between the transport protocol and the network adapter card driver so that an NDIS-compliant protocol stack can operate with an NDIS-compliant adapter driver.

- To define a method for binding multiple protocols to a single driver so that the adapter can simultaneously support communications under multiple protocols. In addition, the method enables you to bind one protocol to more than one adapter.

The Open Data-Link Interface (ODI), developed by Apple and Novell, serves the same function as NDIS. Originally, ODI was written for NetWare and Macintosh environments. Like NDIS, ODI provides rules that establish a vendor-neutral interface between the protocol stack and the adapter driver. This interface also enables one or more network drivers to support one or more protocol stacks.

PLANNING

The planning section on the exam tests your ability to apply networking components and standards when designing a network.

Select the Appropriate Media for Various Situations

Media choices include:

- Twisted-pair cable
- Coaxial cable
- Fiber-optic cable
- Wireless

Situational elements include:

- Cost
- Distance limitations
- Number of nodes

Summary Table 1 outlines the characteristics of the cable types discussed in this section.

Summary Table 2 compares the different types of wireless communication media in terms of cost, ease of installation, distance, and other issues.

SUMMARY TABLE 1   COMPARISON OF CABLE MEDIA

Cable Type	Cost	Installation	Capacity	Range	EMI
Coaxial Thinnet	Less than STP	Inexpensive/ easy	10Mbps typical	185m	Less sensitive than UTP
Coaxial Thicknet	Greater than STP Less than Fiber	Easy	10Mbps typical	500m	Less sensitive than UTP
Shielded Twisted-Pair (STP)	Greater than UTP Less than Thicknet	Fairly easy	16Mbps typical up to 500Mbps	100m typical	Less sensitive than UTP
Unshielded twisted-pair (UTP)	Lowest	Inexpensive/ easy	10Mbps typical up to 100Mbps	100m typical	Most sensitive
Fiber-optic	Highest	Expensive/ difficult	100Mbps typical	Tens of Kilometers	Insensitive

The summary table below compares the different types of wireless communication media in terms of cost, ease of installation, distance, and other issues.

SUMMARY TABLE 2   COMPARISON OF WIRELESS MEDIA

Cable Type	Cost	Installation	Distance	Other Issues
Infrared	Cheapest of all the wireless	Fairly easy; may require line of sight	Under a kilometer	Can attenuate due to fog and rain
Laser	Similar to infrared	Requires line of sight	Can span several kilometers	Can attenuate due to fog and rain
Narrow band radio	More expensive than Infrared and laser; may need FCC license	Requires trained technicians and can involve tall radio towers	Can span hundreds of kilometers	Low power devices can attenuate; can be eaves-dropped upon; can also attenuate due to fog, rain, and solar flares
Spread spectrum radio	More advanced technology than Narrow band radio, thus more expensive	Requires trained technicians and can involve tall radio towers	Can span hundreds of kilometers	Low power devices can attenuate; can also attenuate due to fog, rain, and solar flares

Cable Type	Cost	Installation	Distance	Other Issues
Microwave	Very expensive as it requires link to satellites often	Requires trained technicians and can involve satellite dishes	Can span thousands of kilometers	Can be eavesdropped upon; can also attenuate due to fog, rain, and solar flares

Select the Appropriate Topology for Various Token-Ring and Ethernet Networks

The following four topologies are implemented by Ethernet and Token-Ring networks:

- Ring. Ring topologies are wired in a circle. Each node is connected to its neighbors on either side, and data passes around the ring in one direction only. Each device incorporates a receiver and a transmitter and serves as a repeater that passes the signal to the next device in the ring. Because the signal is regenerated at each device, signal degeneration is low. Most ring topologies are logical, and implemented as physical stars. Token-Ring networks follow a ring topology.

- Bus. Star topologies require that all devices connect to a central hub. The hub receives signals from other network devices and routes the signals to the proper destinations. Star hubs can be interconnected to form tree or hierarchical network topologies. A star physical topology is often used to physically implement a bus or ring logical topology that is used by both Ethernet and Token-Ring networks.

- Star. Star topologies require that all devices connect to a central hub. The hub receives signals from other network devices and routes the signals to the proper destinations. Star hubs can be interconnected to form tree or hierarchical network topologies. A star physical topology is often used to physically implement a bus or ring logical topology that is used by both Ethernet and Token-Ring networks.

- Mesh. A mesh topology is really a hybrid model representing a physical topology because a mesh topology can incorporate all of the previous topologies. The difference is that in a mesh topology every device is connected to every other device on the network. When a new device is added, a connection to all existing devices must be made. Mesh topologies can be used by both Ethernet and Token-Ring networks.

Select the Appropriate Network and Transport Protocol or Protocols for Various Token-Ring and Ethernet Networks

Protocol choices include:

- DLC
- AppleTalk
- IPX
- TCP/IP
- NFS
- SMB

Data Link Control (DLC)

The Data Link Control (DLC) protocol does not provide a fully functioning protocol stack. In Windows NT systems, DLC is used primarily to access to Hewlett-Packard JetDirect network-interface printers. DLC also provides some connectivity with IBM mainframes. It is not a protocol that can be used to connect Windows NT or 95 computers together.

AppleTalk

AppleTalk is the computing architecture developed by Apple Computer for the Macintosh family of personal computers. Although AppleTalk originally supported only Apple's proprietary LocalTalk cabling system, the suite has been expanded to incorporate both Ethernet and Token-Ring Physical layers. Within Microsoft operating systems, AppleTalk is only supported by Windows NT Server. Windows NT Workstation and Windows 95 do not support AppleTalk. AppleTalk cannot be used for Microsoft to Microsoft

operating system communication, only by NT servers supporting Apple clients.

The LocalTalk, EtherTalk, and TokenTalk Link Access Protocols (LLAP, ELAP, and TLAP) integrate AppleTalk upper-layer protocols with the LocalTalk, Ethernet, and Token-Ring environments.

Apple's Datagram Deliver Protocol (DDP) is a Network layer protocol that provides connectionless service between two sockets. The AppleTalk Transaction Protocol (ATP) is a connectionless Transport layer protocol. Reliable service is provided through a system of acknowledgments and retransmissions. The AppleTalk File Protocol (AFP) provides file services and is responsible for translating local file service requests into formats required for network file services. AFP directly translates command syntax and enables applications to perform file format translations. AFP is responsible for file system security and verifies and encrypts logon names and passwords during connection setup.

IPX

The Internetwork Packet Exchange Protocol (IPX) is a Network layer protocol that provides connectionless (datagram) service. (IPX was developed from the XNS protocol originated by Xerox.) As a Network layer protocol, IPX is responsible for internetwork routing and maintaining network logical addresses. Routing uses the RIP protocol (described later in this section) to make route selections. IPX provides similar functionality as UDP does in the TCP/IP protocol suite.

IPX relies on hardware physical addresses found at lower layers to provide network device addressing. IPX also uses sockets, or upper-layer service addresses, to deliver packets to their ultimate destinations. On the client, IPX support is provided as a component of the older DOS shell and the current DOS NetWare requester.

TCP/IP

TCP/IP is a broad protocol that covers many different areas. This summary presents some of the most important protocols within the TCP/IP protocol suite.

Internet Protocol (IP)

The Internet Protocol (IP) is a connectionless protocol that provides datagram service, and IP packets are most commonly referred to as IP datagrams. IP is a packet-switching protocol that performs the addressing and route selection.

IP performs packet disassembly and reassembly as required by packet size limitations defined for the Data Link and Physical layers being implemented. IP also performs error checking on the header data using a checksum, although data from upper layers is not error-checked.

Transmission Control Protocol (TCP)

The Transmission Control Protocol (TCP) is an internetwork connection-oriented protocol that corresponds to the OSI Transport layer. TCP provides full-duplex, end-to-end connections. When the overhead of end-to-end communication acknowledgment isn't required, the User Datagram Protocol (UDP) can be substituted for TCP at the Transport (host-to-host) level. TCP and UDP operate at the same layer.

TCP corresponds to SPX in the NetWare environment (see the NetWare IPX/SPX section). TCP maintains a logical connection between the sending and receiving computer systems. In this way, the integrity of the transmission is maintained. TCP detects any problems in the transmission quickly and takes action to correct them. The

tradeoff is that TCP isn't as fast as UDP, due to the number of acknowledgments received by the sending host.

TCP also provides message fragmentation and reassembly and can accept messages of any length from upper-layer protocols. TCP fragments message streams into segments that can be handled by IP. When used with IP, TCP adds connection-oriented service and performs segment synchronization, adding sequence numbers at the byte level.

Windows Internet Naming Services (WINS)

Windows Internet Naming Service (WINS) provides a function similar to that of DNS, with the exception that it provides a NetBIOS name to IP address resolution. This is important because all of Microsoft's networking requires the capability to reference NetBIOS names. Normally NetBIOS names are obtained with the issuance of broadcasts, but because routers normally do not forward broadcasts, a WINS server is one alternative that can be used to issue IP addresses to NetBIOS name requests. WINS servers replace the need for LMHOSTS files on a computer.

Domain Name System (DNS)

The Domain Name System (DNS) protocol provides host name and IP address resolution as a service to client applications. DNS servers enable humans to use logical node names, utilizing a fully qualified domain name structure to access network resources. Host names can be up to 260 characters long. DNS servers replace the need for HOSTS files on a computer.

Network File System (NFS)

Network File System (NFS), developed by Sun Microsystems, is a family of file-access protocols that are a considerable advancement over FTP and Telnet. Since Sun made the NFS specifications available for public use, NFS has achieved a high level of popularity.

Server Messaging Blocks (SMB)

One protocol that is slightly independent is Microsoft's Server Messaging Blocks (SMB). SMBs are Microsoft's equivalent to NCP packets. Like NCP packets, SMBs operate at the Application layer of the OSI model.

SMBs allow machines on a Microsoft network to communicate with one another. Through the use of SMBs, file and print services can be shared. SMBs can use TCP/IP, NWLink (IPX/SPX), and NetBEUI because SMBs utilize a NetBIOS interface when communicating. For more information on NetBIOS names, see the following section.

Select the Appropriate Connectivity Devices for Various Token-Ring and Ethernet Networks

Connectivity devices include:

- Repeaters. Repeaters regenerate a signal and are used to expand LANs beyond cabling limits.

- Bridges. Bridges know the side of the bridge on which a node is located. A bridge passes only packets addressed to computers across the bridge, so a bridge can thus filter traffic, reducing the load on the transmission medium.

- Routers. Routers forward packets based on a logical (as opposed to a physical) address. Some routers can determine the best path for a packet based on routing algorithms.

- Brouters. A brouter is a device that is a combination of a bridge and a router, providing both types of services.

- Gateways. Gateways function under a process similar to routers except that gateways can connect dissimilar network environments. A gateway replaces the necessary protocol layers of a packet so that the packet can circulate in the destination environment.

List the Characteristics, Requirements, and Appropriate Situations for WAN Connection Services

WAN connection services include:

- X.25
- ISDN
- Frame relay
- ATM

X.25

X.25 is a packet-switching network standard developed by the International Telegraph and Telephone Consultative Committee (CCITT), which has been renamed the International Telecommunications Union (ITU). The standard, referred to as Recommendation X.25, was introduced in 1974 and is now implemented most commonly in WANs.

At the time X.25 was developed, this flow control and error checking was essential because X.25 was developed around relatively unreliable telephone line communications. The drawback is that error checking and flow control slow down X.25. Generally, X.25 networks are implemented with line speeds up to 64Kbps, although actual throughput seems slower due to the error correction controls in place. These speeds are suitable for the file transfer and terminal activity that comprised the bulk of network traffic when X.25 was defined, most of this traffic being terminal connections to mainframes. Such speeds, however, are inadequate to provide LAN-speed services, which typically require speeds of 1Mbps or better. X.25 networks, therefore, are poor choices for providing LAN application services in a WAN environment. One advantage of X.25, however, is that it is an established standard that is used internationally. This, as well as lack of other services throughout the world, means that X.25 is more of a connection service to Africa, South America, and Asia, where a lack of other services prevails.

ISDN

The original idea behind ISDN was to enable existing phone lines to carry digital communications, and it was at one time touted as a replacement to traditional analog lines. Thus, ISDN is more like traditional telephone service than some of the other WAN services. ISDN is intended as a dial-up service and not as a permanent 24-hour connection.

ISDN separates the bandwidth into channels. Based upon how these channels are used, ISDN can be separated into two classes of service:

- Basic Rate (BRI).   Basic Rate ISDN uses three channels. Two channels (called B channels) carry the digital data at 64Kbps. A third channel (called the D channel) provides link and signaling information at 16Kbps. Basic Rate ISDN thus is referred to as 2B+D. A single PC transmitting through ISDN can use both B channels simultaneously, providing a maximum data rate of 128 Kbps (or higher with compression).

- Primary Rate (PRI).   Primary Rate supports 23 64Kbps B channels and one 64Kbps D channel. The D channel is used for signaling and management, whereas the B channels provide the data throughput.

In a BRI line, if the line was currently being used for voice, this would only allow one of the B channels to be available for data. This effectively reduces the throughput of the BRI to 64Kbps.

Frame Relay

Frame Relay was designed to support the Broadband Integrated Services Digital Network (B-ISDN), which was discussed in the previous section. The specifications for Frame Relay address some of the limitations of X.25. As with X.25, Frame Relay is a packet-switching network service, but Frame Relay was designed around newer, faster fiber-optic networks.

Unlike X.25, Frame Relay assumes a more reliable network. This enables Frame Relay to eliminate much of the X.25 overhead required to provide reliable service on less reliable networks. Frame Relay relies on higher-level protocol layers to provide flow and error control.

Frame Relay typically is implemented as a public data network and, therefore, is regarded as a WAN protocol. The scope of Frame Relay, with respect to the OSI model, is limited to the Physical and Data Link layers.

Frame Relay provides permanent virtual circuits that supply permanent virtual pathways for WAN connections. Frame Relay services typically are implemented at line speeds from 56Kbps up to 1.544Mbps (T1).

Customers typically purchase access to a specific amount of bandwidth on a frame-relay service. This bandwidth is called the committed information rate (CIR), a data rate for which the customer is guaranteed access. Customers might be permitted to access higher data rates on a pay-per-use temporary basis. This arrangement enables customers to tailor their network access costs based on their bandwidth requirements.

To use Frame Relay, you must have special Frame Relay-compatible connectivity devices (such as frame-relay-compatible routers and bridges).

Asynchronous Transfer Mode (ATM)

Asynchronous Transfer Mode (ATM) is a high-bandwidth switching technology developed by the ITU Telecommunications Standards Sector (ITU-TSS). An organization called the ATM Forum is responsible for defining ATM implementation characteristics. ATM can be layered on other Physical layer technologies, such as Fiber Distributed Data Interface (FDDI) and SONET.

Several characteristics distinguish ATM from other switching technologies. ATM is based on fixed-length 53-byte cells, whereas other technologies employ frames that vary in length to accommodate different amounts of data. Because ATM cells are uniform in length, switching mechanisms can operate with a high level of efficiency. This high efficiency results in high data transfer rates. Some ATM systems can operate at an incredible rate of

622Mbps; a typical working speed for an ATM is around 155Mbps.

The unit of transmission for ATM is called a cell. All cells are 53 bytes long and consist of a 5-byte header and 48 bytes of data. The 48-byte data size was selected by the standards committee as a compromise to suit both audio- and data-transmission needs. Audio information, for instance, must be delivered with little latency (delay) to maintain a smooth flow of sound. Audio engineers therefore preferred a small cell so that cells would be more readily available when needed. For data, however, large cells reduce the overhead required to deliver a byte of information.

Asynchronous delivery is another distinguishing feature of ATM. "Asynchronous" refers to the characteristic of ATM in which transmission time slots don't occur periodically but are granted at irregular intervals. ATM uses a technique called label multiplexing, which allocates time slots on demand. Traffic that is time-critical, such as voice or video, can be given priority over data traffic that can be delayed slightly with no ill effect. Channels are identified by cell labels, not by specific time slots. A high-priority transmission need not be held until its next time slot allocation. Instead, it might be required to wait only until the current 53-byte cell has been transmitted.

IMPLEMENTATION

The Implementation section of the exam tests your knowledge of how to implement, test, and manage an installed network.

Choosing an Administrative Plan to Meet Specified Needs, Including Performance Management, Account Management, and Security

Administrative plans can be broken down into three areas: performance management, account management, and security.

Performance Management

Performance management is best done through the establishment of a baseline of the network performance and a baseline of a computer's performance. Based upon the information in a baseline, the administrators of the network can establish when network or computer performance is abnormal.

Account Management

Account management within Windows NT is done through the use of groups. In a workgroup model, there exist local groups, or groups that are local to the computer. These groups are not seen on other machines in the network. Users are placed into these local groups and assigned permissions to resources, such as printers, shares, or files and directories.

Windows 95 computers do not have built-in groups. There also is no account database on a Windows 95 computer to provide user accounts.

Windows NT domain models do make use of user accounts and groups. Like the workgroup model, the domain model has user accounts and local groups. A domain model also has global groups. Global groups reside on a domain controller and can be referenced as a resource user by any Windows NT computer within the domain sharing resources.

Security

Windows 95 computers have the capability to provide share-level security, which involves password protecting resources.

Windows NT computers can provide user-level security, in which users are granted access to resources on a user or local group basis (workgroups and domains support this) and a global group basis (only domains support this).

Choosing a Disaster Recovery Plan for Various Situations

Disaster recovery applies to many different components on the network. The following sections describe the most common issues and solutions used in a disaster recovery program.

Uninterruptible Power Supply (UPS)

An uninterruptible power supply (UPS) is a special battery (or sometimes a generator) that supplies power to an electronic device in the event of a power failure. UPSs commonly are used with network servers to prevent a disorderly shutdown by warning users to log out. After a predetermined waiting period, the UPS software performs an orderly shutdown of the server. Many UPS units also regulate power distribution and serve as protection against power surges. Remember that in most cases, a UPS generally does not provide for continued network functionality for longer than a few minutes. A UPS is not intended to keep the server running through a long power outage, but rather to give the server time to do what it needs before shutting down. This can prevent the data loss and system corruption that sometimes result from sudden shutdown.

Tape Backup

Tape backups are done to store data offline in the event that the hard drive containing the data fails. There are three types of tape backups:

- Full backup. Backs up all specified files.

- Incremental backup. Backs up only those files that have changed since the last backup.

- Differential backup. Backs up the specified files if the files have changed since the last backup. This type doesn't mark the files as having been backed up, however. (A differential backup is somewhat like a copy command. Because the file is not marked as having been backed up, a later differential or incremental backup will back up the file again.)

RAID 1

In level 1, drives are paired or mirrored with each byte of information being written to each identical drive. You can duplex these devices by adding a separate drive controller for each drive. Disk mirroring is defined as two hard drives (one primary, one secondary) that use the same disk channel or controller cards and cable. Disk mirroring is most commonly configured by using disk drives contained in the server. Duplexing is a form of mirroring that involves the use of a second controller and that enables you to configure a more robust hardware environment.

RAID 5

RAID 5 uses striping with parity information written across multiple drives to enable fault-tolerance with a minimum of wasted disk space.

This level also offers the advantage of enabling relatively efficient performance on writes to the drives, as well as excellent read performance.

Striping with parity is based on the principle that all data is written to the hard drive in binary code (ones and zeros). RAID 5 requires at least three drives because this version writes data across two of them and then creates the parity block on the third. If the first byte is 00111000 and the second is 10101001, the system computes the third by adding the digits together using this system:

$$1+1=0, \ 0+0=0, \ 0+1=1, \ 1+0=1$$

The sum of 00111000 and 10101001 is 10010001, which would be written to the third disk. If any of the disks fail, the process can be reversed and any disk can be reconstructed from the data on the other two. Recovery includes replacing the bad disk and then regenerating its data through the Disk Administrator. A maximum of 32 disks can be connected in a RAID 5 array under Windows NT.

Given the Manufacturer's Documentation for the Network Adapter, Install, Configure, and Resolve Hardware Conflicts for Multiple Network Adapters in a Token-Ring or Ethernet Network

The following resources are configurable on network adapter cards:

- IRQ

- Base I/O port address

- Base memory address

- DMA channel

- Boot PROM
- MAC address
- Ring speed (token-ring cards)
- Connector type

Not all network adapter cards have all of these resources available for configuration. These resource settings on the network adapter card must be different than the settings found on other components used within the computer.

Some network adapter cards use jumper settings to configure these settings, others use software, and others can have this done through the operating system software, such as Windows 95 and Windows NT. The method of configuration is dependent upon the manufacturer.

Implementing a NetBIOS Naming Scheme for All Computers on a Given Network

NetBIOS is an interface that provides NetBIOS-based applications with access to network resources. Every computer on a Windows NT network must have a unique name for it to be accessible through the NetBIOS interface. This unique name is called a computer name or a NetBIOS name.

On a NetBIOS network, every computer must have a unique name. The computer name can be up to 15 characters long. A NetBIOS name can include alphanumeric characters and any of the following special characters:

! @ # $ % ^ & ( ) - _ ' { } . ~

Note that you cannot use a space or an asterisk in a NetBIOS name. Also, NetBIOS names are not case sensitive.

Selecting the Appropriate Hardware and Software Tools to Monitor Trends in the Network

The hardware and software tools described in the next five sections are used to monitor trends in a network.

Protocol Analyzer

This can be a hardware or software tool to analyze the traffic in a network. Protocol analyzers capture packets on a network and display their contents. The software version of this tool supplied by Microsoft is Network Monitor. Network Monitor ships with Windows NT as a scaled-down version that can only capture data between the host computer and those to which the host talks.

Event Viewer

This software tool is found on Windows NT. It reports one of three event types:

- System Events. Those generated by the operating system.
- Application Events. Those generated by any application that is programmed to make event calls to the Event Viewer.
- Auditing. Any auditing being performed on NTFS partitions or by users interacting with the network.

Performance Monitor

Windows NT's Performance Monitor tool lets you monitor important system parameters for the computers on your network in real time. Performance Monitor can keep an eye on a large number of system parameters, providing a graphical or tabular profile of system and network trends. Performance Monitor also can save performance data in a log for later reference. You can use Performance Monitor to track statistical measurements (called counters) for any of several hardware or software components (called objects).

System Monitor

Windows 95 includes a program called System Monitor that also allows information to be collected on the Windows 95 machine in real time. System Monitor collects information on different categories of items on the system. System Monitor is not as detailed as Windows NT's Performance Monitor.

Simple Network Management Protocol (SNMP)

SNMP is a TCP/IP protocol used to perform management operations on a TCP/IP network. SNMP-enabled devices allow for information to be sent to a management utility (this is called a trap). SNMP devices also allow for the setting and extraction of information (this is done by the issuance of a set or get command) found in their Management Information Base (MIB).

TROUBLESHOOTING

The Troubleshooting section of the exam covers many of the topics covered in previous sections.

Emphasis of this section is to test your understanding of what can cause problems, and how to fix them.

Identifying Common Errors Associated with Components Required for Communications

The utilities described in the next four sections can be used to diagnose errors associated with components required for communications.

Protocol Analyzers

Protocol analyzers are either hardware or software products used to monitor network traffic, track network performance, and analyze packets. Protocol analyzers can identify bottlenecks, protocol problems, and malfunctioning network components.

Digital Volt Meter (DVM)

Digital volt meters are handheld electronic measuring tools that enable you to check the voltage of network cables. They also can be used to check the resistance of terminators. You can use a DVM to help you find a break or a short in a network cable.

DVMs are usually inexpensive battery-operated devices that have either a digital or needle readout and two metal prongs attached to the DVM by some wires a foot or more in length. By sending a small current through the wires and out through the metal prongs, resistance and voltages of terminators and wires can be measured.

Time-Domain Reflectometers (TDR)

Time-domain reflectometers send sound waves along a cable and look for imperfections that might be caused by a break or a short in the line. A good TDR can detect faults on a cable to within a few feet.

Oscilloscope

An oscilloscope measures fluctuations in signal voltage and can help find faulty or damaged cabling. Oscilloscopes are often more expensive electronic devices that show the signal fluctuations on a monitor.

Several diagnostic software tools provide information on virtually any type of network hardware, as well. A considerable number of diagnostic software packages are available for a variety of prices.

A common software tool distributed with most network cards is a Send/Receive package. This software tool allows two computers with network cards and cables to connect to each other. This tool does not rely on a networked operating system, nor can it be used to send data. It simply sends packets from one computer to the other, establishing that the network cards and underlying transmission media are connected and configured properly.

Diagnosing and Resolving Common Connectivity Problems with Cards, Cables, and Related Hardware

Most network problems occur on the transmission media or with the components that attach devices to the transmission media. All of these components operate at the Physical, DataLink, or Network levels of the OSI model. The components that connect PCs and enable them to communicate are susceptible to many kinds of problems.

Troubleshooting Cables and Connectors

Most network problems occur at the OSI Physical layer, and cabling is one of the most common causes. A cable might have a short or a break, or it might be attached to a faulty connector. Tools such as DVMs and TDRs help search out cabling problems.

Cabling problems can cause three major problems: An individual computer cannot access the network, a group of computers cannot access the network, or none of the computers can access the network.

On networks that are configured in a star topology, an individual cable break between the computer and hub or MSAU causes a failure in communication between that individual computer and the rest of the network. This type of cable break does not cause problems between all of the other computers on the network.

A cable break in cables connecting multiple hubs causes a break in communications between the computers on one side of the cable break and the computers on the other side of the cable break. In most cases, the communications between computers within the broken segment can continue.

In the case of MSAU, the breakage of a cable connecting MSAUs often causes all computers on the ring to fail because the ring is not complete. A break in the cable on a bus topology also causes all computers on the network segment to be unable to communicate with any other computers on the network.

Try the following checks when troubleshooting network cabling problems:

- With 10BASE-T, make sure the cable used has the correct number of twists to meet the data-grade specifications.

- Look for electrical interference, which can be caused by tying the network cable together with monitor and power cords. Fluorescent lights, electric motors, and other electrical devices can cause interference if they are located too close to cables. These problems often can be alleviated by placing the cable away from devices that generate electromagnetic interference or by upgrading the cable to one that has better shielding.

- Make sure that connectors are pinned properly and crimped tightly.

- If excess shielding on coaxial cable is exposed, make sure it doesn't ground out the connector.

- Ensure that coaxial cables are not coiled tightly together. This can generate a magnetic field around the cable, causing electromagnetic interference.

- On coaxial Ethernet LANs, look for missing terminators or terminators with improper resistance ratings.

- Watch out for malfunctioning transceivers, concentrators, or T-connectors. All of these components can be checked by replacing the suspect devices.

- Test the continuity of the cable by using the various physical testing devices discussed in the previous section or by using a software-based cable testing utility.

- Make sure that all the component cables in a segment are connected. A user who moves his client and removes the T-connector incorrectly can cause a broken segment.

- Examine cable connectors for bent or broken pins.

- On Token-Ring networks, inspect the attachment of patch cables and adapter cables. Remember, patch cables connect MSAUs, and adapter cables connect the network adapter to the MSAU.

One advantage of a Token-Ring network is its built-in capability to monitor itself. Token-Ring networks provide electronic troubleshooting and, when possible, actually make repairs. When the Token-Ring network can't make its own repairs, a process called beaconing narrows down the portion of the ring in which the problem is most likely to exist.

Troubleshooting Network Adapter Cards

Network problems often result from malfunctioning network adapter cards. The process of troubleshooting the network adapter works like any other kind of troubleshooting process: Start with the simple. The following list details some aspects you can check if you think your network adapter card might be malfunctioning:

- Make sure the cable is properly connected to the card.

- Confirm that you have the correct network adapter card driver and that the driver is installed properly. Be sure the card is properly bound to the appropriate transport protocol.

- Make sure the network adapter card and the network adapter card driver are compatible with your operating system. If you use Windows NT, consult the Windows NT hardware compatibility list. If you use Windows 95 or another operating system, rely on the adapter card vendor specifications.

- Test for resource conflicts. Make sure another device isn't attempting to use the same resources. If you think a resource conflict might be the problem, but you can't pinpoint the conflict using Windows NT Diagnostics, Windows 95's Device Manager, or some other diagnostic program, try removing all the cards except the network adapter and then replacing the cards one by one. Check the network with each addition to determine which device is causing the conflict.

- Run the network adapter card's diagnostic software. This will often indicate which resource on the network card is failing.

- Examine the jumper and DIP switch settings on the card. Make sure the resource settings are consistent with the settings configured through the operating system.

- Make sure the card is inserted properly in the slot. Reseat if necessary.

- If necessary, remove the card and clean the connector fingers (don't use an eraser because it leaves grit on the card).

- Replace the card with one that you know works. If the connection works with a different card, you know the card is the problem.

Token-Ring network adapters with failure rates that exceed a preset tolerance level might actually remove themselves from the network. Try replacing the card. Some Token-Ring networks also can experience problems if a Token-Ring card set at a ring speed of 16Mbps is inserted into a ring using a 4Mbps ring speed, and vice versa.

Troubleshooting Hubs and MSAUs

If you experience problems with a hub-based LAN, such as a 10BASE-T network, you often can isolate the problem by disconnecting the attached workstations one at a time. If removing one of the workstations eliminates the problem, the trouble may be caused by that workstation or its associated cable length. If removing each of the workstations doesn't solve the problem, the fault may lie with the hub. Check the easy components first, such as ports, switches, and connectors, and then use a different hub (if you have it) to see if the problem persists. If your hub doesn't work properly, call the manufacturer.

If you're troubleshooting a Token-Ring network, make sure the cables are connected properly to the MSAUs, with ring-out ports connecting to the ring-in ports throughout the ring. If you suspect the MSAU, isolate it by changing the ring-in and ring-out cables to bypass the MSAU. If the ring is now functional again, consider replacing the MSAU. In addition, you might find that if your network has MSAUs from more than one manufacturer, they are not wholly compatible. Impedance and other electrical characteristics can show slight differences between manufacturers, causing intermittent network problems. Some MSAUs (other than the 8228) are active and require a power supply. These MSAUs fail if they have a blown fuse or a bad power source. Your problem also might result from a misconfigured

MSAU port. MSAU ports using the hermaphrodite connector need to be reinitialized with the setup tool. Removing drop cables and reinitializing each MSAU port is a quick fix that is useful on relatively small Token-Ring networks.

Isolating problems with patch cables, adapter cables, and MSAUs is easier to do if you have a current log of your network's physical design. After you narrow down the problem, you can isolate potential problem areas from the rest of the network and then use a cable tester to find the actual problem.

Troubleshooting Modems

A modem presents all the potential problems you find with any other device. You must make sure that the modem is properly installed, that the driver is properly installed, and that the resource settings do not conflict with other devices. Modems also pose some unique problems because they must connect directly to the phone system, they operate using analog communications, and they must make a point-to-point connection with a remote machine.

The online help files for both Windows NT and Windows 95 include a topic called the Modem Troubleshooter. The Modem Troubleshooter leads you to possible solutions for a modem problem by asking questions about the symptoms. As you answer the questions (by clicking the gray box beside your answer), the Modem Troubleshooter zeroes in on more specific questions until (ideally) it leads you to a solution.

Some common modem problems are as follows:

- Dialing problems. The dialing feature is improperly configured. For instance, the modem isn't dialing 9 to bypass your office switchboard, or it is dialing 9 when you're away from your office. The computer also could be dialing an area code or an international code when it shouldn't. Check the dialing properties for the connection.

- Connection problems. You cannot connect to another modem. Your modem and the other modem might be operating at different speeds. Verify that the maximum speed setting for your modem is the highest speed that both your modem and the other modem can use. Also make sure the Data Bits, Parity, and Stop Bits settings are consistent with the remote computer.

- Digital phone systems. You cannot plug a modem into a telephone line designed for use with digital phone systems. These digital phone systems are commonplace in most office environments.

- Protocol problems. The communicating devices are using incompatible line protocols. Verify that the devices are configured for the same or compatible protocols. If one computer initiates a connection using PPP, the other computer must be capable of using PPP.

Repeaters, Bridges, and Routers

Issues dealing with repeaters, bridges, and routers are often more technically advanced than those covered in a book such as Networking Essentials. Companies such as Cisco, Bay Networks, and 3Com have their own dedicated books and courses on dealing with the installation, configuration, and troubleshooting of repeaters, bridges, and routers. In general, there are some basic troubleshooting steps you can do when working with these three devices.

Repeaters are responsible for regenerating a signal sent down the transmission media. The typical problem with repeaters is that they do not work—that is, the signal is not being regenerated. If this is the case, the signal being sent to devices on the other side of the repeater from the sending device will not receive the signal.

Problems with bridges are almost identical to that of a repeater. The signal being sent to devices on the other side of the bridge from the sending device will be received. Other issues with bridges are that the table of which devices are on which interface of the bridge can get corrupt. This can lead from one to all machines not receiving packets on the network. Diagnostic utilities provided by the bridge's manufacturer can resolve this type of problem.

Problems with routers can be complex, and troubleshooting them often involves a high level of understanding of the different protocols in use on the network, as well as the software and commands used to program a router. There are generally two types of router problems.

The first router problem that is commonly found is that packets are just not being passed through because the router is "dead" or simply not functioning. The second common problem with routers is that the routing tables within the routers are corrupted or incorrectly programmed. This problem either leads to computers on different networks being unable to communicate with each other or to the fact that certain protocols simply do not work.

Resolve Broadcast Storms

A broadcast storm is a sudden flood of broadcast messages that clogs the transmission medium, approaching 100 percent of the bandwidth. Broadcast storms cause performance to decline and, in the worst case, computers cannot even access the network. The cause of a broadcast storm is often a malfunctioning network adapter, but a broadcast storm also can be caused when a device on the network attempts to contact another device that either doesn't exist or for some reason doesn't respond to the broadcast.

If the broadcast messages are viable, a network-monitoring or protocol-analysis tool often can determine the source of the storm. If the broadcast storm is caused by a malfunctioning adapter throwing illegible packets onto the line, and a protocol analyzer can't find the source, try to isolate the offending PC by removing computers from the network one at a time until the line returns to normal.

Identify and Resolve Network Performance Problems

If your network runs slower than it used to run (or slower than it ought to run), the problem might be that the present network traffic exceeds the level at which the network can operate efficiently. Some possible causes for increased traffic are new hardware (such as a new workstation) or new software (such as a network computer game or some other network application). A generator or another mechanical device operating near the network could cause a degradation of network performance. In addition, a malfunctioning network device could act as a bottleneck. Ask yourself what has changed since the last time the network operated efficiently, and begin there with your troubleshooting efforts.

A performance monitoring tool, such as Windows NT's Performance Monitor or Network Monitor, can help you look for bottlenecks that are adversely affecting your network. For instance, the increased traffic could be the result of increased usage. If usage exceeds the capacity of the network, you might want to consider expanding or redesigning your network. You also might want to divide the network into smaller segments by using a router or a bridge to reduce network traffic. A protocol analyzer can help you measure and monitor the traffic at various points on your network.

Index

SYMBOLS

A

Q-R

printers, 170, 177
protocol analyzers, 292
RAS servers, dial-up connections, 169, 173
repeaters, 189, 194, 297
resources
  conflicts, 295
  file server bottlenecks, 16, 22
  sharing, 169-170, 176-177
routers, 297
segments
  connections, 180, 183
  viewing computers on other segments, 169, 174
servers
  cable connections, 180, 184
  domain connections, 180, 184
  initializing networking components, 181, 185-186
service performance, 200, 205
Token-Ring networks, 85
  communications, 84
  response time, 198, 203
user downtime, 200, 205
Windows NT Event Viewer, 184
trunks, bus networks, 12
tuning performance of routers, 141
tunneling protocol, PPTP, 48
twisted-pair cable, 281

U

UDP (User Datagram Protocol), connectionless mode, 278
UNC paths (Universal Naming Convention), 124
UNIX
  clients, print protocol, 92, 97
  servers, file sharing protocols, 92, 96
unshielded twisted-pair (UTP) cable, 207
updates, network adapter card drivers, 145
UPSs (Uninterruptible Power Supplies), 132, 137
upstream computer, Token-Ring networks, 88
user-level permissions, 24, 120
user-level security, 26, 29, 276
  compatible operating systems, 33, 38
  permissions, 28
  resource sharing, 27
usernames, 128

users
  accounts
    lockouts, 121, 126
    resource sharing, Windows NT Workstation, 14, 18
    security, 125
    validating, 176
  domain controller validation problems, 170, 176
  downtime, troubleshooting, 200, 205
  global groups, 127
  monitoring network usage, 13
  tracking network usage, 5
UTP (unshielded twisted-pair) cable, 8, 75, 79, 207, 282

V

validation, domain controllers
  NIC problems, 171, 178
  troubleshooting, 170, 176
viewing
  hardware conflicts, 141, 146
  other computers, 139
virtual circuits, 113
  port numbers, 99
  WANs, 109
voice/data/video connection services, WANs, 110, 115

W

WANs (wide area networks), 1, 276
  ATM, 288
  backups, 134
  broadcast storms, 104
  connections
    100Mbps throughput, 110
    ATM, 115
    error correction services, 108
    Frame Relay, 113
    greatest overhead, 109, 114
    intercontinental, 108
    ISDN, 114
    leased-line speeds, 116
    least overhead, 109, 114

TRAINING GUIDES

Complete, Innovative, Accurate, Thorough

Our next generation *Training Guides* have been developed to help you study and retain the essential knowledge that you need to pass the MCSE exams. We know your study time is valuable, and we have made every effort to make the most of it by presenting clear, accurate, and thorough information.

In creating this series, our goal was to raise the bar on how MCSE content is written, developed, and presented. From the two-color design that gives you easy access to content, to the new software simulator that allows you to perform tasks in a simulated operating system environment, we are confident that you will be well-prepared for exam success.

Our New Riders Top Score Software Suite is a custom-developed set of full-functioning software applications that work in conjunction with the Training Guide by providing you with the following:

Exam Simulator includes over 150 fact-based and situational-based questions.
Electronic Study Cards really test your knowledge with explanations that are linked to an electronic version of the *Training Guide.*
Electronic Flash Cards help you retain the facts in a time-tested method.
An Electronic Version of the Book provides quick searches and compact, mobile study.
Customization Capabilities allow you to adapt Top Score to the way you want to learn.

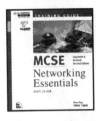

MCSE Training Guide: Networking Essentials, Second Edition

1-56205-919-X, $49.99, 9/98

MCSE Training Guide: TCP/IP, Second Edition

1-56205-920-3, $49.99, 11/98

MCSE Training Guide: Windows NT Server 4, Second Edition

1-56205-916-5, $49.99, 9/98

MCSE Training Guide: SQL Server 7 Administration

0-7357-0003-6, $49.99, Q2/99

MCSE Training Guide: Windows NT Server 4 Enterprise, Second Edition

1-56205-917-3, $49.99, 9/98

MCSE Training Guide: SQL Server 7 Design and Implementation

0-7357-0004-4, $49.99, Q2/99

MCSE Training Guide: Windows NT Workstation 4, Second Edition

1-56205-918-1, $49.99, 9/98

MCSD Training Guide: Solution Architectures

0-7357-0026-5, $49.99, Q2/99

MCSE Training Guide: Windows 98

1-56205-890-8, $49.99, 1/99

MCSD Training Guide: Visual Basic 6

0-7357-0002-8, $59.99, Q1/99

NEW RIDERS CERTIFICATION TITLES

TRAINING GUIDES
FIRST EDITIONS

Your Quality Elective Solution

MCSE Training Guide: Systems Management Server 1.2, 1-56205-748-0

MCSE Training Guide: SQL Server 6.5 Administration, 1-56205-726-X

MCSE Training Guide: SQL Server 6.5 Design and Implementation, 1-56205-830-4

MCSE Training Guide: Windows 95, 70-064 Exam, 1-56205-880-0

MCSE Training Guide: Exchange Server 5, 1-56205-824-X

MCSE Training Guide: Internet Explorer 4, 1-56205-889-4

MCSE Training Guide: Microsoft Exchange Server 5.5, 1-56205-899-1

MCSE Training Guide: Internet Information Server 4, 1-56205-823-1

MCSD Training Guide: Visual Basic 5, 1-56205-850-9

MCSD Training Guide: Microsoft Access, 1-56205-771-5

TESTPREPS

MCSE TestPrep: Networking Essentials, Second Edition

0-7357-0010-9, $19.99, 12/98

MCSE TestPrep: Windows 95, Second Edition

0-7357-0011-7, $19.99, 12/98

MCSE TestPrep: Windows NT Server 4, Second Edition

0-7357-0012-5, $19.99, 12/98

MCSE TestPrep: Windows NT Server 4 Enterprise, Second Edition

0-7357-0009-5, $19.99, 11/98

MCSE TestPrep: Windows NT Workstation 4, Second Edition

0-7357-0008-7, $19.99, 12/98

MCSE TestPrep: TCP/IP, Second Edition

0-7357-0025-7, $19.99, 12/98

MCSE TestPrep: Windows 98

1-56205-922-X, $19.99, 11/98

TESTPREPS
FIRST EDITIONS

Your Quality Elective Solution

MCSE TestPrep: SQL Server 6.5 Administration, 0-7897-1597-X

MCSE TestPrep: SQL Server 6.5 Design and Implementation, 1-56205-915-7

MCSE TestPrep: Internet Explorer 4, 0-7897-1654-2

MCSE TestPrep: Exchange Server 5.5, 0-7897-1611-9

MCSE TestPrep: Internet Information Server 4, 0-7897-1610-0

FAST TRACK SERIES

The Accelerated Path to Certification Success

Fast Tracks provide an easy way to review the key elements of each certification technology without being bogged down with elementary-level information.

These guides are perfect for when you already have real-world, hands-on experience. They're the ideal enhancement to training courses, test simulators, and comprehensive training guides. *No fluff—simply what you really need to pass the exam!*

LEARN IT FAST

Part I contains only the essential information you need to pass the test. With over 200 pages of information, it is a concise review for the more experienced MCSE candidate.

REVIEW IT EVEN FASTER

Part II averages 50–75 pages, and takes you through the test and into the real-world use of the technology, with chapters on:

1) Fast Facts Review Section
2) The Insider's Spin (on taking the exam)
3) Sample Test Questions
4) Hotlists of Exam-Critical Concepts
5) Did You Know? (real-world applications for the technology covered in the exam)

MCSE Fast Track:
Networking Essentials

1-56205-939-4,
$19.99, 9/98

MCSE Fast Track:
Windows 98

0-7357-0016-8,
$19.99, 12/98

MCSE Fast Track:
Windows NT Server 4

1-56205-935-1,
$19.99, 9/98

MCSE Fast Track:
Windows NT Server 4
Enterprise

1-56205-940-8,
$19.99, 9/98

MCSE Fast Track:
Windows NT
Workstation 4

1-56205-938-6,
$19.99, 9/98

MCSE Fast Track:
TCP/IP

1-56205-937-8,
$19.99, 9/98

MCSE Fast Track:
Internet Information
Server 4

1-56205-936-X,
$19.99, 9/98

MCSD Fast Track:
Solution Architectures

0-7357-0029-X,
$19.99, Q2/99

MCSD Fast Track:
Visual Basic 6,
Exam 70-175

0-7357-0018-4,
$19.99, 12/98

MCSD Fast Track:
Visual Basic 6,
Exam 70-176

0-7357-0019-2,
$19.99, 12/98

HOW TO CONTACT US

IF YOU NEED THE LATEST UPDATES ON A TITLE THAT YOU'VE PURCHASED:

1) Visit our Web site at www.newriders.com.

2) Click on the DOWNLOADS link, and enter your book's ISBN number, which is located on the back cover in the bottom right-hand corner.

3) In the DOWNLOADS section, you'll find available updates that are linked to the book page.

IF YOU ARE HAVING TECHNICAL PROBLEMS WITH THE BOOK OR THE CD THAT IS INCLUDED:

1) Check the book's information page on our Web site according to the instructions listed above, or

2) Email us at support@mcp.com, or

3) Fax us at (317) 817-7488 attn: Tech Support.

IF YOU HAVE COMMENTS ABOUT ANY OF OUR CERTIFICATION PRODUCTS THAT ARE NON-SUPPORT RELATED:

1) Email us at certification@mcp.com, or

2) Write to us at New Riders, 201 W. 103rd St., Indianapolis, IN 46290-1097, or

3) Fax us at (317) 581-4663.

IF YOU ARE OUTSIDE THE UNITED STATES AND NEED TO FIND A DISTRIBUTOR IN YOUR AREA:

Please contact our international department at international@mcp.com.

IF YOU WISH TO PREVIEW ANY OF OUR CERTIFICATION BOOKS FOR CLASSROOM USE:

Email us at pr@mcp.com. Your message should include your name, title, training company or school, department, address, phone number, office days/hours, text in use, and enrollment. Send these details along with your request for desk/examination copies and/or additional information.

WE WANT TO KNOW WHAT YOU THINK

To better serve you, we would like your opinion on the content and quality of this book. Please complete this card and mail it to us or fax it to 317-581-4663.

Name _____

Address _____

City _____ State _____ Zip _____

Phone _____ Email Address _____

Occupation _____

Which certification exams have you already passed? _____
_____
_____
_____

Which certification exams do you plan to take? _____
_____
_____
_____

What influenced your purchase of this book?
❏ Recommendation   ❏ Cover Design
❏ Table of Contents   ❏ Index
❏ Magazine Review   ❏ Advertisement
❏ Reputation of New Riders ❏ Author Name

How would you rate the contents of this book?
❏ Excellent   ❏ Very Good
❏ Good   ❏ Fair
❏ Below Average   ❏ Poor

What other types of certification products will you buy/have you bought to help you prepare for the exam?
❏ Quick reference books   ❏ Testing software
❏ Study guides   ❏ Other

What do you like most about this book? Check all that apply.
❏ Content   ❏ Writing Style
❏ Accuracy   ❏ Examples
❏ Listings   ❏ Design
❏ Index   ❏ Page Count
❏ Price   ❏ Illustrations

What do you like least about this book? Check all that apply.
❏ Content   ❏ Writing Style
❏ Accuracy   ❏ Examples
❏ Listings   ❏ Design
❏ Index   ❏ Page Count
❏ Price   ❏ Illustrations

What would be a useful follow-up book to this one for you?_____

Where did you purchase this book? _____

Can you name a similar book that you like better than this one, or one that is as good? Why?_____
_____
_____

How many New Riders books do you own? _____

What are your favorite certification or general computer book titles? _____
_____

What other titles would you like to see New Riders develop? _____
_____

Any comments? _____
_____
_____
_____

MCSE TestPrep: Networking Essentials, Second Edition

Fold here and Scotch tape to mail

Place
Stamp
Here

New Riders
201 W. 103rd St.
Indianapolis, IN 46290